Women as Leaders in Education

Women as Leaders in Education

SUCCEEDING DESPITE INEQUITY, DISCRIMINATION, AND OTHER CHALLENGES

VOLUME 1: WOMEN'S LEADERSHIP IN HIGHER EDUCATION

Jennifer L. Martin, Editor

Women and Careers in Management
Michele A. Paludi, Series Editor

PRAEGER

AN IMPRINT OF ABC-CLIO, LLC
Santa Barbara, California • Denver, Colorado • Oxford, England

Library of Congress Cataloging-in-Publication Data

Women as leaders in education : succeeding despite inequity, discrimination, and other challenges / Jennifer L. Martin, editor.

p. cm. — (Women and careers in management)

Includes bibliographical references and index.

ISBN 978–0–313–39169–9 (hard copy : alk. paper) — ISBN 978–0–313–39170–5 (ebook)

1. Women school administrators—United States. 2. Women college administrators—United States. 3. Sex discrimination in higher education—United States. 4. Educational leadership—United States. I. Martin, Jennifer L. II. Title. III. Series.

LC212.862.W64   2011

378.1′2082—dc22   2011009216

ISBN: 978–0–313–39169–9
EISBN: 978–0–313–39170–5

15 14 13 12 11   1 2 3 4 5

This book is also available on the World Wide Web as an eBook.
Visit www.abc-clio.com for details.

Praeger
An Imprint of ABC-CLIO, LLC

ABC-CLIO, LLC
130 Cremona Drive, P.O. Box 1911
Santa Barbara, California 93116-1911

Contents

Series Foreword

Ma muaka kite a muri
Ma muri ka ora a mua
(Those who lead give sight to those who follow,
Those who follow give life to those who lead)
—Pauline Tangiora

Welcome to the *Women and Careers in Management* Series at Praeger. This series examines the status of women in management and leadership and offers discussions of issues women managers and leaders face, including:

Differences in leadership styles

Traditional gender roles reinforcing women's subordinate status in the workplace

Obstacles to advancement and pay

Benefit and resource inequity

Discrimination and harassment

Work/life imbalance

This series acknowledges that gender is one of the fundamental factors influencing the ethics, values, and policies of workplaces and that the discrimination against women managers and leaders explains the pervasiveness of institutionalized inequality. This series also discusses interconnections among equality issues: sex, race, class, age, sexual orientation, religion, and disability. Thus, this series brings together a multidisciplinary and multicultural discussion of women, management, and leadership.

Women and Careers in Management encourages all of us to think criti-cally about women managers and leaders, to place value on cultural expe-riences, and to integrate empirical research and theoretical formulations with experiences of our family, friends, colleagues, and ourselves. It is my hope that the books in *Women and Careers in Management* serve as a "life raft" (Klonis, Endo, Crosby, & Worrell, 1997), especially for the Millennial and subsequent generations.

I am honored to have Dr. Jennifer Martin's two-volume set published in the *Women and Careers in Management Series*. Dr. Martin was instrumen-tal in bringing together noted educators and scholars to address women as leaders in K–12 and in higher education. The volumes are essential read-ing for students preparing for a career in teaching and education administration, school and college administrators, and human resource personnel. Dr. Martin offers her readers a "paper mentor" in her edited volumes. As such, these volumes share Pauline Tangiora's sentiment:

> Those who lead give sight to those who follow, Those who follow give life to those who lead.

—Michele A. Paludi
Series Editor

Reference

Klonis, S., Endo, J., Crosby, F., & Worrell, J. (1997). Feminism as life raft. *Psychology of Women Quarterly, 21,* 333–45.

Acknowledgments

Do not follow where the path may lead. Go instead where there is no path and leave a trail.

—Muriel Strode

I dedicate this book set to veteran feminist leaders. I thank you for making the road a little less rocky for the women behind you. I honor your work and celebrate your strength. Your work informs and inspires mine and has led me to this point in my thinking about women and leadership. You have carved your own path; because of your work, mine is possible. It is with you in mind that I bring together this group of diverse voices.

I have had the distinct pleasure of collaborating with colleagues, friends, students, and mentors on this project. I have also been given the unique opportunity to meet many feminist scholars who were interested in sharing their work. These new colleagues have taught me much from their writing and their scholarship. I thank you for your contributions to this book set. This process has been a true collaboration in the spirit of transformational leadership; all of the authors have brought much to the discussion on women and leadership and have assisted me greatly throughout this process.

I thank my parents, John and Dolores Martin, and my sister Elizabeth Martin for their help and support throughout this process. Tremendous thanks go to my husband Peter Midtgard, my greatest sounding board, cheerleader, and provider of reassurance and support; no one believes in me as much as he.

I acknowledge several special friends whose encouragement has been instrumental throughout this process: Annie James, Elizabeth Schuch, and Karissa Williams. Special thanks go to Alice Kondraciuk for technological support without which this project would have been much more laborious, and Ken VanDerworp for his keen wordsmithing. I also thank the Women of Words writer's group, especially Coralie Johnson and Karen Simpson, for allowing me to share my thoughts and providing me with guidance, feedback, friendship, and mentoring.

My students continue to inspire me and make me strive to be a better person and educator. I thank my students from the Women and Gender Studies and Education Specialist programs at Oakland University and my high school students at Tinkham Alternative High School. My students have informed my praxis, my research, and my writing.

I have been fortunate enough to have many mentors throughout my career. These inspiring people continue to help me and advise me in my work. I honor and thank Dr. Duane Moore, Dr. Heather Neff, Dr. Mary Otto, Dr. Dawn Pickard, Dr. Julia Smith, and especially Dr. Jo Reger and Dr. Dyanne Tracy.

To my friends at Michigan NOW, thank you for your support and wisdom. Your feminist leadership continues to inspire me.

I thank Brian Romer, Senior Acquisitions Editor at Praeger, for supporting my work and my vision for this project. His helpful guidance has been instrumental in the completion of this series.

Finally, I give special thanks to my mentor and friend Dr. Michele Paludi, who always believed in my abilities as a scholar, teacher, and writer. She has provided me with tremendous opportunities to grow as a person and as a professional. Without her, this book set would not have been possible.

—Jennifer L. Martin

Introduction

How much are you prepared to risk of what is familiar, comfortable, safe, and perhaps working well for you, in the name of better education for others?

—Roland Barth

Woman must write herself: must write about women and bring women to writing, from which they have been driven away as violently as from their bodies—for the same reasons, by the same law, with the same fatal goal.

—Helene Cixoux

There is much to learn through the sharing of struggle. Both the reader and the writer can be moved, transformed, inspired to action. The process can be counter-hegemonic as well as instructive. This two-volume set provides a forum for such sharing with these goals in mind: to examine the challenges that women leaders in education experience and to unravel their successes despite a labyrinth of obstacles. Leadership as experienced by women in academe is unique; they face many challenges that men do not. White patriarchal hegemony affects women's coming to voice, the percentage of women in positions of leadership, and the levels of success women experience within these positions. The essays in this volume, written by a diverse group of scholars who bring together an interdisciplinary approach, capture the difficulty of grappling with these issues. The contributors examine a variety of discourses through nondominant lenses including their own frequent marginalization within higher education. However, this is not a narrative of despair, but one of hope: a didactic account of the transition from margin to mainstream.

Leadership has been defined and refined in American educational thought for centuries. One of the most enduring paradigms is the "great man" leading the organization to success. We feel the repercussions of this image today, for leaders who deviate from the reticent but aggressive solitary leader may be viewed negatively. For example, leaders who are more transformational tend to have more difficulty achieving authenticity. The personal qualities that are valued in a leader still stem from the "great man" paradigm: agency and assertiveness. When these qualities are exhibited by women, they are often viewed with disdain or mistrust. Additionally, many women scholars engaging in social justice work (those who strive for the inclusion of feminist and other nondominant discourses) can be marginalized within higher education based upon the perception that they are too controversial or political. Thus, feminist and social justice scholars are frequently bypassed for tenure and promotion or their research is ignored or trivialized because their work does not accord with hegemonic discourse.

Women leaders in higher education face many challenges; perhaps the most prominent is that of representation. We know that women in academe have not yet reached equity with their male counterparts. According to the American Association of University Professors 2006 equity study, women hold only 24 pecent of full professor positions in the United States. Despite the gains women have made in higher education over the past few decades, they are underrepresented in tenure-track positions. In fact, women in higher education face more obstacles to career advancement than in the corporate world (West & Curtis, 2006). The areas with the fewest women in higher education are the most prestigious and most highly paid. Women make far less than men in higher education because they are more likely to hold positions at institutions that pay lower salaries and are less likely to gain senior rank. Women are also more likely to remain in the rank of instructor, a low-paid, low-prestige position.

For those women who possess double minority status (based upon race, class, disability, sexuality, etc.), the disparities are even more pronounced. For example, women of color represent 14 percent of those attaining bachelor's degrees, 13 percent of master's degrees, and 9 percent of doctoral degree recipients, yet they account for only 6 percent of faculty; the problem of women's representation is exacerbated when rank increases: women of color account for 10 percent of instructors, 9 percent of assistant professors, and 3 percent of professors (The White House Project Report, 2009).

The trend of low representation for women in higher education is perhaps most striking in administrative positions. According to research conducted by the Association of Governing Boards of Universities and Colleges (AGB), less than one-third of board members with voting privileges and 4.4 percent of college presidents are women. These inequities are reflected in personal lives as well: only 63 percent of women college presidents are married and only 68 percent have children (89 percent of male college presidents are married and 91 percent have children; The White House Project Report, 2009). The decision of marriage and children is not a measure of a fulfilled life, but a choice; a choice that is simply easier for a man.

Childbearing and rearing affect tenure and career advancement for many women and are issues that require advocacy and cultural change. "The average age that a woman gets a PhD is 34, which means the five to seven years of racing the tenure clock fall right in the middle of her peak reproductive and child-rearing years" (The White House Project Report, 2009, p. 26). Marriage for women can complicate or stall career goals by adding the additional stress of achieving work/life balance. Women are still responsible for the majority of the household chores and for kin keeping at work and in the home. Hochschild (2005) estimates that women in heterosexual relationships are responsible for 70 percent of household duties; this increases stress and disadvantages them in terms of career advancement. The choice of marriage itself is typically one that can only be contemplated within a heterosexual relationship, which illustrates further inequities, especially if universities do not offer partner benefits.

The above statistics do not account for the discrimination that women and double-minority-status women face within higher education, making it difficult for them to perform the most basic obligations, let alone blossom and attain personal career fulfillment and satisfaction. Most higher education institutions are run based upon white male hegemony; issues such as racism, sexism, homophobia, sexual harassment, and microaggressions are real issues for women that may not affect men, particularly white men, as frequently. It is clear that more social justice work within the academy is required in general in order to bring issues disproportionately affecting women to light and to increase women's representation at all levels.

This volume contains chapters describing the situation of women leaders in a variety of areas within higher education: in the teaching ranks, in administration, and on higher education boards. All of the chapters work in concert to present a detailed analysis of what women leaders in higher education face today. It is important for women to tell these truths, to have their voices heard in education. As Adrienne Rich once stated, we have to "claim an education." We have to fight to have our voices included in the dialogues to create change within our institutions. We have to sound our voices, remain visible, and resist "the forces in society which say that women should be nice, play safe, have low professional expectations, drown in love and forget about work, live through others, and stay in the places assigned to us" (1979, p. 26). We must advocate for the inclusion of diverse voices in these dialogues, even if we feel they do not serve our direct interests. I began this writing with a quotation from Barth that sets the tone for this volume; he implores us to look beyond what is easy, what is comfortable, and engage in the difficult work that is a requirement of advancing equity. We must realize that our "direct interest" in education is in serving the needs of all. This is the true goal of feminist and social justice work. These are the voices that speak within this volume: those who have made it "on the page," and those who remain "in the margins."

As Audre Lorde once stated (1984), "your silence will not protect you" (p. 41). It is in the spirit of Lorde that women, through our telling, can bridge our narratives and work toward advancing equity at all levels. This volume is but one of many steps in that journey, the journey of coming to voice. It takes bravery to tell these stories, stories that are fraught with marginalization, silencing, racism, and discrimination, "For we have been socialized to respect fear more than our own needs for language and definition" (Lorde, p. 44). It is my hope that this language will be transformed into action and that these words will inspire others to tell their stories and to advocate for the inclusion of nondominant discourses within higher education. The contributors to this volume implore us to examine our positions and to think critically about what it means to be a leader. It is my hope that readers will continue our work: to resist discourses of exclusion and to continue to share our struggles so that together we can work to put them to an end.

—Jennifer L. Martin

References

Cixous, H. (1981). The laugh of the medusa. In E. Marks & I. de Courtivron (Eds.), *New French feminisms* (pp. 245–264). New York: Schocken Books.

Hochschild, A. R. (2005). *The second shift*. New York: Penguin Books.

Lorde, A. (1984). The transformation of silence into language and action. In *Sister outsider: Essays and speeches by Audre Lorde* (pp. 40–44). Freedom, CA: Crossing Press.

Rich, A. (2009/1979). Claiming an education. In S. Shaw & J. Lee (Eds.), *Women's voices, feminist visions: Classic and contemporary readings* (4th ed.; pp. 25–27). Boston: McGraw Hill.

West, M. S., & Curtis, J. W. (2006). *AAUP faculty gender equity indicators 2006*. Washington, DC: American Association of University Professors.

The White House Project. (2009, November). *The White House project report: Benchmarking women's leadership*. Retrieved February, 2, 2010, from http://www.thewhitehouseproject.org/documents/Report.pdf.

1

Trials and Triumphs of Women Leaders in Higher Education

Eugenia Proctor Gerdes

The 1970s as a Turning Point

Women who began academic careers in the early 1970s experienced a transformation in American higher education. Women's representation in the faculty had reached 28 percent by the end of the 1930s, then actually dipped through the 1940s, 1950s, and 1960s, and only began to rise again in the 1970s (NCES, 1998). From 1976 to 2007, women's representation increased from 25 percent to 42 percent of full-time faculty members and, likewise, from 26 percent to 53 percent of full-time executive-administrative-managerial positions (NCES, 2010). This turnaround in numbers was related to other crucial developments in the early 1970s. Legislation enacted in 1972 extended affirmative action as well as protection from discrimination to women in higher education (Astin & Snyder, 1982; Glazer-Raymo, 1999, 2008). Women's collective action supported passage and implementation of this legislation; on many campuses, commissions on the status of women appeared in the late 1960s and 1970s and allowed feminist activists to address inequities (Glazer-Raymo, 1999, 2008). And the first official women's studies programs were founded in 1970, with increasing numbers of women faculty thereafter fostering development of the new discipline as well as feminist perspectives within traditional disciplines (Boxer, 1998). Whether we women who entered academe in the early 1970s realized it or not, we were present at a crucial juncture. Moreover, we not only

1

experienced dramatic changes in the academic environment; we were responsible for many of them. Thus, our careers provide valuable narratives for understanding women's progress in higher education. When my institution's Women's Resource Center sponsored a panel of women who had arrived in the 1970s as part of its 1996 tenth anniversary celebration, panel members emphasized contrasts between our situations as senior administrators and professors and the beginnings of our careers. Younger women in our audience were surprised that many of us had no women professors in our own education and most of us had no courses on women's issues, that we developed our intentions to become professors out of confidence based partly on naïveté regarding barriers to women, and that we described our hiring as resulting from affirmative action rather than purely from our own qualifications. They would have been even more surprised to hear the negative incidents from our early careers that we felt unable to share in this public setting. Our context also limited our discussion of barriers remaining for women. I began to imagine collecting a fuller version of career stories from a broader sample of women, before those women who entered higher education in the 1970s began to retire.

Survey of Senior Academic Women

In the spring of 1997, I began to ask a broad sample of senior academic women to describe their careers and their perceptions of changes in higher education over their careers. Consistent with feminist scholarship's emphasis on hearing women's voices, I developed an open-ended, qualitative survey so that women could answer in their own words (see Kitzinger, 2004; Marshall & Rossman, 2006). I e-mailed a letter of explanation and open-ended questionnaire to women identified through acquaintances and listservs, soliciting confidential responses from faculty and administrators who had begun their careers with faculty positions in the 1970s or a few years earlier. Using snowball sampling (Gobo, 2004; Patton, 2002), I also asked recipients to forward my request to other academic women who might meet these requirements. Of the ninety-eight respondents, eleven were current or recent presidents or chancellors; forty were academic deans, vice presidents for academic affairs/provosts, or their associates working in academic or faculty affairs; nine were other administrators; and thirty-eight were faculty members. Respondents' disciplinary backgrounds spanned the humanities, social sciences, and natural sciences including medicine. They were located across the country (plus several in Canada) and at institutions that represented every Carnegie classification and that included some women's colleges. (For details of the sample, see Gerdes, 2003a, 2006.)

Except when categories were predetermined by the question and were mutually exclusive and exhaustive (e.g., better, worse, neither, or both), an inductive form of qualitative content analysis was used to form categories that were distinct and internally consistent (Marshall & Rossman, 2006; Patton, 2002). After skimming the answers to each question to determine preliminary categories, new categories were added when elements of an answer did not fit any existing categories; and categories were combined when elements appeared to fit either of two categories. Each respondent was counted in each of the categories she mentioned; the percentage of respondents who fit each category could be calculated by dividing the number of respondents represented in that category by the total number of respondents answering the question. (The percentages of all categories do not sum to 100% for questions where respondents could give multiple answers; category percentages do sum to 100%, except as a result of rounding, where categories are mutually exclusive and exhaustive.) The synopsis below includes the most frequent responses from the content analyses and those that link the analyses together; further information is available in the cited sources.

Early Career

The first two questions on the survey asked respondents to consider the beginning of their academic careers: whether they were treated differently than men in comparable positions and whether there were shortcomings in their preparation or incidents, expectations, policies, treatment, or specific people that caused difficulties for them as women. Respondents did not distinguish these two questions, so they were analyzed together. A few women (7%) believed that they were treated better than men due to their department's or institution's need to recruit and retain women, and some (17%) did not believe any difficulties they experienced were due to gender or felt they were treated the same as men in the same position. In contrast, 76 percent described negative treatment, policies, or incidents that disadvantaged them in their early careers. Common themes were poor mentoring in graduate school, less help getting a job, lower pay, worse teaching assignments, being isolated as the first or one of few women, being left out of men's activities, paternalistic expectations, lack of respect, being explicitly told they would not succeed or were not wanted, lack of maternity leave and expectations that they would quit when they got married or became pregnant, being the brunt of jokes or rumors, and sexual harassment. Most women noted multiple differences between male colleagues' situations and their own. It is important to share some of these early experiences because the beginning of their careers provides the starting point for these senior women's other answers dealing with later experiences and perceptions of changes. Typical examples of early-career difficulties, some mild and some severe, were reported by five women who made clear the psychological effects of their treatment:

> There was occasional skepticism (usually from people who did not know me well) that someone could handle a demanding academic position as well as responsibilities of having a small (two-year-old) child. Male colleagues also seemed to think of me as capable of doing departmental and committee "scut work" or willing to assume inconvenient class schedules that they avoided. There was a very sorry episode of providing me with a condescending nickname that I continually said I hated and that only male colleagues thought endearing. It took repeated and increasingly angry responses to wipe it out, and my blood still boils at the recollection!

> There were assumptions that my income was disposable (when I actually was the primary breadwinner) and I was treated accordingly. I continually pointed out the true nature of my situation and that I was being treated unfairly, and most issues were resolved quickly once folks were aware. An example is that when I became pregnant with my second child, I was told that I could only work into the 5th month—I informed my supervisor that I couldn't quit, that this was silly and discriminatory, and he got the policy changed. ... Some polices caused difficulty, although the biggest problem I have always faced is general treatment: being patronized, excellence in performance not acknowledged, ideas appropriated, doors closed (or never opened to me). Perhaps the most insidious problem was that these men never considered that the door should be opened, which made me continually question whether it should be myself—a significant problem for a young woman.

When I applied to graduate school in the 1967–68 academic year, I was asked questions that no graduate school would dare ask today. [Ivy League institution] wanted to know what my husband was going to do if I came and [another Ivy League institution] wanted to know if I was on the pill! I was the first person ever hired by the ... department at the [large public institution], starting in the fall 1973. At least half the department didn't want me there and made it abundantly clear to me. The experience sent me to [another institution] to study [a different discipline].

I was the first woman hired as faculty in two different [science] departments. Until other women were hired, I was a constant "spectacle" and source of jokes, innuendos, etc., especially at faculty meetings. The response of the male faculty indicated an extreme degree of nervousness and discomfort. I was the target of unwanted sexual advances by my Chair. I was not included in get-togethers and lunches with the boys. Probably the most destructive was the perception that I was the "mistress of the Chair." ... The most destructive aspect of this was the hostile response of other faculty who were certain I received preferential treatment in terms of workload, pay, promotion, etc. Consequently, other faculty shunned and responded negatively to me for about three years. Another difficulty was at the national, international as well as local level where I was put on different committees as a "token female." In many cases I had no idea what the committee was about or what the expectations were for being on this committee. In the process, I felt inadequate, alone, alienated and incompetent. Only much later did I realize that many of the men on these committees had extensive knowledge and preparation and had networked in advance. This made them seem much more competent.

I discovered that newly minted male Assistant Professors had been hired at $1000 more than the females. ... The male department chair to whom I addressed my inquiry about the salary differential explained that men needed more money to support families. He was deaf to further discussion. I was sufficiently angry to find immediately another Assistant Professor position ..., which I consequently deferred to accept an endowed one-year chair. ... Ironically, I got the chair by virtue of being a woman ... but the professor who selected (and supervised) the chair turned out to be the most blatant sexual harasser I have ever encountered. So much for my pride in blazing gender trails: it was the year from hell.

At the risk of understatement, such experiences obviously disadvantaged entry-level women and required extra effort—and courage—on their part as they struggled to establish their careers. In response to a third question, more than two-thirds (70%) of respondents reported that there were no policies early in their careers that helped them deal with such issues or helped them in general. Of the few helpful policies mentioned, the most frequent were affirmative action or the institution's attempts to achieve gender balance or salary equity, reported by 19 percent of respondents. In response to whether being a woman helped, hurt, or both as their career developed, 8 percent responded that there were no differences due to gender as their careers developed; 26 percent mentioned only ways in which they were disadvantaged; 19 percent mentioned only ways in which they were advantaged; and 46 percent mentioned both advantages and disadvantages. Most of the stated advantages involved higher visibility as the only or one of few women in their situation or being sought for affirmative action or to improve gender balance, or for positions at women's colleges. In fact, most of the advantages arose from programs or practices to remediate past inequities, whereas the disadvantages were continued biases in expectations or treatment. Two administrators expressed common versions of being both helped and hurt:

> I was recruited and hired . . . by men seeking a woman administrator for their team. But I hit the glass ceiling as vp, and watched as about half a dozen similarly placed men moved up . . . but not a single woman.

> I have been asked to be on/nominated for lots of things because of my gender, especially as a woman in science. I have often felt like a token presence in such situations, and have dealt with that feeling by being as professional as I can and ignoring the gender vibrations. Sometimes that has been easy, sometimes, when facing overt hostility or distain, very difficult and painful. But I have felt it was important to face and deal with this, for me, and for women who come after me. I have taken great pleasure and pride in being the dissertation sponsor of four women Ph.D. students, and have tried to be a role model woman scientist/wife/mother/administrator (crazy person). So in answer to whether it helped

or hurt, I was there when they needed women bodies and that gave me opportunities I might not have had—it helped. But I still had to deal with a very male-dominated, variably hostile environment.

Other women reported being helped by their networks or expectations of women, but also reported experiencing less consideration or power than men. In the words of two deans:

> I found women's networks immensely helpful, had wonderful friends, found support from regional and national women's studies associations and from women's caucuses within organizations . . . received grants and fellowships associated with women's studies . . . ; but mostly it was the friendships and networks! . . . Men still find it hard to listen to women and sometimes to take them as seriously as they take themselves.

> [I]n academic administration, gender helped in the appointment and subsequent promotions. It also helped in projecting a sense of integrity in my dealings with constituents. The last few years brought significant changes at the highest levels—all male, and very power oriented. These men were unable to share institutional power with administrators below their level—most certainly not when these administrators were female.

Lack of true gender neutrality was expressed by all the women who cited disadvantages, including this social science faculty member:

> Even at [large university], I was for a long time "the most senior woman." Being alone is hard. Most practices were officially gender neutral but in fact favored males (e.g., it's male to count publications, there's a male way to flaunt your achievements and show someone else is flawed). As a woman, I'm still added to some committees for balance. As a woman, I'm still treated as shrill when I object to various actions.

Changes and Constancies over the Career

Going beyond the respondents' personal experiences of inequities, I solicited their observations concerning how the overall situation of women in higher education had changed and how it had not changed over the course of their careers (Gerdes, 2006). All of the respondents who answered these two questions noted some positive changes. Identifying several changes, an associate dean stated:

> The changes for women have been significant. Affirmative Action in the academy has had an effect. A more open and democratic process of evaluation and review also has changed things significantly. Having more women in professional positions has halted the "token woman" issues at least in the Arts and Sciences. There seems to be more support and understanding of family issues.

The majority (53%) of respondents cited increased numbers of women or increased access to positions and leadership opportunities. Changes in sensitivity, perceptions, or acceptance regarding women in higher education, including women's own beliefs, were cited by 43 percent. Overt, observable changes in institutions' policies or individuals' behavior were cited by 42 percent. Many women stated interrelationships among these types of changes (e.g., increased numbers yielding greater acceptance); and the belief that women have helped themselves was implicit in many answers. For example, one president included numbers of women, perceptions of women's situation, and affirmative action, as well as emphasizing women's own influence:

Most obviously, there are many more mentors for women these days and much more has been studied and written about the experience of women in academe. It's hard to emerge from graduate school, in particular, without a keen understanding of the challenges ahead and also the resources available. More women occupy senior roles and provide models for others as well as the ability to change institutional cultures. The importance of women's studies is established. Affirmative Action had much to do with this positive evolution. Descriptions of positive changes often included qualifications. Mixed feelings by one faculty member were expressed as, "More women are being hired, more women are being asked to compromise themselves for success, more women are resisting." Addressing leadership, one president stated, "Women are more frequently (but not THAT much more frequently) in positions of leadership." An associate provost provided another less-than-enthusiastic example: "Many more institutions now consider women as appropriate candidates for senior positions; in some cases, women are treated equitably. My current institution is on the low end of the equitable continuum."

Consistent with such qualifications, more than two-thirds (69%) of the respondents cited remaining bias against women in addressing the separate question on factors that had not changed. Aside from the most commonly mentioned bias, salary inequities (mentioned by 15% of respondents), most of the biases described were not overt discrimination but less obvious biases intrinsic to higher education as a traditionally masculine enterprise. Examples of phrases used by several women follow: subtle or underground discrimination; male rules, male standards, or male hierarchy; glass ceiling; having to work harder or be better in order to succeed; and tenure, promotion, or advancement being harder to achieve. In addition, almost half (46%) of the respondents cited unchanged family issues, such as balancing career with family or personal demands, childcare problems, lack of family-friendly policies, conflict of the tenure clock with prime childbearing years, and two-career problems. Many discussed conflict between work and family roles as irresolvable given real time constraints; others pointed to traditional expectations that make this role conflict worse for women than men. Some also looked to institutions for changes in their expectations, such as this science faculty member, who stated:

> Child care is still an issue . . . It is still not acceptable for fathers to be the primary care-givers or even to be active sharing care-givers—this is not an issue for women per se but for families. Institutions have not changed their expectations of faculty, which may have been more appropriate when women were unmarried or men had full-time wives at home, but are now unrealistic.

In addition to the two major constancies reported, remaining bias and family issues, 24 percent of women pointed out greater underrepresentation of women in nontraditional disciplinary areas, in leadership positions, or for non-white and lesbian women.

Personal Challenges

Positive changes and remaining barriers in higher education together constituted the general background for these women as they progressed through their own unique careers. Additional questions (Gerdes, 2003b) dealt with each woman's experience of difficulties in her own career. One question asked whether factors in the respondent's personal life, such as family, made it easier or harder for her to succeed in her career. A related question asked whether the career had made it necessary to give up or compromise other goals in the respondent's life. On the first question, answers were split: 37 percent harder, 31 percent easier, and 33 percent neither or both harder and easier. The fairly even split obscures the overwhelmingly negative effect *on careers* reported for children, in spite of the many women who carefully stated that their *lives overall* were better due to their children. Negative effects of having children on their careers or advantages of being childless were mentioned by almost two-thirds (65%), who cited delay in the career, lower mobility, less time devoted to career, and lower productivity. A dean's answer exemplifies some of these perceptions:

> Having children definitely made it harder for me to go "up the ladder" in my career. It took me longer to complete the work to get to the rank of full professor. I postponed going into administration until my children were older. Nevertheless, I have no regrets. My role as a mother is crucially important to me, and to this day, my children would come before my job if I were forced to choose. Fortunately, I feel that I have been able to combine career and motherhood. Having a supportive spouse has been tremendously helpful, but despite his support, the major responsibility for child-rearing was definitely mine.

Anticipated difficulties generally did not prevent women who wanted children from having them; being a mother was mentioned in answering these two questions by 66 percent of the women, and only 14 percent of those answering the question on sacrificing other goals for the career mentioned not having children or having only one child as a consequence of their careers. Although the survey did not specifically ask whether respondents had a spouse or partner, various answers indicated that at least 85 percent and possibly as many as 93 percent of respondents had at some point been married or had domestic partners. Negative effects on the career, such as lack of mobility, antinepotism rules, commuting or moving to follow a spouse/ partner, or time or attention needed by the partner, were cited by 20 percent of the respondents. On the other hand, 39 percent reported that their spouse's or partner's support facilitated their success. Only 11 percent of the respondents described divorce or loss of a long-term relationship or difficulty forming committed relationships as a sacrifice due to their careers. Overall, 67 percent of the women who answered the question on sacrifices reported that they had given up or compromised other goals due to their careers; 29 percent believed that they had not done so; and the rest were uncertain. Notwithstanding the life-altering problems of maintaining committed relationships and limitations on having children, the most commonly reported sacrifices were simply reduced time for other life goals: for family (spouse/partner, children, or both), reported by 26 percent, and for personal interests and social life, reported by 18 percent. One faculty member emphatically addressed both:

> I've had to deal nervously with my kids. ["Hurry Up!!"] My male colleagues have wives, if they have children; their wives either handle, or organize, home and family. I also have missed out on developing friendships. NO TIME! [I WANT A WIFE!]

Respondents were asked to rate the degree of stress in their current positions (which generally constituted their highest level of advancement and leadership) from very low to very high. Administrators reported extremely high stress, averaging 4.2 (between high and very high). Faculty members reported considerable but significantly lower stress, averaging 3.6 (between moderate and high), although it should be noted that several mentioned that their stress had been higher earlier in their careers when their jobs were less secure and career and childrearing demands overlapped. Of those reporting sources of stress, 56 percent of faculty members and 48 percent of administrators mentioned time/workload pressures. Specifically, faculty members emphasized difficulty balancing teaching, research, service, and occasional administrative commitments; whereas administrators described the simple but severe situation of too much work for the time available. Another large category of stressors for administrators was responsibilities to others and for others, others' expectations, and interpersonal conflict, reported by 56 percent of administrators as compared to 31 percent of faculty members. Examples of both time pressure and interpersonal stress are illustrated by this provost's answer:

Sources of stress, include, in random order: responsibility for faculty with problems both inside and outside the classroom, that are resistant to solution but need to be solved; too much work and too little staff support; no time to do things carefully or right; negative personnel decisions; e-mail.

In answering another question about their greatest sources of dissatisfaction or disappointment in their careers (Gerdes, 2010), 30 percent of these senior women returned to the issue of time: time pressure, workload, lack of time to do everything well or to have a balanced life. The other large category of dissatisfaction/disappointment was lack of support for themselves or their agendas on the personal level, the institutional level, or the level of higher education or society (such as lack of respect for women or women's issues in academe, too few senior women, society's negative opinion of discipline or academe, backlash against affirmative action), reported by 31 percent. This was the most frequent source of dissatisfaction identified by the least satisfied women—those who rated their overall satisfaction with their careers as moderate, low, or very low.

Accomplishments

Although the barriers remaining in higher education and the challenges faced over the span of these women's careers must not be forgotten, their successes overcoming those negative factors moved them into positions of influence and moved higher education in the direction of equity for women (Gerdes, 2010). In spite of high stress and willingness to identify some dissatisfactions, these women leaders expressed high overall satisfaction with their careers, averaging between high and very high (4.3) on a scale from very low to very high. In fact, 86 percent of these women rated their satisfaction with their careers as either high or very high. When asked to list their accomplishments, the answers of current faculty members and administrators naturally diverged. Excellent teaching, including mentoring, or scholarly achievements were mentioned by 87 percent of faculty members and 44 percent of administrators. Many answers made clear that these were innovations rather than traditional academic successes. One faculty member's answer is a good example of teaching and research innovations as well as a programmatic accomplishment (a new conference):

> I have done major writing on feminist practice in [applied discipline], on rethinking research practices, and on looking more closely at curricular issues related to race and gender. I have founded (with others) a major national conference, am editor of a book series, and have established a national reputation in my field as a feminist.

Programmatic accomplishments, such as success in completing institutional projects, their role in improving their institution or the quality of education delivered, institutional or national programs that they had developed or fostered, or being effective administrators, were mentioned by 85 percent of administrators and 50 percent of faculty women. Another important category included 49 percent of administrators and 21 percent of faculty women who described their skills and style as integral to their achievements, most often using descriptors such as nurturant, cooperative, empowering others, building consensus. Looking over all the categories of accomplishments, 39 percent of women described successes in advancing women's issues or equity or diversity more broadly. These accomplished women also were asked whether their contributions would have been made by a man in the same position. The belief that some of their accomplishments might not have been made by a man was expressed explicitly or implicitly by 69 percent of the respondents; only 13 percent stated explicitly that they did not know, could not or would not compare or generalize, or that men's accomplishments were equivalent. One provost's answer illustrates a programmatic accomplishment, the dependence of this accomplishment on interpersonal skills and style, and the belief that a man would not have achieved the same result:

> One of my accomplishments, perhaps not major, as an administrator has been to repair some damaged relations between academic and administrative "branches" of the college; I suspect this was partly possible because as a woman I am less interested in fighting battles, taking stands, more willing to compromise and seek consensus, and more able to work with admittedly difficult personalities.

These senior women were also asked to consider what had motivated them over their careers, whether their goals and priorities had been any different from men on similar career paths, and whether women's issues had been a priority. Their motivations corresponded closely to their reported sources of satisfaction, which will not be reported separately. The most frequently mentioned category of motivations was the desire to make a difference, to be a change agent, to solve problems, to be of service, or to help others, reported by 57 percent of respondents. Nine (82%) of the presidents as well as 63 percent of the academic vice presidents and deans reported this motivation. One president made a keen distinction, "My goals have been more to make a difference than to make a reputation." Another president explained:

> I think I got into administration out of some desire to serve and some desire to build things. My motivations have been to create things and to see change and improvements. I am now heavily motivated by how much of a difference I can make to the institution and energized by seeing the changes I have been able to make.

More than half (53%) of these senior women mentioned their own intrinsic traits or characteristics as motivating their careers, for example, love of ideas, learning, knowledge, challenges, or desire to use talents. Another, more specific, intrinsic motivation involved love of one's discipline, teaching, and/or research, reported by 19 percent of respondents, primarily faculty members. Surprisingly, only 13 percent expressed extrinsic motivations such as ambition or desire for rewards such as money, power, status, success, or recognition. Almost three-quarters (72%) of the women who addressed whether their motivations were different from men's did report a difference, with the majority (55%) of those who reported a difference giving the opinion that men tended to be more self-interested or competitive. This difference between men and women was described in two ways: (1) men being more motivated by power, advancement, status, recognition, or money or less motivated to help others or solve problems, or (2) men having a style that is more authoritarian, competitive, or confrontational or less likely to nurture others or work collaboratively. The only answer that used both explanations provides good examples of each:

I think my teaching and research have been very much influenced by my gender and by my gradually increasing consciousness of gender issues. I think my teaching style and my interactions with students have always been, if you like, more nurturing than confrontational. ... Fame and scholarly recognition have never been a big value for me; for some reason (I suspect gender-related) I just don't seem to have the same kind of ambition my male contemporaries have.

Moreover, almost all (93%) of the women who addressed whether women's issues had been a priority stated that such issues were a priority, an interest, important, or present in their careers.

Advice

Given their own success and perceptions of improvements for women, on the one hand, combined with their stresses and sacrifices and perceptions of remaining barriers, on the other hand, were these women leaders optimistic or pessimistic about the future? As well as assessing their own careers as of the late 1990s, they were asked to look toward the future: to report what we should be teaching women students about the situation of women in institutions of higher education and what advice they would give to women beginning their careers in higher education (Gerdes, 2003a). Most women answered these questions together and gave several pieces of advice, and many gave both optimistic and pessimistic advice. The most pessimistic advice was represented by either cautions or unpleasant facts of life; almost half (47%) of respondents gave such advice. For example, women were explicitly warned to "Be wary of everyone, everything," "Be aware of negative, hidden attitudes about women in academe," or against more specific "dangers" such as getting dragged into service activities that would not count in evaluations. Facts of life were more subtle reminders of the situation for women, with descriptions of specific barriers or the inherent bias of higher education toward male issues and interests. An even higher percentage (63%) of respondents acknowledged downsides yet advised women to adopt strategies for coping with ongoing gender disadvantages or to make life choices that would facilitate success. Advice on life choices was given by 21 percent of respondents, including the 15 percent of respondents giving advice concerning marriage and family. Aside from advice about life choices, a majority (51%) of these successful women gave instrumental advice for coping with gender disadvantages, giving 73 separate pieces of advice. Most striking, given the open-ended opportunity to offer any type of advice, 35 percent of respondents mentioned mentoring and/or networking as a strategy to cope with gender disadvantages. Other coping advice from multiple respondents could be classified as follows: not thinking too much about discrimination, avoiding either being too strident a feminist/woman or emulating men, adapting to the situation in the short run to change it in the long run, and standing up for oneself. In the most optimistic answers, 53 percent of respondents proclaimed good news about higher education or offered personal wisdom. Some good news was unqualified, such as "It's a great profession," and, more fully: "There is much less of a 'glass ceiling' in academe than in almost any other profession, and more accommodation to women's special needs than in most other professions, and relatively more acknowledgement that 'women's problems' are 'people's problems.' "

Other good news was qualified but still more positive than facts of life, such as: "Excellent women can usually do about as well as excellent men in academia." Advice categorized as personal wisdom was more proscriptive and motivational than pronouncements of good news (and less strategic than coping with gender disadvantages) and included these subtypes: do what is good for oneself, identify one's own values and follow them, do what one loves, have high aspirations, work hard and excel, help others, and have fun and a sense of humor. In considering optimistic advice, it must be remembered that these respondents were successful senior women; surveying women who had left academe due to unsatisfactory experiences certainly would have changed the balance of discouraging and encouraging advice. And, as noted previously, few answers gave only optimistic advice. Advice spanning several categories and combining acknowledgement of barriers with optimism about the potential for success if those barriers are addressed was common. Such complex yet coherent advice is illustrated by two academic administrators, who advised:

> Rely on your instincts, follow your natural style, develop a strong network of other women (and men), follow the literature on leadership and gender differences, be introspective, learn to deal with situations of conflict, expect others to expect more of you.

Assume you can do it, and if you are lucky you can. Pick the right husband, if you want a husband. Try to ignore the criticism, or at least
don't take it too seriously. Find women friends, listen to other wom-
en's stories, both inside and outside academe. Do what you have to
do to get tenure; find a problem you love to work on and work very
hard on it. Don't try to change things until you are in a position of
strength; if you get to such a position, try to remember what it is like
not to have power.

The idea that women should not simply adapt to the traditionally masculine environment or measure their success by traditional male standards
was implicit in many answers, such as the above, and explicit in some
answers, such as these statements by two faculty members indicating their
reluctance to urge women to be self-serving:

If women were advised to pick the most successful male colleagues as
role models, they would in general see very self-centered individuals
who do little or nothing for their departments or institution, who dump
service and teaching on females and junior faculty, and who have
achieved top ranks and pay based on bringing in money and receiving
national recognition for scholarly activity.

I think there is a general difficulty here, in that the kinds of enthusiastic
commitments to teaching and service that women often show are really
valuable, and also are needed for the healthy functioning of the university. To encourage women to be more prudently self-concerned about
their research is, in a way, to urge them not to be so devoted to these
other aspects of university life.

This perspective on the traditional male model of success and its inap-
propriateness for academic women is not surprising. Recall that the majority of these women reported their own career motivation as serving,
helping, or producing positive change, and the majority of women who
believed men's motivations to be different described men as more self-
interested or competitive than women. It is not clear, however, whether
these senior women believe it will be as necessary for their successors to
work to advance women's issues as it was for their own cohort; in spite
of their concerns about remaining inequities and the fact that almost all

of them made women's issues a priority, very few explicitly urged younger women to work on women's issues.

Moving Forward

These women leaders overcame differential treatment and incidents in their early careers that included hostile sexism and overt discrimination as well as benevolent sexism and insensitivity (see Cikara & Fiske, 2009). Most continued to experience some disadvantages as women as their careers progressed. They were aware of the tremendous changes for women over their careers; but, unlike observers who are falsely reassured by comparisons with the past (see Schmitt, Spoor, Danaher, & Branscombe, 2009), they remained quite aware of continuing problems, particularly subtle biases and family issues. They described their own careers as balancing acts. Family demands compromised career goals, and career demands required sacrificing time for family and personal life. Dissatisfaction with time pressure/workload and with support over their careers was common. High stress levels were reported, especially by those in administrative positions; and time/workload pressures were significant for both administrators and faculty. Although their descriptions of higher education included the environmental constraints and structural barriers emphasized by many authors (e.g., Eagly & Carli, 2007; Glazer-Raymo, 1999; see also Ward & Wolf-Wendel, 2008), they described their own paths in terms of choices in their careers and personal lives. Much of their advice for the next generation of women in higher education was instrumental, including cautions about the remaining barriers but also strategies for overcoming problems as well as emphatic optimism about current prospects for women if appropriate strategies were followed. Perhaps most importantly for the future of women in higher education, these senior women's assessment of their achievements fit more with their sense of agency and optimism concerning women's progress than with their high stress and the cautionary aspect of their perceptions of higher education. A majority of them cited the desire to serve or make a difference and sought personal fulfillment in their work; most saw men's motivations as dissimilar, typically as more self-interested and competitive in seeking external rewards or recognition. Overall, these women described themselves as successful, and they did not describe themselves as having assimilated to the masculine expectations of their workplace (see Martin, 1997, 2000). Many mentioned helping women; many mentioned a collaborative, nurturing style as integral to their success and as different from their typical male colleagues. In short, they described their motivations and accomplishments in terms more consistent with the advantages of transformational models of leadership than with more stereotypically masculine models of leadership (see Eagly, 2005; Eagly & Carli, 2003, 2007). Indeed, these women leaders, who now have either retired or are near the end of their careers, transformed the terrain of higher education. Their sacrifices and unselfish motivations should be a reminder to women rising to leadership positions in higher education today. However, caution still is appropriate. Although women working in higher education have come a long way toward equity since the 1970s, a stubborn gender gap remains. The improvement in women's representation in faculty and administrative positions, although forced by affirmative action in the 1970s, was facilitated by dramatic expansion in professional positions in American higher education—full-time equivalent professional positions increased 63 percent between 1976 and 1997, when responses were collected for this study, and increased another 41 percent between 1997 and 2007 (NCES, 2010). In comparison, the percentages of full-time faculty and administrators who were women increased less than 1 percent per year, on average, over the same period. And it can be argued that progress has been slowing relative to the increasing number of women in the higher education pipeline. That is, women have been the majority of undergraduate students since 1978 and the majority of post-baccalaureate students since 1988; most relevant to academic positions, the proportion of doctoral degrees awarded to women has increased steadily, surpassing the number awarded to men in 2006–2007 (NCES, 2010). Notwithstanding improvement in the pipeline, women still lag in advancement and leadership. Women are most underrepresented in full-time positions, tenure-track and tenured positions, higher faculty ranks, higher administrative positions, traditionally male fields in the faculty or administration, and more prestigious institutions; and women earn less than men in comparable positions (Glazer-Raymo, 1999, 2008; NCES, 2010). In the absence of the compensatory mechanisms of earlier times, women will have trouble climbing out of the bottom of the distribution onto the leadership track in this era of retrenchment. Women are held back by institutions' increasing reliance on part-time and temporary positions to reduce expenses and by other aspects of commercialization, or academic capitalism, that favor traditionally male fields and market-driven decisions (Glazer-Raymo, 2008; Metcalfe & Slaughter, 2008). Wise women predicted such problems in 1997: "I am troubled by how fast and to what extent society's support for affirmative action has shifted—and what this may mean in terms of few opportunities for women and minorities." "But it could go bad, with retrenchment—no hiring and the over-reliance on lecturers." "Individual situations may be better, . . . but collectively we still fight the same battles." Nevertheless, general lack of awareness of current inequities is suggested not only by the backlash against affirmative action and other remedial measures (Glazer-Raymo, 2008) but also by lack of attention to women's issues in the major higher education journals (Hart, 2006). It is much easier to believe that the playing field is now level and women's problems in higher education have been successfully resolved. Fortunately, projects such as the current volume can reveal continuing disadvantages for women and additional paths to leadership as well as drawing attention to women's impressive accomplishments.

References

Astin, H. S., & Snyder, M. B. (1982). Affirmative action 1972–1982: A decade of response. *Change, 14*(5), 26–31, 59.

Boxer, M. J. (1998). *When women ask the questions: Creating women's studies in America.* Baltimore: Johns Hopkins.

Cikara, M., & Fiske, S. T. (2009). Warmth, competence, and ambivalent sexism: Vertical assault and collateral damage. In M. Barreto, M. K. Ryan, & M. T. Schmitt (Eds.), *The glass ceiling in the 21st century: Understanding barriers to gender equality* (pp. 73–96). Washington, DC: American Psychological Association.

Eagly, A. H. (2005). Achieving relational authenticity: Does gender matter? *Leadership Quarterly, 16,* 459–74.

Eagly, A. H., & Carli, L. L. (2003). The female leadership advantage: An evaluation of the evidence. *Leadership Quarterly, 14,* 807–34.

Eagly, A. H., & Carli, L. L. (2007). *Through the labyrinth: The truth about how women become leaders.* Boston: Harvard Business School.

Gerdes, E. P. (2003a). Do it your way: Advice from senior academic women. *Innovative Higher Education, 27,* 253–76.

Gerdes, E. P. (2003b, Spring). The price of success: Senior academic women's stress and life choices. *Advancing Women in Leadership Journal.* Retrieved June 1, 2010 from http://www.advancingwomen.com/awl/spring2003/GERDES%7E1.HTML.

Gerdes, E. P. (2006, Summer). Women in higher education since 1970: The more things change, the more they stay the same. *Advancing Women in Leadership Journal.* Retrieved June 2, 2010 from http://www.advancingwomen.com/awl/summer2006/Gerdes.html.

Gerdes, E. P. (2010). We did it our way: Motivations, satisfactions, and accomplishments of senior academic women. *Advancing Women in Leadership Journa, 30* (21). Retrieved November 23, 2010 from http://advancingwomen.com/awl/awl_wordpress/.

Glazer-Raymo, J. (1999). *Shattering the myths: Women in academe.* Baltimore: Johns Hopkins.

Glazer-Raymo, J. (2008). The feminist agenda: A work in progress. In J. Glazer-Raymo (Ed.), *Unfinished agendas: New and continuing challenges in higher education* (pp. 1–34). Baltimore: Johns Hopkins.

Gobo, G. (2004). Sampling, representativeness, and generalizability. In C. Seale, G. Gobo, J. F. Gubrium, & D. Silverman (Eds.), *Qualitative research practice* (pp. 435–56). Thousand Oaks, CA: Sage.

Hart, J. (2006). Women and feminism in higher education scholarship: An analysis of three core journals. *Journal of Higher Education, 77,* 40–61.

Kitzinger, C. (2004). Feminist approaches. In C. Seale, G. Gobo, J. F. Gubrium, & D. Silverman (Eds.), *Qualitative research practice* (pp. 125–40). Thousand Oaks, CA: Sage.

Marshall, K., & Rossman, G. B. (2006). *Designing qualitative research* (4th ed.). Thousand Oaks, CA: Sage.

Martin, J. R. (1997). Bound for the promised land: The gendered character of higher education. *Duke Journal of Gender Law & Policy, 4*(3), 3–26.

Martin, J. R. (2000). *Coming of age in academe: Rekindling women's hopes and reforming the academy.* New York: Routledge.

Metcalfe, A. S., & Slaughter, S. (2008). The differential effects of academic capitalism on women in the academy. In J. Glazer-Raymo (Ed.),

Unfinished agendas: New and continuing challenges in higher education (pp. 80–111). Baltimore: Johns Hopkins.

National Center for Education Statistics. (1998). *E. D. tabs: Fall staff in postsecondary institutions, 1995,* NCES 98-228, by S. Roey & R. Rak. Washington, DC: U.S. Department of Education. Retrieved July 26, 2010 from http://nces.ed.gov/pubs98/98228.pdf.

National Center for Education Statistics. (2010). *Digest of education statistics 2009*, NCES 2010-013, by T. D. Snyder & S. A. Dillow. Washington, DC: U.S. Department of Education. Retrieved July 26, 2010 from http://nces.ed.gov/pubs2010/2010013.pdf.

Patton, M. Q. (2002). *Qualitative research and evaluation methods* (3rd ed.). Newbury Park, CA: Sage.

Schmitt, M. T., Spoor, J. R., Danaher, K., & Branscombe, N. R. (2009). Rose-colored glasses: How tokenism and comparisons with the past reduce the visibility of gender inequality. In M. Barreto, M. K. Ryan, & M. T. Schmitt (Eds.), *The glass ceiling in the 21st century: Understanding barriers to gender equality* (pp. 49–72). Washington, DC: American Psychological Association.

Ward, K., & Wolf-Wendel, L. (2008). Choice and discourse in faculty careers: Feminist perspectives on work and family. In J. Glazer-Raymo (Ed.), *Unfinished agendas: New and continuing challenges in higher education* (pp. 253–72). Baltimore: Johns Hopkins.

2

Historical Constructs of Gender and Work: Informing Access and Equity in U.S. Higher Education

Amber L. Vlasnik

In recent years, administrators, the press, scholars, and the public have paid increased attention to women's changing demographics in U.S. higher education. Now the majority of two-year and four-year college students, women have moved in large numbers into almost all sectors of higher education since the 1970s (Snyder, Dillow, & Hoffman, 2009). They have also moved in greater numbers into the workforce, with 59.5 percent of all women working in 2008 (U.S. Department of Labor, 2009); of these women laborers aged 25 to 64, 36 percent have college degrees, a percentage that has more than tripled from 11 percent in 1970 (U.S. Department of Labor, 2009).

Women have clearly gained momentum both in college enrollment and the postgraduation labor force since the 1970s, and institutions of higher education have been deeply affected by their presence. In the words of Wilkerson (1989):

> On one hand, colleges and universities, unprepared for this radical change [majority women], have felt beleaguered by a staggering range of new demands, from curriculum reform to child care, while on the other hand, women—claiming a subtle form of gender apartheid—often find themselves treated as a minority, despite their greater numbers. (p. 27)

The higher education literature has explored the various experiences of women and men and the implications for their shifting demographics in the academy (e.g., Allen, Dean, & Bracken, 2008; Pearson, Shavlik, & Touchton, 1989; Sax, 2008); however, institutional responses to changing student demographics have ranged widely. While some campuses have enacted few or no changes in how students are taught, served, or supported, others have become concerned with how to better provide programs and services for men, who find themselves in the minority on most college campuses.

Through my work in campus-based women's centers, I participate in conversations that cover this range of reactions, during which I typically express concern for continued gender inequity despite women's growing numbers. In these discussions, I generally raise three points: First, we must identify which women and men we are discussing and attend to how intersecting identities change access and equity in higher education; second, the *quantity* of women in higher education is a different discussion than the *quality* of their experiences, and; third, the many histories of women's access to higher education are critical to understanding their current status, opportunities, and challenges.

This final point is the central focus of this chapter, which evolves from my interest in understanding higher education's shifting demographics as part of an ongoing journey for women and men. While much attention has been given to the result—women becoming the numerical majority—I want to focus on the historical contexts that continue to inform and shape women's experiences in higher education today as well as the social and historical dialogues about women and work that affect their lives. I believe that this understanding is critical for higher education administrators dedicated to women's success, particularly as administrators who witnessed firsthand and often advocated for the great changes in women's higher education since the 1970s are retiring and younger professionals are filling their roles. As younger women dedicated to careers in higher education, we must understand the histories, complexities, and contexts for the higher education structures, policies, and practices we are inheriting, particularly as they relate to our diverse women students.

In order to pursue this understanding, this chapter will examine how arguments about gender and labor roles have determined U.S. women's exclusion from or acceptance to the academy in the twentieth century. Feminist theory helps provide a framework for understanding this history;

specifically, I employ materialist feminist theory as an analytical lens through which to recognize and understand the roles of gender and work in determining possibilities for women's participation in higher education in the twentieth century. The chapter begins with a discussion of the three most common structural means of educating women in the 1900s—women's colleges, annexes, and coeducation—as well as how legislation changed educational opportunities for women. The chapter continues with exploration of period arguments about women and work, as well as how these arguments influenced access and experiences in higher education. The chapter concludes with implications for current practice as it relates to serving women, our new majority in higher education.

As a final note, I continue my commitment to being explicit about "which women" by focusing this chapter on the experiences of and arguments surrounding educational opportunities for black and white women. Regularly compared in contemporary higher education, black and white women represent demographic groups that experienced wide gaps in labor and educational opportunities for most of United States history due to slavery, racism, discrimination, and the institutionalization of white privilege. I focus on these two groups of women knowing that I cannot do justice to their incredible diversity of class, age, sexual orientation, ability, and leadership styles in this chapter. However, my goal is to complicate and interrupt current discussions about women in higher education, which often ignore women's immense diversity and their many intersecting identities, as well as their sometimes drastically different histories in the academy.

Women, Education, and Work in the Twentieth Century

Women's Colleges, Annexes, and Coeducation: Strategies for the Education of Women

In an essay posthumously published in a volume with her husband (Palmer & Palmer, 1908), Alice Freeman Palmer wrote about the options for women's higher education at the beginning of the twentieth century:

> These, then—coeducation, the woman's college, and the annex—are the three great types of college in which the long agitation in behalf of women's education has thus far issued. Of course they are but types—that

is, they do not always exist distinct and entire; they are rather the central forms to which many varieties approximate. (Palmer, 1908, p. 319)

Palmer's viewpoint for her naming and analysis of these three forms of women's education is unique, for she was intimately acquainted with these three forms of women's education. One of the first women graduates of the University of Michigan in 1876, Palmer's own college years were coeducational. She taught at and later became the second president of Wellesley College from 1881–1887 (Wellesley College, 2009), a women's college. After her marriage to Harvard professor George Herbert Palmer—through which she became acquainted with the Harvard Annex (Palmer, 1908)—Palmer was heavily pursued by University of Chicago president William Rainey Harper to become Dean of Women (Schwartz, 1997). She accepted the post in 1892 after negotiating an arrangement in which she would work part time and commute between Chicago and Boston, becoming "the first significant appointment of a woman to be a dean of women" (Schwartz, 1997, p. 506). Her unusual career as a professor and administrator who advocated for the education of women is often forgotten in the history books, but her words, at the beginning of the twentieth century, remain largely accurate descriptions of the higher educational opportunities for women during the past 100 years. These three options for structuring the education of women are the focus of this section, which will explore them in turn.

Women's Colleges

While few colleges for women were in operation before the Civil War, by 1900 there were an estimated 150 women's colleges (Rudolph, 1962); in 1960, women's colleges peaked at an estimated 300 institutions (Wolf-Wendel, 2003). This leap in educational opportunity was in part due to increased encouragement for women to earn a college degree. However, women's colleges also benefited from generous donors. In the rising philanthropic atmosphere of higher education in the late 1800s, women's colleges such as Vassar secured founding donations, and many others received sizeable gifts (Thelin, 2004). Westward expansion also accounted for the founding of many women's colleges in the Midwest and West.

The first generation of graduates from women's colleges finished their studies in the 1880s. As undergraduates, students at women's colleges:

... played aggressive team sports, organized meetings, politicked among classmates, handled budgets, solicited advertisements. For men, such elements of college life confirmed patterns of socialization that led to the world of business; for women, learning the routes of power contrasted with feminine upbringing and led to no known future. (Horowitz, 1987, p. 197)

As a result of the skills practiced through their undergraduate opportunities, many of the women college graduates participated in public life. Jane Addams, founder of the Hull House in Chicago and Nobel Peace Prize winner, was an 1881 Rockford College graduate. An 1880 Vassar graduate, Julia Lathrop, became Chief of the Children's Bureau at the U.S. Department of Education. Sophonisba Breckinridge, an 1888 Wellesley College alumna, was Vice President of the National American Woman's Suffrage Association and president of several social workers' organizations. Even if subsequent generations of graduates might not have exhibited the same social agenda (Gordon, 1990), these women and other women's college alumnae led the first generation of women's college graduates in fighting for social justice and women's rights (Harwarth, Maline, & DeBra, 1997).

The first classes of women graduates, in particular, saw falling marriage rates for college women. From 1880 to 1900, almost half of all women graduates did not marry, a number in stark contrast to similarly aged, non-college-educated women who averaged a marriage rate of almost 90 percent (Horowitz, 1987). Higher education created financial opportunities that lessened the economic need for marriage, exactly the intent of society when it pushed women to attend college after the Civil War. Horowitz (1987) illustrates the choice of some college-educated women: "They could enter into the female community of reformers and professional women, a subculture that provided them with companionship and love and respected their choices and achievements" (p. 198). However, some male detractors proclaimed that women's colleges were producing too many spinsters. Palmieri (1997) explains, "They believed the women's colleges were 'institutions for the promotion of celibacy,' producing a disappearing class of intellectual women who were not marrying and hence were committing race suicide" (p. 177).

Also important to note is that women's colleges in the late nineteenth century and early twentieth century achieved a reputation for educating the privileged elite. While some women from lower-income families and

African American women attended women's colleges, the campuses of women's colleges were largely for economically privileged white women. Perkins (in Thelin, 2004) estimates that the Seven Sisters—Barnard, Bryn Mawr, Mount Holyoke, Radcliffe, Smith, Vassar, Wellesley—graduated more than 10,000 women but only a few hundred African American women before World War II. While early women's colleges encouraged women's higher education opportunities, they primarily benefited white women.

There are two notable exceptions: Bennett and Spelman Colleges and their missions to advance the education of black women. Founded in 1881, Spelman College is the oldest institution for the education of black women in the United States (Guy-Sheftall & Bell-Scott, 1989; Tidball, Smith, Tidball, & Wolf-Wendel, 1999). Bennett College was founded in 1873 as a coeducational institution but became a women's college in 1926 after experiencing financial difficulties that led to its reorganization (Tidball et al., 1999). The only two colleges to carry the distinction of being both women's colleges and HBCUs (Historically Black Colleges and Universities), Spelman and Bennett Colleges provided environments where the success and education of black women were the primary mission (Gary, 2008; Guy-Sheftall & Bell-Scott, 1989; Tidball et al., 1999).

Overall, women's colleges contribute important lessons to the successful higher education of women. Wolf-Wendel (2003) describes how higher education can benefit from the seven successful actions of women's colleges to "clarify and communicate a mission that puts women at the center," "believe women can achieve and hold them to high expectations," "make students feel like they matter," "provide strong, positive role models," "provide ample opportunities for women to engage in leadership activities," "include women in the curriculum," and "create safe spaces in which women can form a critical mass" (p. 41). Wolf-Wendel argues that women's colleges have a future in higher education because they continue to be effective at creating "structures, policies, practices and curriculum that are attuned to the needs of women" (p. 49), and that coeducational institutions can learn from these successes.

Annexes, Affiliate, and Coordinate Campuses

At the end of the nineteenth century, a new phenomenon began to occur at the leading white U.S. institutions: affiliate campuses for women, which were sometimes called annexes or coordinate campuses. Rather than admit women, universities opted to create a separate campus for them, usually geographically connected to the parent institution. By sponsoring an affiliate campus, colleges and universities could simultaneously accommodate women students and keep them separate from men.

One of the first affiliate campuses was at Harvard, which though it was founded in 1636 and had educated African American men since 1865 (Titcomb, 1993), chose to create the Harvard Annex in 1879 rather than admit women. Despite its name, "the Annex" had no official affiliation with the university; rather, it was started by thirteen Harvard faculty members who agreed to repeat their lectures to groups of female students but had no authority to grant Harvard degrees or honors (Schwager, 2004). However, this distinction was not clearly made to the public, and most regarded the Harvard Annex as an important step for women in higher education, even though Harvard officials had no intention to admit women. In 1894, the Annex was rechartered by the state and named Radcliffe College, which had permission to grant degrees to women (Morison, 1936). The college admitted black women, and in 1898 Alberta V. Scott became Radcliffe's first black graduate (Titcomb, 1993); regardless, Radcliffe women were still denied a Harvard education and degree.

Major universities across the United States began to follow Harvard's lead, and affiliate institutions such as H. Sophie Newcomb Memorial College in 1886 (affiliated with Tulane University) and Pembroke College (affiliated with Brown University shortly after they admitted women in 1891) were founded in the late 1800s (Brubacher & Rudy, 1997). Overall, affiliate campuses for women helped to bridge the divide between men's colleges and the admission of women: It became only a matter of time before financial concerns and societal pressure encouraged most institutions to combine their campuses into one. In the case of Harvard and Radcliffe, discussed earlier, Harvard admitted women in 1943 (President and Fellows of Harvard College, 2007), when war made their admission a financial necessity (Faust, 2004). Yet women in Harvard's entering class of 1999 were the first women since Harvard-Radcliffe's wartime agreement to be admitted to Harvard proper, instead of Harvard-Radcliffe (Faust, 2004). Many of the former annexes or affiliate campuses—as evidenced in the case of Harvard and Radcliffe—had long histories with their institutions, and many continue today, transformed into institutes for research on women or to promote women's advanced study.

Coeducation

When Oberlin College was founded in 1833, it was the first institution of higher education to admit both women and students of color (Oberlin College, 2007). However, many decades passed before coeducation could be considered even remotely mainstream. The opportunities for coeducation first took hold in the pioneering American West: in 1872 there were ninety-seven coeducational colleges in the United States, and sixty-seven of them were in the West (Rudolph, 1962). By the early twentieth century, these opportunities were beginning to mainstream: In 1910 only 27 percent of U.S. institutions of higher education barred women from entering; twenty years later, only 15 percent barred entrance to women (Carnegie Commission on Higher Education, 1973).

The mass movement to coeducation in the twentieth century affected former women's colleges differently than men's institutions. According to Thelin (2004), all-men institutions gained the best and brightest women candidates, who would have otherwise attended women's colleges. Women's colleges that chose to become coeducational not only lost their best women candidates but also experienced male candidates with lower academic qualifications; this phenomenon was widely noted at Vassar (Thelin, 2004), which admitted men in 1969 (Vassar College, n.d.).

Coeducation was not without its difficulties. It quickly became apparent that while universities might open their doors to women, this did not necessarily indicate that campus climates were welcoming (Brubacher & Rudy, 2003; Wolf-Wendel, 2003). Women struggled during the beginning years of coeducation to fit into campus structures that were not designed to accommodate them and to interact with men who were not accustomed to women's presence. While women were present on campus in the early 1900s, they were unlikely to achieve leadership positions on campus (Miller-Bernal, 2004) and often were "tracked" into certain academic programs or discouraged from others (Thelin, 2004). Furthermore, coeducational institutions often did not provide equitable resources to women students, such as the housing opportunities, medical care, and physical education facilities that they offered to male students (Nidiffer, 2003). Poulson and Miller-Bernal (2004) write, "It was as though women were expected to fit into the existing situation without disturbing the status quo" (p. 312).

Clearly, the road to coeducation was not quickly or easily traveled and institutions created various strategies for serving women students.

Beginning in the early to mid 1800s at institutions like Oberlin and Antioch, coeducational institutions appointed deans of women to look after the unmarried women students (Nidiffer, 2003). While the administration largely viewed the Dean of Women as disciplinarian and watchperson in these early years, the position evolved in the late 1800s to demand the deans' responsibility for meeting women's educational and college-related needs (Brooks, 1988; Nidiffer, 2003). Deans of women were focused professionals committed to doing their best for women on campus. Schwartz (1997) explains:

> Far from "spinsterly battle axes," the first deans were well-respected academic women who had committed themselves to their disciplines. While they were determined to provide counsel and support to young women, they also focused on the prerequisites of scholarship as the road to respect in academe. Accordingly, the early deans wrote books, conducted research, published articles, and established professional associations. In turn, the associations developed journals and held annual conferences for the further dissemination of knowledge and the advancement of the profession. (p. 509)

After years of debate, the positions "Dean of Men" and "Dean of Women" were recombined in the 1950s and 1960s, often with deans of men assuming the title of "Dean of Students" (Brooks, 1988). Schwartz (1997) claims that "in many respects, coeducation was successful because of the work of the deans of women" (p. 518), illustrating the importance and legacy of their roles on campus.

As deans of women faded into the annals of higher education, women's centers were beginning to be founded on college campuses in the 1960s and 1970s as a result of the women's movement and as a response to the continued difficulties with the incorporation of women into previously men's institutions of higher education (Clevenger, 1988). The link between deans of women and women's centers is important to note. Brooks (1988) calls deans of women "the foremothers of the women's centers of today" (p. 20), though she describes deans of women and women's centers as having parallel goals rather than centers becoming the new deans of women. Women's centers were founded with the goal "to provide or help institutions to provide programs and services which would enable women to achieve equity in all aspects of their education, work, and life" (Gould, 1989, p. 219).

While there is no one model of a women's center, women's centers tend to serve women in five key categories: safety, education and awareness, support and advocacy, equity, and community (Kunkel, 1994, 2002); additional foci include leadership, internationalization, and technology (Davie, 2002). Despite the enormous diversity among the more than 500 campus women's centers across the nation today (National Women's Studies Association, n.d.), women's centers share commitments to the success and equity of women. For example, the Women's Centers Committee of the Southwestern Ohio Council on Higher Education and the Greater Cincinnati Consortium of Colleges and Universities recently engaged in a writing project to develop their shared statement of philosophy:

> Women's centers reflect the unique needs of their institutions and communities, yet share a commitment to historically underserved individuals and groups. Additionally, women's centers play a leadership role in understanding the changing workplace and preparing members of the university community to engage successfully with an increasingly complex world. Women's centers are integral to transforming institutions into inclusive environments; through community-building, advocacy, education, support, and research, they encourage the full participation and success of women. (Vlasnik, 2010)

The philosophy statement delineates women's centers' commitments to expanding opportunities for women students and creating more inclusive institutions. Their commitment to women of color, one of many historically underserved groups, is also reflected in the statement, and women's centers have employed varying strategies for serving women of color in the academy (see Buford, 1988; DiLapi & Gay, 2002).

Women's centers and other units and individuals working for women's equity in coeducational settings were aided by several key court cases and legislative actions in the mid to late 1900s, particularly related to integration. While the twentieth century saw advances for women in the areas of women's colleges, annexes, and coeducation, these advances differed based on race. Black higher education was slowed by decades of segregation, institutionalized racism, and underfunding. While private black colleges were growing in numbers and the law mandated state support for black education, only Alabama, Maryland, North Carolina, and Virginia had established institutions funded with tax dollars for African Americans prior to 1900 (Anderson, 2002); however, these institutions were "colleges" and "universities" in name only, as their curricula and facilities did not measure up to white institutions of higher education (Anderson, 2002). In the 1900s, legislation meant to open higher education opportunities, such as the GI Bill, actually did little to help African Americans who served in the armed forces: the bill made no provisions for nondiscrimination, and African American veterans (some of who were, presumably, women) were not granted access to white public institutions (Thelin, 2004). On the other hand, black veteran enrollment at HBCUs increased dramatically in the postwar years, spurring considerable growth for HBCUs as well as straining their finite resources (Wilson, 2008).

It wasn't until the 1954 *Brown v. Board of Education* decision that there was a legal foundation for equal education according to race. The majority opinion of the Court reads, "We conclude that in the field of public education the doctrine of 'separate but equal' has no place. Separate educational facilities are inherently unequal" (*Brown v. Board of Education*, 1954). When the Supreme Court remanded *Hawkins v. Board of Control* to the Florida Supreme Court in 1956, the *Brown* decision was applied to higher education. *Hawkins* addressed the complaints of African American students who applied to the University of Florida Law School and were denied admission based on race; the Florida ruling stipulated that qualified candidates, regardless of race, must be admitted to the program (*Hawkins v. Board of Control*, 1956). These two cases laid the legal groundwork for the integration of public educational institutions.

It was the Civil Rights Act of 1964, however, that enforced these court rulings at public institutions, making higher education at previously white institutions a possibility for African American students (Teddlie & Freeman, 2002). Overall African American enrollment increased dramatically in the years that followed. Nonetheless, Allen and Jewell's 1968 study noted that 80 percent of all African American undergraduates still received degrees from HBCUs (in Anderson, 2002). While advances were made for African Americans, black men benefited disproportionately from these cases, as black women still faced discrimination based on their gender.

A final piece of legislation, Title IX of the Education Amendments (1972), gave legal footing to gender-based inequities in higher education. Title IX states, "No person in the United States shall, on the basis of sex, be excluded from participation in, be denied the benefits of, or be subjected to discrimination under any educational program or activity receiving Federal financial assistance . . ." (Education Amendments, 1972). While Title IX is most famous for its application in the area of collegiate sports, the act was not created merely to facilitate women's movement onto the court, green, or field or into the pool; rather, Title IX intended to remove barriers to women's participation in all aspects of federally funded programs and events.

Varying institutional structures, administrators and units dedicated to serving women, legislation, and court cases—there were many challenges and advances in women's access to higher education in the twentieth century. These changes often paralleled discussions of women's roles as laborers in the home and the market. The next section explores women, work, and their relationships with higher education.

"Working Women" and the Academy

While women have always worked, the term *working women* took on new meaning in the twentieth century. These social changes regarding women and work informed the continuing debate about women's participation in higher education. This section highlights major changes regarding women, labor, and family, as well as discusses how the identities of "working women" shaped women's experiences in the academy.

Women's efforts to enter more areas of the workforce were challenged by fresh debate about women's bodies and their roles as wives and mothers in the twentieth century. Changing ideas about family size were important to the debate. Between 1800 and 1900, the average number of children born to white women fell from 7 to 3.5 due to advances in birth control methods over the course of the century (Cott, 1994). In the early 1900s, contraceptive options were enlarged by the work of Margaret Sanger. A nurse, sexual health advocate, and birth control pioneer, Sanger advocated medical research about contraceptives and promoted their usage among women. In 1920 she wrote, "Millions of women are asserting their right to voluntary motherhood. They are determined to decide for themselves whether they shall become mothers, under what conditions and when" (p. 5). Despite a general sense that lowering marital fertility was acceptable, the use of birth control itself was highly controversial (Cott, 1994), and Sanger was censored, arrested, and fined for her teachings.

However, Sanger's radical medical and social arguments for birth control were taking hold, and college campuses reflected the changes in sexual attitudes and expectations. Thelin (2004) writes that the "college woman" between the two World Wars was considered to be in the same category of misbehaving, promiscuous women as the flapper and the "new woman." Horowitz (1987) further explains, "According to [the canons of conventional coeds] they could enjoy sexual activity—to a point—along with certain symbols of the new freedom: bobbed hair, short skirts, cigarettes, jazz, and automobiles" (p. 208). Nevertheless, the general public mistrusted these symbols, and college women were often deemed dangerous women.

Working women also fell into the category of dangerous women. Working women were "trying to have it all" by having husbands and children while also working outside the home. Women began to move in significant numbers out of the private home and into the public workforce in the twentieth century. The numbers started small, with the U.S. Census reporting in 1930 that less than 12 percent of married women worked for pay outside the home (Cott, 1994); overall, just 23.6 percent of all women were working for wages. These numbers do not reveal whether women worked full time or part time or if they had children, but regardless, women were making their mark as laborers.

World War II had a profound effect on women's work opportunities. Jacobsen (1998) explains that women moved into manufacturing positions "as men were conscripted and production of war-related goods increased . . . both to fill the slack in labor supply left by the men and as a response to both reduced income and reduced nonmarket work responsibilities" (p. 439). World War II demanded that 2.5 million women enter the workforce for the first time, 1.3 million of whom were hired by war industries (in Jacobsen, 1998). Black women, in particular, benefited from wartime labor opportunities, experiencing a rise in remuneration for their efforts as they shifted from overrepresentation in domestic work to factory jobs (Matthews, 1992).

However, when the war ended and men returned to civilian life, they were often able to reclaim their previous jobs from women because of pre-existing union agreements or because employers felt inclined to hire veterans due to their military service (Blau, Ferber, & Winkler, 1998). Women's participation in the labor market therefore suffered, as they were either laid off to make room for returning soldiers or lost their jobs due to decreasing production of wartime supplies. Just two years after the war ended, the number of working women dropped from 35.8 percent in 1945—the highest number yet seen for women—to 31.5 percent in 1947 (U.S. Census figures, cited in Blau, Ferber, & Winkler, 1998); again these numbers do not tell us if women worked full time or part time.

Materialist feminist arguments are helpful in understanding this phenomenon. Women were accepted and actually praised as workers in the labor market during the war years, but as soon as men returned to the labor market, traditional arguments about women and work resurfaced. The media largely contributed to this shift in social messages, as during the War, women were encouraged to emulate the government's propaganda icon Rosie the Riveter, whose rallying cry "We can do it!" ushered women into the factories; however, men's return to the labor force after the war resulted in many women returning to the home to engage in domestic labor and childrearing. Marriage rates soared after World War II, accompanied by a lowering of women's ages at the time of their first marriage and a rise in fertility (Jacobsen, 1998).

Veterans also displaced women on college campuses after returning from World War II. Overall, women comprised 40 percent of undergraduate enrollment in 1939 to 1940 but by 1950 composed just 32 percent of enrollment, which reveals how the GI Bill worked to "masculinize the postwar campus" (Thelin, 2004, p. 267) and made higher education, even on coeducational campuses, "a man's world once again" (Schwartz, 1997, p. 517). After veterans came to campus, "it took a certain independence of mind for a college woman to envision a future career" (Horowitz, 1987, p. 216).

Yet some women—married and unmarried, college-educated and non-college-educated—did enter the workforce. Labor force participation rates reveal that 34.5 percent of white women and 46.1 percent of black women worked in 1955 (in Blau, Ferber, & Winkler, 1998), again demonstrating the longstanding trend that more black women worked outside their homes than white women (Davis, 1981). However, Evans (1989) points out that 1950s society feared that women would abandon their "natural" roles; in order to counter this argument, working women were quick to declare the "primacy of marriage and family in professional women's lives" (p. 262).

Just one example of the emphasis on family and home life made at that time by working women is a 1956 *Fortune* magazine study of women executives in which all participants valued family above work yet believed that they could satisfactorily complete the demands of both "if they want to badly enough" (quoted in Evans, 1989, p. 262).

Despite these proclamations by working women about the importance of family, they were constantly responding to sharp criticism. In 1955, journalist Elizabeth Pope wrote in *McCall's* magazine:

> Working women have been blamed for everything from juvenile delinquency to divorce. They have been charged with neglecting their babies, bulldozing their husbands, neglecting their homes. It's hard to think of a social problem ranging from inadequate breakfasts to world unrest which someone at some time or another hasn't dumped into their laps. (1955/1999, p. 231)

College-educated women in particular faced difficulties with their careers and labor in their homes. Working women graduates often felt the need to assert their domesticity even more strongly than those who did not attend college in order to assure society that the privilege of higher education had not altered their commitment to home and family. In a seeming effort to prove that family was more important, more and more women did not finish college. By the mid-1950s, 60 percent of college women were dropping out in order to marry or to improve their chances for marriage (Friedan, 1963).

Despite this backlash against college-educated working women, marriage ages increased and birthrates began to fall beginning in 1957. The 1960 FDA approval of the birth control pill created the possibility of recreational sex without the risk of pregnancy (Evans, 1989). Sanger, in the words of Michel and Muncy (1999), "participated in creating the modern, sexualized woman, a new gender identity altogether, and one that made women seem more like men than before" (p. 119). Helen Gurley Brown's 1962 how-to book *Sex and the Single Girl* demonstrates the emergence of this modern, sexually liberated woman:

> Theoretically a "nice" single woman has no sex life. What nonsense! She has a better sex life than most of her married friends. She need

never be bored with one man per lifetime. Her choice in partners is endless and they seek *her*. They never come to her bed duty-bound. Her married friends refer to her pursuers as wolves, but actually many of them turn out to be lambs—to be shorn and worn by her. (Brown, 1962/2003, p. 7)

This book and many other publications created a new identity for single women, who for the first time could choose to postpone or reject their reproductive capacity.

In 1963, many married women received a new message as well: Betty Friedan published *The Feminine Mystique*, and millions of housewives realized that they were not alone in their feelings of loneliness, dissatisfaction, and restlessness. Arguing that the "happy housewife" was a myth created by society and a mask for the underlying social problem of sexism, Friedan writes, "In the fifteen years after World War II, this mystique of feminine fulfillment became the cherished and self-perpetuating core of contemporary American culture" (p. 14). Friedan called attention to women's disillusion with housewifery and their complex, unpaid labor in the home.

Arguments about women's capabilities and responsibilities, as well as their educational, work, and familial opportunities continued to dominate the latter part of the twentieth century. Hochschild and Machung's book *The Second Shift* (2003) exposes the ongoing reality of the majority of working women, not just those in higher education. The women in their study contributed a full day's work at the office and then arrived home to cook, clean, and care for their children. Hochschild and Machung (2003) argue that this work at home constitutes another full shift of labor. Responding to the dual demands of work and home, the "Super-Mom" was born. Hochschild and Machung (2003) implicate women's transition to the workforce as the means by which the heterosexual family could adapt to deindustrialization and declining men's wages. And, more and more, women are doing both shifts as single parents. In 1960, 74.5 percent of households in the United States were married couples living with children; by 1995, only 54.5 percent of the 99 million total households fit this description (Jacobsen, 1998).

The social, economic, and political forces described in this section illuminate part of the journey for women—specifically white and black women—related to work and higher education in the twentieth century.

These historical arguments, higher education structures, and responses to women's growing numbers as workers and students deeply inform women's access and opportunities today. As educators invested in the success of women, these histories can also inform our understandings of and responses to women's needs on contemporary college campuses.

Access and Equity in U.S. Higher Education: Moving Forward with Intention

In the early twenty-first century, women have established their place as the majority of students in higher education. As the emphasis on the demographics of women and men in the academy continues, we as educators have a unique opportunity to discuss gender issues in a new way. The discussions in this chapter have multiple implications for policy and practice related to women in higher education. For practitioners, particularly younger professionals, it is imperative that the histories explored in this chapter—and also the histories that were not discussed—are considered when exploring how to best serve college women. New conversations that are more firmly rooted in an understanding of how historical contexts inform and shape the present day will encourage different dialogues about the majority of women in higher education and perhaps offer fresh suggestions for improving educational access and equity. Practitioners also benefit from a deeper understanding of the institutional structures they inherited; from women's colleges to women's centers and beyond, the structures present in higher education today are embedded in historical discussions and traditions about the education of women.

References

Allen, J. K., Dean, D. R., & Bracken, S. J. (Eds.). (2008). *Most college students are women: Implications for teaching, learning, and policy.* Sterling, VA: Stylus.

Anderson, J. D. (2002). Race in American higher education: Historical perspectives on current conditions. In W. A. Smith, P. G. Altbach, & K. Lomotey (Eds.), *The racial crisis in American higher education: Continuing challenges for the twenty-first century* (pp. 3–21). Albany: State University of New York Press.

Blau, F. D., Ferber, M. A., & Winkler, A. E. (1998). *The economics of women, men, and work* (3rd ed.). Upper Saddle River, NJ: Prentice Hall.

Brooks, K. H. (1988, Summer). The women's center: The new dean of women? *Initiatives, 51*(2/3), 17–21.

Brown, H. G. (2003). *Sex and the single girl*. Fort Lee, NJ: Barricade Books. (Original work published 1962)

Brown v. Board of Education, 347 U.S. 483 (1954).

Brubacher, J. S., & Rudy, W. (1997). *Higher education in transition: A history of American colleges and universities* (4th ed.). New Brunswick, NJ: Transaction Publishers.

Buford, C. (1988, Summer). Multicultural programming in a university women's center. *Initiatives, 51*(2/3), 31–35.

Carnegie Commission on Higher Education. (1973, September). *Opportunities for women in higher education: Their current participation, prospects for the future, and recommendations for action*. New York: McGraw-Hill.

Clevenger, B. M. (1988, Summer). Women's centers on campus: A profile. *Initiatives, 51*(2/3), 3–9.

Cott, N. F. (1994). The modern woman of the 1920s, American style (A. Goldammer, Trans.). In G. Duby & M. Perrot (Series Eds.) & F. Thébaud (Vol. Ed.), *A history of women in the West: Vol. V. Toward a cultural identity in the twentieth century* (pp. 76–91). Cambridge, MA: Harvard University Press.

Davie, S. L. (2002). Drawing new maps. In S. L. Davie (Ed.), *University and college women's centers: A journey toward equity* (pp. 447–58). Westport, CT: Greenwood Press.

Davis, A. Y. (1981). *Women, race and class*. New York: Random House.

DiLapi, E. M., & Gay, G. M. (2002). Women's centers responding to racism. In S. L. Davie (Ed.), *University and college women's centers: A journey toward equity* (pp. 203–26). Westport, CT: Greenwood Press.

Education Amendments, 20 U.S.C. § 1681 et seq. (1972).

Evans, S. M. (1989). *Born for liberty: A history of women in America*. New York: Free Press.

Faust, D. G. (2004). Mingling promiscuously: A history of women and men at Harvard. In L. T. Ulrich (Ed.), *Yards and gates: Gender in Harvard and Radcliffe history* (pp. 317–27). New York: Palgrave Macmillan.

Friedan, B. (1963). *The feminine mystique.* New York: Dell.

Gary, S. (2008). Bennett and Spelman Colleges: Creating Black female PhDs in the sciences. In M. Gasman & C. L. Tudico (Eds.), *Historically black colleges and universities: Triumphs, troubles, and taboos* (pp. 41–52). New York: Palgrave Macmillan.

Gordon, L. D. (1990). *Gender and higher education in the progressive era.* New Haven, NH: Yale University Press.

Gould, J. S. (1989). Women's centers as agents of change. In C. S. Pearson, D. L. Shavlik, & J. G. Touchton (Eds.), *Educating the majority: Women challenge tradition in higher education* (pp. 219–29). New York: American Council on Education & Macmillan.

Guy-Sheftall, B., & Bell-Scott, P. (1989). Black women's studies: A view from the margin. In C. S. Pearson, D. L. Shavlik, & J. G. Touchton (Eds.), *Educating the majority: Women challenge tradition in higher education* (pp. 205–18). New York: Macmillan.

Harwarth, I., Maline, M. S., & DeBra, E. (1997, June). *Women's colleges in the United States: History, issues, and challenges.* Washington, DC: U.S. Government Printing Office.

Hawkins v. Board of Control, 350 U.S. 413 (1956).

Hochschild, A. R., & Machung, A. (2003). *The second shift* (2nd ed.). New York: Penguin.

Horowitz, H. L. (1987). *Campus life: Undergraduate cultures from the end of the eighteenth century to the present.* Chicago: University of Chicago Press.

Jacobsen, J. P. (1998). *The economics of gender* (2nd ed.). Oxford, England: Blackwell.

Kunkel, C. A. (1994). Women's needs on campus: How universities meet them. *Initiatives, 56*(2), 15–28.

Kunkel, C. A. (2002). Starting a women's center: Key issues. In S. L. Davie (Ed.), *University and college women's centers: A journey toward equity* (pp. 65–78). Westport, CT: Greenwood Press.

Matthews, G. (1992). *The rise of public woman: Woman's power and woman's place in the United States, 1630–1970.* New York: Oxford University Press.

Michel, S., & Muncy, R. (Eds.). (1999). *Engendering America: A documentary history, 1865 to the present.* Boston: McGraw-Hill.

Miller-Bernal, L. (2004). Coeducation: An uneven progression. In L. Miller-Bernal & S. L. Poulson (Eds.), *Going coed: Women's experiences in formerly men's colleges and universities, 1950–2000* (pp. 3–21). Nashville, TN: Vanderbilt University Press.

Morison, S. E. (1936). *Three centuries of Harvard: 1636–1936.* Cambridge, MA: Harvard University Press.

National Women's Studies Association. (n.d.). *NWSA campus women's centers database.* Retrieved July 1, 2010 from http://www.nwsa.org/research/centerguide/index.php.

Nidiffer, J. (2003). From whence they came: The contexts, challenges, and courage of early women administrators in higher education. In B. Ropers-Huilman (Ed.), *Gendered futures in higher education: Critical perspectives for change* (pp. 15–34). Albany: State University of New York Press.

National Women's Studies Association. (n.d.). *NWSA campus women's centers database.* Retrieved April 24, 2010, from http://www.nwsa.org/research/centerguide/index.php.

Oberlin College. (2007). *About Oberlin.* Retrieved June 8, 2010, from http://www.oberlin.edu/newserv/facts.html.

Palmer, A. F. (1908). Three types of women's colleges. In G. H. Palmer & A. F. Palmer (Eds.), *The teacher: Essays and addresses on education* (pp. 313–36). Boston: Houghton Mifflin.

Palmer, G. H., & Palmer, A. F. (Eds.). (1908). *The teacher: Essays and addresses on education.* Boston: Houghton Mifflin.

Palmieri, P. A. (1997). From republican motherhood to race suicide: Arguments on the higher education of women in the United States, 1820–1920. In L. F. Goodchild & H. S. Wechsler (Eds.), *The history of higher education* (2nd ed., pp. 173–82). Boston: Pearson Custom.

Pearson, C. S., Shavlik, D. L., & Touchton, J. G. (Eds.). (1989). *Educating the majority: Women challenge tradition in higher education.* New York: American Council on Education and Macmillan.

Pope, E. (1999). Working women have been blamed for everything. In S. Michel & R. Muncy (Eds.), *Engendering America: A documentary history, 1865 to the present* (pp. 231–34). Boston: McGraw-Hill. (Original work published 1955)

Poulson, S. L., & Miller-Bernal, L. (2004). Coeducation and gender equal education. In L. Miller-Bernal & S. L. Poulson (Eds.), *Going coed: Women's experiences in formerly men's colleges and universities, 1950–2000* (pp. 309–16). Nashville, TN: Vanderbilt University Press.

President and Fellows of Harvard College. (2007). *The Harvard guide: Recent history.* Retrieved June 8, 2010, from http://www.news.harvard.edu/guide/intro/hist3.html.

Rudolph, F. (1962). *The American college and university: A history.* New York: Knopf.

Sanger, M. (1920). *Woman and the new race.* New York: Blue Ribbon Books.

Sax, L. J. (2008). *The gender gap in college: Maximizing the potential of women and men.* San Francisco, CA: Jossey-Bass.

Schwager, S. (2004). Taking up the challenge: The origins of Radcliffe. In L. T. Ulrich (Ed.), *Yards and gates: Gender in Harvard and Radcliffe history* (pp. 87–115). New York: Palgrave Macmillan.

Schwartz, R. A. (1997, September/October). Reconceptualizing the leadership roles of women in higher education: A brief history on the importance of deans of women. *The Journal of Higher Education, 68*(5), 502–22.

Snyder, T. D., Dillow, S. A., & Hoffman, C. M. (2009, March). *Digest of education statistics 2008* (NCES 2009-020). Washington, DC: National Center for Education Statistics, Institute of Education Sciences, U.S. Department of Education.

Teddlie, C., & Freeman, J. A. (2002). Twentieth-century desegregation in U.S. higher education: A review of five distinct historical eras. In W. A. Smith, P. G. Altbach, & K. Lomotey (Eds.), *The racial crisis in American higher education: Continuing challenges for the twenty-first century* (pp. 77–99). Albany: State University of New York Press.

Thelin, J. R. (2004). *A history of American higher education.* Baltimore: Johns Hopkins University Press.

Tidball, M. E., Smith, D. G., Tidball, C. S., & Wolf-Wendel, L. E. (1999). *Taking women seriously: Lessons and legacies for educating the majority.* Phoenix, AZ: American Council on Education and Oryx Press.

Titcomb, C. (1993). The black presence at Harvard: An overview. In W. Sollors, C. Titcomb, & T. Underwood (Eds.), *Blacks at Harvard: A documentary history of African-American experience at Harvard and Radcliffe* (pp. 1–7). New York: New York University Press.

U.S. Department of Labor, Bureau of Labor Statistics. (2009, September). *Women in the labor force: A databook* (Report No. 1018). Retrieved July 12, 2010, from http://www.bls.gov/cps/wlf-databook-2009.pdf.

Vassar College. (n.d.). *About Vassar: History.* Retrieved June 8, 2010, from http://admissions.vassar.edu/about_hist.html.

Vlasnik, A. L. (2010, May). *Ohio women's centers: Statement of philosophy* (Issue Brief No. 01). Retrieved May 28, 2010, from Southwestern Ohio Council for Higher Education website: http://www.soche.org/ and Greater Cincinnati Consortium of Colleges and Universities website: http://www.gcccu.org/.

Wellesley College (2009, January). *Wellesley College presidents.* Retrieved June 8, 2010, from http://www.wellesley.edu/Welcome/wcpres.html.

Wilkerson, M. B. (1989). Majority, minority, and the numbers game. In C. S. Pearson, D. L. Shavlik, & J. G. Touchton (Eds.), *Educating the majority: Women challenge tradition in higher education* (pp. 25–31). New York: Macmillan.

Wilson, M. (2008). The forgotten GI: The Servicemen's Readjustment Act and black colleges, 1944–54. In M. Gasman & C. L. Tudico (Eds.), *Historically black colleges and universities: Triumphs, troubles, and taboos* (pp. 93–104). New York: Palgrave Macmillan.

Wolf-Wendel, L. (2003). Gender and higher education: What should we learn from women's colleges? In B. Ropers-Huilman (Ed.), *Gendered futures in higher education: Critical perspectives for change* (pp. 35–52). Albany: State University of New York Press.

3

"Many Phantoms and Obstacles . . . Looming in Her Way": Women Faculty in Academe

Michele A. Paludi and Florence L. Denmark

Introduction: Systematic Oppression of Women Faculty

> Even when the path is nominally open—when there is nothing to prevent a woman from being a doctor, a lawyer, a civil servant—there are many phantoms and obstacles . . . looming in her way.
>
> —Virginia Woolf

> When I spoke up for women's issues, I was made to feel unwelcome in my own department, kept off crucial committees, ridiculed, ignored. . . . Ironically, my name in the catalogue gave Columbia a reputation for encouraging feminist studies in modernism. Nothing could be further from the truth.
>
> —Carolyn Heilbrun

In *Death in a Tenured Position* (Cross, 1986), protagonist Professor Kate Fansler tries to solve the death of the first woman to hold a full professorship in Harvard University's English department. Prior to coming to Harvard to help solve Janet's murder, a colleague informs her: "I'll send you a nice fat packet about women at Harvard. It's a particularly depressing collection of materials" (p. 25).

The mystery novel is set in 1978; the recipient of the endowed chair is Professor Janet Mandelbaum, who states she is determined to succeed at her professorship based on merit, not on the fact that she is a woman.

45

The Chair of the English Department notes, "Most of our best students are women; that's true everywhere in graduate studies ... so it seems only right that they should have at least one representative of their sex on the faculty of the department" (p. 128). He further notes: "I was glad that Janet ... wasn't a real feminist" (p. 128). He also declares, "Of course, given a choice, I'd have chosen not to have a woman professor in the department. It's bound to cause problems" (p. 128).

Professor Mandelbaum finds herself ostracized by colleagues who consider women's studies to be faddish and an unnecessary part of the liberal arts curriculum. Eventually, Professor Mandelbaum is found drugged, dead, and in a compromising position in a women's room at Harvard.

While the mystery novel *Death in a Tenured Position* is fiction, the issues raised by Cross (Carolyn Heilbrun's pen name) are accurate reflections of universities being gatekeepers toward women professors in order to limit the advancement of women in their careers. Gatekeepers believe, for example, that women have no place in university teaching and research; however, they rationalize that their resistance to women in the profession is based on "facts," for example, women are not viewed as being committed to their careers as are men; they are rather interested in marrying and raising families (Betz & Schifano, 2000).

These discriminatory behaviors stemming from stereotypic attitudes toward women faculty as described by Cross existed long before her critique of universities in the late 1970s. For example, the first generation of American women psychologists was caught in the middle of two conflicting stereotypes (Rossiter, 1982). On one hand, they were stereotyped as "soft, delicate, emotional, noncompetitive, and nurturing kinds of feelings and behavior" (p. xv). On the other hand, they were scientists, who were portrayed as "tough, rigorous, rational, impersonal, masculine, competitive, and unemotional" (p. xv).

When compared to their male peers, these women psychologists were similar in age and training. However, they were less likely to achieve equivalent professional status. Furthermore, according to the American Psychological Association (2009), with respect to the first generation of American women psychologists, "the mantle of scientific psychology was used to justify discrimination against them" (p. 1).

According to Furumoto and Scarborough (1986), "Certain gender-specific factors profoundly affected the women's experience: exclusion from important educational and employment opportunities, the responsibility of daughters to their families, and the marriage-versus-career dilemma" (p. 39).

These issues are those that many women in the second generation of American psychologists and other professionals and modern-day women academicians and scholars face, supporting Hanisch's (1969) conclusion: "the personal is political." The personal problems faced by early women scholars and academicians just as today are political problems, the result of *systematic oppression.*

Women Faculty as "Outsiders" Looking In

The Modern Language Association (cited in *Inside Higher Ed*, 2008) reported from its Associate Professor Survey (also included full professors) the following findings:

a. On every measure of job satisfaction, male professors are more satisfied than female professors in English and foreign languages.
b. Women spend an average of 1.5 hours more per week than do men on grading student work.
c. Male faculty work an average of 2 hours more per week on research than do female faculty.
d. It takes women faculty longer than men to earn the promotion from associate to full professor.
e. The sole area in which women are overwhelmingly very satisfied with their faculty responsibilities (but still not as satisfied as men) is their autonomy in the college classroom.

Quotations from survey respondents highlighted these statistical results. For example, respondents tended to "love their jobs" but simultaneously "struggle to meet the various demands they face" (p. 1). Some women professors noted they value teaching because "teaching can be a kind of refuge" (p. 2) in that their classroom is the one place where they have the most control over professional decisions impacting their academic career.

Results from surveys by the Center for Workforce Studies of the American Psychological Association (2008) and the 2008–2009 American Psychological Association Faculty Salaries in Graduate Departments of Psychology Survey indicated:

a. In 2005, 72 percent of new Ph.D.s in psychology were women, an increase of 6 percent in the last ten years and 20 percent in the last 20 years. In 1976, the percentage of women Ph.D.s was thirty-three.
b. The majority of women Ph.D.s were on the faculty at two-year colleges or in hospital settings; the majority of men Ph.D.s were on the faculty of universities with graduate programs.
c. More women than men were lecturers or assistant or associate professors in academic institutions; more men were full professors.
d. More men than women achieved tenure in psychology graduate departments each selected year studied (from 1985 to the present).

Bernstein and Russo (2008) and Bilimoria, Joy, and Liang (2008) also noted that women faculty in STEM careers (science, technology, engineering, and mathematics) represent less than 5 percent of full professorships in the top fifty departments in math, statistics, and electrical, civil, mechanical, and chemical engineering. They further noted that the ratio of women earning Ph.D.s in a STEM field to full professorships is approximately 4 to 1. According to Bernstein and Russo (2008):

> ... there is growing evidence that even women who have the appropriate credentials and experience for entering STEM careers leave their positions significantly more often than men.... one study estimated 6-year attrition in the information technology workforce at 40% for women compared to 25% for men. (p. 2)

Similar results were obtained by the National Academies (2009). For example:

a. In every scientific, medical and engineering field, women were underrepresented among candidates for tenure relative to the number of women assistant professors. "In chemistry, for example, women made up 22 percent of assistant professors, but only

15 percent of the faculty being considered for tenure. Women also spent a significantly longer time as assistant professors" (p. 2).

b. Men faculty had greater access to equipment needed for research and to administrative support.

Carter (cited in *Inside Higher Ed*, 2010) reported comparable results for women professors in business schools in the United States. She utilized data from 1988 to 2004 that were provided by the National Study of Postsecondary Faculty. She noted that in the first year of her study, 1988, the largest proportion of women and men professors were at the instructor level. However, a review of the 2004 data indicated that the largest proportion of women faculty were instructors while the majority of men were full professors.

Mason (2010) recently noted that when the nineteen Canada Excellence Research Chairs were awarded to men, women professors were concerned about this obvious bias. The Canadian Association of University Teachers reported that in 2007 (the most recent data), 41 percent of new faculty appointments were filled by women. They further noted that 46 percent of Ph.D.s were earned by women. Mason (2010) reported that in 2007, women represented approximately 20 percent of full professors at Canadian universities. According to Mason: "Women occupy just 30 percent of tenured positions on our campuses; while filling 45 percent of non-tenured jobs" (p. 2).

Multiple Marginality

When we consider race as well as sex, we find women of color experience more discrimination as professors than do white women. Turner (2002) noted:

Faculty women of color experience multiple marginality, characterized by lived contradiction and ambiguous empowerment. Their lives are often invisible, hidden within studies that either examine experiences of women faculty or faculty of color. (p. 74)

De la Luz Reyes and Halcon (1988) argued that women of color have been more disadvantaged in psychology than white women as a consequence of their participation in a culture that has valued neither women nor nonwhite individuals. Beale (1970) referred to this as "double jeopardy." De la Luz Reyes and Halcon (1988) noted that many gatekeepers operate under the "one-minority-per-pot" syndrome in academia:

> We believe that implicit in this practice is a deep-seated belief that minorities are not as qualified as non-minorities. This conviction stems from an unspoken fear that the presence of more than one minority . . . in a mainstream, traditional department might reduce the department's . . . reputation. . . . (pp. 305–15)

Hune (1998) reported findings with Asian Pacific American women in academe "contest a popular conception that Asian Pacific Americans in higher education, especially women, are a 'model minority' and a racial 'success' story. Asian Pacific Americans have yet to achieve parity with whites in access and accommodation in the academy" (p. 1). Hune noted how Asian Pacific American women faculty are ostracized in the academy and treated as "strangers" and "outsiders." According to Hune:

> Asian Pacific American female faculty often experience unwanted and unwarranted overattention as racial minority group represen-tatives and may be treated as "tokens." They find underattention as well in the devaluation of their research and teaching, and in the dismissal of issues they deem important. (p. 2)

Nelson (2007) conducted the first national demographic analysis of ten-ured and tenure-track professors in the top 100 departments of engineer-ing and science in the United States. Nelson reported that:

> There are relatively few tenured and tenure-track underrepresented minority faculty in these research university departments, even though a growing number and percentage of minorities are completing their PhDs. . . . In most disciplines, underrepresented minority faculty are so few that a minority student can get a B.S. or Ph.D. without being taught by or having access to an underrepresented minority professor in that discipline. However, there is a disproportionate number of White male professors as role models for White male students. (p. 1)

Recently, Newsom (reported in Hernandez, 2010) stated at the American Association of University Professors' annual national conference the following:

> The dismal truth is academe doesn't really want a racially-diverse faculty . . . it's totally a myth. . . . If you are an African-American, American Indian or Latina/o with a Ph.D., your odds of ever receiving tenure at a Research I school are between slim and none. (p. 1)

Discrimination By Any Other Name . . .

Halpern (2004) noted that "we now do a better job of encouraging women to play sports than we do with women in tenured full professor faculty positions" (p. 2). She urged colleges/universities to consider the underrepresentation of women in full professorships "another civil-rights issue" (p. 1), noting gender bias in equal compensation, hiring, promotion, and tenure decisions. In this description, Halpern echoes Hall and Sandler's (1982) finding of a "chilly climate" for women faculty in academia. We discuss several examples of "chilly academic climates" for women faculty in this chapter, specifically: salary discrepancies, career/family conflict, biased evaluations by students, and lack of access to mentoring and networking. We offer recommendations to campuses for making women faculty, including minority women faculty, central, not marginal, to academic life.

Salary Discrepancies

> Women should have equal pay for equal work and they should be considered equally eligible to the offices of principal and superintendent, professor and president. So you must insist that qualifications, not sex, shall govern appointments and salaries
>
> —Susan B. Anthony

While the Equal Pay Act was passed into law in 1963, the salary gap between women's and men's wages is still a major issue in all disciplines (Paludi, Martin, Paludi, Boggess, Hicks, & Speech, 2010). Furthermore, the wage gap is more severe for women of color (Gee, 2006; Kim, 2006). According to Paludi et al. (2010):

> ... salary discrimination reduces total career lifespan earnings, reduces benefits from Social Security and pension plans, and inhibits the ability to save money for retirement, to purchase a home, to pay for college education for children and/or for themselves, and to cover medical expenses throughout their lives, especially during their elderly years. (p. 148)

Carter's (cited in *Inside Higher Ed*, 2010) review of faculty in business schools revealed that women faculty, both tenured and nontenured, earn less than men. Banerji's (2006) review of the American Association of University Professors data on gender and tenure and salary comparisons indicated universities are " ... still reluctant to hire women or pay them in parity with their male hires" (p. 1). The salary data in 2006 suggest no changes since the 1970s. According to Banerji:

> In 2005–06, across all ranks and all institutions, the average salary for women faculty was 81 percent of the amount earned by men. Among all full professors at all types of institutions in 2005–06, women earned on average 88 percent of what men earned. For associate and assistant professors, the overall national figure for women was 93 percent. (p. 2)

Results from surveys by the Center for Workforce Studies of the American Psychological Association (2008) and the 2008–2009 American Psychological Association Faculty Salaries in Graduate Departments of Psychology Survey indicated that the median starting salary in 2005 was $55,206. Women reported earning a median salary approximately $4,000 less than earned by men. The National Academies (2009) reported that women faculty were paid on average 8 percent less than men.

Recently, PhysOrg.com (2010) reported that within the discipline of academic medicine, women faculty are paid substantially less than their male colleagues. This report cited research by DesRoches, who reported that with respect to this discipline and controlling for differences in academic rank and publications, women faculty were paid between $6,000 to $15,000 less than men per year. According to DesRoches:

These differences may seem modest ... but over a 30-year career, an average female faculty member with a PhD would earn almost $215,000 less than a comparable male. If that deficit were invested in a retirement account earning 6 percent per year, the difference would grow to almost $700,000 over a career. For department of medicine faculty, that difference could be almost twice as great. (p. 2)

The wage gap also has implications for adequately caring for children and elderly parents, an issue we address in the next section.

Paludi et al. (2010) and Porter, Toutkoushian, and Moore (2008) noted that wage discrimination against women can be explained by stereotypes about women, women and work, and the meaning of money for women. According to Paludi et al., " ... part of the inequity in salaries is due to the cultural stereotype that men must earn more than women because men are the primary 'breadwinners' of the family" (p. 160).

This interpretation, however, must be countered with the realities of women faculty's lives. For example, more women than men report they decided to remain single in order to meet their career demands (Sonnert & Holton, 1995). Bernstein and Russo (2008) further noted that women who earned tenure are approximately twice as likely as men to be single twelve years after completing their Ph.D. Finally, Mason and Goulden (2006) found that faculty women who were married when they began their academic career are more likely than their male colleagues to separate and/or divorce from their spouses. Thus, the reality is that women faculty tend to be the primary breadwinners of their families.

Career/Family Conflict

Working outside the home is not progress if women must also continue with full-time responsibility for housekeeping and motherhood, performing "double duty" or the "second shift."

—Arlie Hochschild

Maternal employment has increased in the past twenty-five years dramatically (Paludi, Vaccariello, Graham, Smith, Allen-Dicker, Kasprzak, & White, 2008). In addition, women with infants have had the fastest growth in labor-force participation of all groups in the United States

(Han, Waldfogel, & Brooks-Gunn, 2001). Furthermore, women are as likely to be employed when they have infants as they are when they have a preschool-aged child.

Recent research also has indicated that in addition to caring for young children, many employed women in the United States are simultaneously caring for their elderly parents. Lockwood (2003) noted that between 40 and 60 percent of women caring for elders also have child care responsibilities in addition to their careers. Lockwood (2003) further noted that women spend approximately seventeen years of their lives caring for children and eighteen years caring for one or both parents. The primary caregiver is the family, most likely the elderly parent's daughter or daughter-in-law (Hammer, Neal, Newsome, Brockwood, & Collton, 2006).

Kanter (1977) brought the issue of work/life balance to the forefront of organizations. Kanter noted the incompatibility between work and family roles, still present thirty-three years later (Paludi & Neidermeyer, 2007; Paludi, Martin, Paludi, Boggess, Hicks, & Speech, 2010; Paludi, Vaccariello, Graham, Smith, Allen-Dicker, Kasprzak, & White, 2007):

1. Women carry more of the workload at home.
2. Employed women do substantially more caregiving to children/and elderly parents than do men.
3. Employed women are more likely than men to lack job flexibility.
4. Salary inequities still remain, especially for women of color.
5. Employed women are more likely to lack basic fringe benefits needed to care for their family than are men.

Employed women continue with full-time responsibility for housekeeping and parenting, performing "double duty" or what Hochschild (1989) referred to as the "second shift."

Furthermore, Gonzalez-Morales et al. (2006) reported that employed women who experience career/family conflict are as much as thirty times more likely to experience a significant mental health problem, for example, depression or anxiety, than women who report no career/family conflicts. Karsten (2006) further noted that women integrating elder (and/or child care) with careers work longer hours than men, impacting their physical as well as emotional well-being.

These realities are experienced by women faculty. Bronstein et al. (1993) noted that "the tenure system in the United States was set up for male faculty, whose wives provided all the homemaking so that their husbands could devote their energies solely to academic career advancement" (cited in Bernstein & Russo, 2007, p. 92). Results from surveys by the Center for Workforce Studies of the American Psychological Association (2008) and the 2008–2009 American Psychological Association Faculty Salaries in Graduate Departments of Psychology Survey indicated:

a. Men were more likely than women to be employed full time (67% vs. 58%). Women were more likely than men to be employed part-time (9.5% vs. 58%). Ninety-two percent of women who worked part time cited family responsibilities as the main reason for this choice.
b. Ninety-seven percent of unemployed doctorates not seeking employment were women, who cited family responsibilities for their decision.

In addition, Mason, Goulden, and Wolfinger (2004) reported that " . . . for women, babies and marriage, particularly in combination, dramatically decrease their likelihood of entering a tenure-track position" (cited in Bernstein & Russo, 2008, p. 105). Bernstein and Russo (2008) noted that with faculty in STEM careers, approximately eight times as many women as men report family responsibilities as the main reason they do not work full time.

Brown, Swinyard, and Ogle (2003) found that with respect to academic medicine:

> . . . the demands of career and personal life are each great enough to extract compromise from the other, and, further, that anticipated support from a partner, the community, and medical center was inadequate to make it possible to succeed in multiple roles at once. (p. 1005)

Furthermore, Preston's results (2004) indicated that women faculty who are mothers, who are also primarily responsible for child care, have to cut back on having lunch with colleagues in their departments and attending academic conferences. While not directly related to teaching, service, and research, these activities are definitely important to advancement in terms of tenure and promotion.

Mason and Goulden (2004) analyzed the National Science Foundation/ National Institutes of Health Survey of Earned Doctorates that follows 160,000 Ph.D.s across all fields until they are seventy-six years of age. They observed that two out of three women professors do not have children. In addition, in the sciences and humanities, 44 percent of women professors are married with children while 70 percent of men professors are married with children. According to Bernstein and Russo (2007), "Career trumping children appears to be a deliberate decision. . . . Among married faculty who decided not to have children, three out of four women cited career considerations compared to fewer than half of the men" (p. 104). Armenti (2004) reported women faculty in a Canadian university indicated they believe having children before earning tenure is detrimental to their professional career.

However, as Bernstein and Russo (2007) noted, there is a perceived incompatibility between motherhood and a career in academia. No matter what path women faculty choose, they will be viewed in a negative light. Furthermore, women faculty have been told to act "more like men" when striving for an academic career, seeking tenure and promotion. However, personality characteristics are not perceived as gender neutral (Ely & Rhode, 2008). When women engage in behaviors stereotypically linked to men, they are not perceived similarly to men and are often evaluated more negatively than when conforming to stereotypes of women faculty. According to Heilman, Wallen, Fuchs, and Tamkins (2004): "The mere recognition that a woman has achieved success on a traditionally male task produces inferences that she has engaged in counternormative behavior and therefore causes similarly negative consequences" (p. 3).

In addition, successful achievement for women is costly. Successful women are described as "cold" vis-à-vis men (Wiley & Eskilson, 1985). Much of the discrimination against women and employment can be traced to stereotypes about women (Basow, 2010).

Course Evaluations: The "Normative Professor is Still a Man"

We find it curious that psychological thought is still heavily influenced by such nineteenth-century theorists as Darwin, Marx, and Freud. As products of their era, they were primarily supportive of the status quo, of upper-class White male privilege with its limited knowledge of and marginal concern for women. If they were alive today, they would be astonished: What? You are still using those old books? Throw them away.

—Rachel Hare-Mustin and Jeanne Marecek

In fact, Kaschak (2006) and Basow (2010) reported that women professors are perceived and evaluated differently by women and men students; men professors are perceived and evaluated similarly by both women and men students. According to Basow (2010):

> Women are marked for gender in ways men are not, especially when women are in non-traditional roles (such as when teaching on the college level, especially in such male-associated fields as science and technology). The normative professor is still a man. When a woman is in this role, students (and others) often note this unusual event by speaking of their "female professor," when their professor is a man, they rarely note his gender. (p. 56)

Women faculty are evaluated on two dimensions by students: whether they meet the expectations for a "good professor" (e.g., up to date on course material, competent, tests fairly) and simultaneously a "good" woman (e.g., caring, understanding, lenient with deadlines). This double bind faced by women faculty is nonexistent for men (Basow, 2010; Smith & Anderson, 2005). When women faculty do not meet both standards perceived to be essential by students, they are evaluated negatively on course evaluations (Eagly & Karau, 2002). Kierstead, D'Agostino, and Dill (1998) and Sanders, Willemsen and Millar (2009) found that for women professors, students rate friendliness, availability, and smiling to be more important than for men professors. When women professors are not perceived by students to be friendlier than men professors, students rate them negatively on course evaluations (Sinclair & Kunda, 2000). Men students evaluate women faculty more negatively than men faculty. In recent years, researchers (e.g., DeSouza & Fansler, 2003; Rospenda, Richman, & Nawyn, 1988) have found men students engage in contrapower sexual harassment toward women faculty, especially in women's studies courses. Examples of contrapower sexual harassment include unwelcomed, negative, nonsexual gender-based verbal and nonverbal behavior. Women faculty's sex is more salient for students than is their organizational power.

Abel and Meltzer (2007) noted that men professors who lectured on gender issues in pay disparities were rated more favorably and less sexist than women professors who provided the exact same lecture. In addition, Abel and Meltzer (2007) found that male students who hold more traditional gender stereotypic attitudes toward women were more sexist in their evaluations of women professors compared to men professors.

Schmidt (2010) recently reported findings by Goodyear, Reynolds, and Bragg that indicated that women faculty are more likely than their male colleagues to be recipients of incivility in the classroom. Incivility has been defined as mistreatment, including bullying, emotional, physical, and psychological abuse, and antisocial behavior (Andersson & Pearson, 1999). Andersson and Pearson (1999) noted that incivility is "low-intensity deviant behavior with ambiguous intent to harm the target, in violation of workplace norms for mutual respect. Uncivil behaviors are characteristically rude and discourteous, displaying a lack of regard for others" (p. 457). Examples of incivility from Goodyear et al.'s study included: sleeping during lectures, texting in class, coming to class late, talking on cell phones during lectures, and open expressions of anger toward women faculty. In addition, their research indicated that women faculty stated the uncivil behavior they experienced from students was severe and they were impacted by it careerwise and in terms of their emotional and physical well-being.

Recently Nadal (2010) has noted that women experience gender and racial microaggressions, which are defined as "brief and commonplace daily verbal, behavioral, or environmental indignities, whether intentional or unintentional, that communicate hostile, derogatory, or negative . . . slights and insults. . . ." (as cited in Sue, Capodilupo, Torino, Bucceri, Holder, & Nadal, 2007, p. 271). Examples of gender microaggressions offered by Nadal (2010, pp. 166–67) include:

Environmental Invalidation:

Women make less money than men.

The majority of university professors in a department are men.

Assumptions of Traditional Gender Roles:

A forty-year-old woman with a successful career is asked why she never had any children.

Invisibility:

A female employee is passed up for a job promotion.

Lack of Access to Mentoring and Networking

A mentor is someone who allows you to see the hope inside yourself.

—Oprah Winfrey

Do not wait for leaders; do it alone, person to person.

—Mother Teresa

The academy is structured by a traditional and stereotypical masculine culture that, in turn, values and rewards men who exhibit these stereotypical traits more so than women (Denmark & Klara, 2010). Women often struggle to find their place within such an organization. As Jandeska and Kraimer (2005) argued:

This "code of conduct" in masculine cultures, while recognizable to males, can be completely alien to females and thus would be considered less hospitable towards women's careers. For example, an "old-boy network" excludes women from centers of influence and valuable sources of information, often trivializing or ignoring their contributions. (p. 465)

Mentoring relationships may be crucial for women faculty in their achievement of career success as well as success within their academic departments and universities (Denmark & Klara, 2010). Because of the unique obstacles women faculty face in the academy, as has been discussed throughout this chapter, it is difficult for them to find mentors. In addition, it is difficult for women faculty to find protégés to pass on the knowledge they have about academic careers. According to Paludi, Martin, Stern, & DeFour (2010), the reason for these findings concerns the belief that women faculty do not have as much organizational power or access to powerful others within their department or universities as do their male colleagues. As Paludi et al. stated, " . . . potential protégés may choose mentoring relationships with men colleagues, thereby reducing the chances for women to pass on their knowledge of the organization as well as their expertise" (p. 80).

Furthermore, Shakeshaft, Brown, Irby, Grogan, & Ballenger (2007) noted that there is a disparity about who receives mentoring within the academy. Mentors thus tend to mentor those most like them: "In a department dominated by white males, white men get most of the mentoring. Women and minorities too often fall through the cracks."

Arguments in favor of women mentors for women stress the importance of women's identification with other women and the positive incentive through women's illustrative success (Miles-Cohen, Keita, Twose, & Houston, 2010). According to Shakeshaft et al. (2007):

> While family support is important for women to be able to gain the time and the approval of those immediately impacted by a decision to work longer hours, professional mentoring is vital to gain the knowledge and political information necessary for a woman to position herself as a viable top-level candidate. (p. 111)

Jandeska and Kraimer (2005) have referred to the factors that bar women from advancing their careers as faculty members as the "opportunity gap." Explanations for the opportunity gap have been offered in this chapter. In addition, the following factors contribute to this gap: sex discrimination, race discrimination, sexual harassment, lack of family-friendly policies, and an academic culture that is not welcoming to women (Martin, 2008; Paludi et al., 2007; Quinlan, 1999; Ward, 2008). Women report feeling marginalized, experiencing incivility and subtle bias, and having their research devalued. Consequently, mentoring for women faculty becomes especially important. However, women may lack access to senior faculty or professional networks (Casto, Caldwell, & Salazar, 2005). According to Martin (2008):

> It is easier for men, with their informal informational networks, to successfully acclimate themselves. Women often have to compensate simply for being women. . . . Women often face tremendous obstacles to gain acceptance in an organizational culture, especially in nontraditional fields. They must deal with negative expectations, gender-roles stereotypes, and doing more than is expected to be seen as

competent. They must try to find a mentor or a way into the informal networks that are often closed to them so that they can learn to navigate the hostile waters of organizational culture. (p. 172)

Women faculty are less likely than their male colleagues to seek out mentors because they assert that their abilities and competence will be sufficient to gain career advancement. The reality for women faculty is that this is often not the case (Collins, Chrisler, & Quina, 1998). Advancement only through merit is rarely achieved. According to Paludi, Martin, Stern, and DeFour (2010), women, especially women of color, are kept out of the loop in terms of what it takes to advance within the academy due to "tacit rules and traditions that are revealed only through informal networks" (p. 83).

In addition, women faculty find it difficult to have male mentors, both because they may find them difficult to approach and because they fear the presumption of a sexual relationship by others (Paludi, Martin, Stern, & DeFour, 2010). Furthermore, attribution factors impact women who are mentored by men. Men mentors perceive a woman's apprenticing herself to them as requiring help or remedial assistance. Men protégés, on the other hand, are perceived by men mentors as individuals whose careers need to be developed and nurtured. LaFrance (1987) noted that this difference raises a serious paradox: As women continue to get the mentoring they need, they will be perceived as needing the mentoring they get.

Collins (2009) noted the following with respect to mentoring and coaching experiences of African American women:

> As outsiders, some black women find their white male counterparts are being groomed for advancement from the date of hire. Meanwhile, by the time management realizes that the black women are just as or even more talented than the individual selected to be groomed due to various commonalities, there is simply no time to provide the visibility and exposure necessary to propel the black women to the next level. (p. 2)

Within their social networks of women, women develop long-term relationships based on emotional ties rather than hierarchical coalitions that are short term, characteristics common to men (Renzulli, Aldrich, & Moody, 2000). This strategy is an alternative to the traditional mentor–protégé hierarchical relationship. Swoboda and Millar (1986) advocated networking mentoring, in which two or more women fulfill the roles of mentor and protégé to each other at different times in the relationship. Networking mentoring is egalitarian rather than hierarchical and is based on belief and commitment to mutual enhancement. Advantages of networking mentoring include the fact that it is open to all faculty who find an individual to mentor them.

This type of mentoring and social networking is more relevant to women's career paths (Paludi, Martin, Stern, & DeFour, 2010). Networking places value on women's unique career paths. One additional benefit of networking mentoring is that it provides an opportunity for the faculty member to learn how to mentor others (Denmark & Klara, 2010). Networking mentoring is akin to (wo)mentoring, which is characterized by a sharing of power, competence, self, and differences (Clifford, 2003).

de Janasz (2006) noted that multiple mentors are beneficial for women and recommended a "constellation of developmental relationships" in order to obtain a variety of perspectives, skills, and knowledge that one person could not possibly fulfill. Thus, having multiple mentors can assist women faculty with providing training and insider/political information about the organization and emotional support (Ragins, 1989).

Conclusion

Women have faced more than their share of trials in order to be a part of the profession. Social forces generated by the Zeitgeist, or the current point of view held by the society as a whole, attempted first to prevent women from educating themselves, then to push them into specific areas of the professional field, approved as women's work, and finally to bury them in obscurity.

—Katharine Swan

Talent is universal, but opportunity is not.

—Hillary Rodham Clinton

van Anders (2004) conducted research with 468 women and men graduate students concerning barriers to pursuing an academic career. van Anders (2004) found that more men than women intended to pursue college/university teaching and research. In addition, parenting was more negatively correlated with an academic career for women, but not for men. Furthermore, van Anders (2004) reported that women were not more interested in being parents than were men. According to this research: " ... women self-select away from academia in response to perceived systemic barriers related to parenthood" (p. 511). van Anders concluded from her research that campuses must adopt their policies and practices to the realities of women faculty members' lives, including the career/life dilemma. This echoes the conclusion of Denmark and Paludi (2010) in their review of the history of feminism in psychology. These researchers demanded that change occur at the college/university level, not the personal level, if women are to ease the conflict of work/life incompatibility, salary inequities, student evaluations, and lack of access to mentoring. We offer the following recommendations for campuses, all based on empirical research in human resource management and the social sciences for meeting this goal.

Human Resource Audits

A human resource audit outlines (1) vulnerability on campus for sex discrimination and harassment and (2) changes that need to be made on the campus so the discriminatory practices are corrected (Smith & Mazin, 2004). Sample audit questions include:

a. Does the university ensure that salaries are based on skill, responsibility, effort, and working conditions?
b. Does the university examine practices to ensure that women and men have equal opportunity for advancement?
c. Does the university examine practices to ensure that white faculty and minority faculty have equal opportunity for advancement?
d. Does the university ensure that its recruitment practices reach the widest array of women and minority applicants?
e. Does the university offer flexible job arrangements for all employees, for example, flex time, career break?

Organizational Culture Climate Surveys

Faculty may be surveyed anonymously about their perceptions of and experiences with the campus's management of gender equity and race equity (Cooper, Cartwright, & Earley, 2001; Driskill & Brenton, 2005). Climate surveys will provide the campus with a metric of the alignment between their stated mission with respect to the recruitment and promotion of women and minority faculty and the actual behaviors of the campus via their policies, procedures, training programs, and tenure/promotion decisions.

Barrier Analysis

A barrier analysis may be used when an employment issue—for example, hiring practices or performance evaluations—limits opportunities for women and minority faculty (Dineen & Bartlett, 2002). Through this analysis, the triggers found in the employment issue are identified and resolved. Triggers include a disparity or trend that suggests a need for an inquiry into an employment issue, for example, the lack of promotions for ethnic minority employees or a high separation rate of women employees. Barriers may be found in all functions of human resource management, including recruitment, hiring, promotions, training, incentive programs, disciplinary actions, and separation from the campus.

Barriers may be institutional, for example, the company may recruit only from within the organization; attitudinal, for example, department chairpersons believe that women faculty are not as committed to their careers as are white male employees; or physical, for example, training materials and faculty handbooks are not available in languages in addition to English, Braille, and so on.

A barrier analysis features six tasks:

1. Review practices, policies, and procedures. Documents include handbooks, directives, staffing charts, hiring records, and tenure and promotion decisions.
2. Analyze the source material.
3. Identify triggers from workplace statistics, complaint data, culture climate surveys, and reports by outside organizations.

4. Determine the root cause of the triggers.

5. If the root cause is a barrier, develop an action plan to remove the barrier.

6. Monitor the action plan periodically.

SWOT Analysis

To evaluate the strengths, weaknesses, opportunities, and threats (SWOT) involved in developing or improving ways women and minority faculty are treated, campuses should conduct a SWOT analysis (Williamson, Cooke, Jenkins, & Moreton, 2003). This analysis provides information that is useful in matching the organization's resources and capabilities to the competitive environment in which it operates. The SWOT analysis filters the information to identify major issues for administrators to address. It classifies internal aspects of the organization as strengths or weaknesses and the external situational factors as opportunities or threats. A completed SWOT analysis may be used for goal setting, strategy formulation, and implementation. This analysis is best conducted with many stakeholders, including the campus president, human resource director, and faculty (Williamson et al., 2003).

Additional Affirmative Responses

The incompatibility between workplace and family demands is exacerbated by a relative lack of provisions that would ease women's integration of these roles. Traditional occupational policies reflect a separation of family from work life and a societal expectation that mothers remain at home to care for their children. Equality of parenting and housekeeping roles has not been achieved (Paludi, Vaccariello, Graham, Smith, Allen-Dicker, Kasprzak, & White, 2007).

The terminology has changed also. *Juggling* was the first term to connote women combining work and family lives. This term was changed to *balancing*, also connoting that it is women's responsibility to excel in both spheres. The term *integration* is currently in vogue. This term has acknowledged the responsibility of organizations to assist women in meeting work and life responsibilities, including parenting and elder care (Paludi & Neidermeyer, 2007).

Such goals include:

a. Reducing women's isolation in male-dominated departments or institutions.
b. Addressing women's experience as outsiders or being marginalized (Gibson, 2006), and providing support for challenges particular to women's career development and advancement (Quinlan, 1999).
c. In addition, there must be a substantial number of women, especially minority women, among the faculty in departments. This has been achieved in certain disciplines, but not in others, including neuropsychology, management, engineering, and other STEM careers (Storm & Gurevich, 2001).
d. The number of women in administrative positions in the academy must be increased so as to make women central, not marginal, to academia.
e. Ensure minority faculty are present to work with minority students. Research by DeFour (1991), Moses (1988), and Vasquez and Daniel (2010) provided compelling evidence of the importance of African American faculty in the retention of African American undergraduate and graduate students. Contact with African American faculty was associated with better academic performance and psychological well-being.
f. Offer family-friendly policies, including career break policies for faculty who need to integrate work and life roles.
g. Train faculty and administrators about hidden biases, incivility, and microaggressions. The goal is to assist campuses in dealing with multiple forms of bias toward women simultaneously rather than independently. We apply the broken windows theory to campus bias against women faculty: If what is perceived by the campus to be trivial isn't handled immediately, more severe forms of discrimination and harassment will result.
h. Establish effective, objective criteria for evaluating applicants and faculty.
i. Develop, monitor, and evaluate tenure clock stop.
j. Offer paid leave and tenure clock stop for women faculty who adopt as well as who give birth to children.
k. Provide child care for women faculty.

l. Provide funds to help women faculty defray child care and/or elder care during attendance at academic conferences.

The American Council on Education, Office of Women in Higher Education (2005) has provided several recommendations for campuses, including:

a. Creating policies for faculty to take multiple-year leaves for professional and/or personal reasons.
b. Providing tenure-tack or tenured faculty to opt to take part-time positions to be used for a certain period of time as personal needs arise.
c. Providing flexible time frames for probationary periods.
d. Establishing tenure-track reentry programs for Ph.D.s who left academia full time to care for family members.

Examples of Redefining the Academy to Value Women and Women's Realities

Bernstein and Russo (2007) noted that "the attrition of talented women from the academy begins early on and continues at each successive step, even after professional goals emerge and women consider graduate programs" (p. 91). Examples of campus attempts to value women faculty include:

a. Harvard University's Dean Light (cited in Merrigan & White, 2010) implemented a policy (which became effective in 2006) by which women professors who gave birth were provided one additional year in the "tenure clock" and extended maternity leave.
b. MIT and Stanford implemented accommodations for their women graduate students (Jaschik, 2005): the option of taking a twelve-week period to take care of third-trimester pregnancies, delivery, and care for newborns. Women remain matriculated during this time-off period and thereby receive financial support. They also are provided a one-term extension to complete their graduation requirements. Similar programs have been implemented by the National Science Foundation ADVANCE program (see Bernstein & Russo, 2007), including extending tenure decisions for women wanting to start their families.

c. The University of Michigan established the STRIDE training program for faculty to learn about the impact of their unexamined stereotypes and bias toward women. STRIDE has recruited full professors to participate in an ongoing committee that provides advice on strategies to recruit a diverse and well-qualified faculty. The university indicates the STRIDE program is related to an increase in new female faculty hires in science and engineering: 14 percent to 34 percent in a period of four years (The Center for WorkLife Law, 2010).

d. The University of California, Davis has developed a policy that explicitly states that faculty who are eligible to stop the clock shall not be arbitrarily disadvantaged for taking childbearing/childrearing leave or for stopping the clock (The Center for WorkLife Law, 2010).

e. The Family Friendly Edge at UC Berkeley facilitates a "School for Chairs." Department chairs throughout the university are instructed in how to (1) discount resume gaps attributable to parenthood; (2) mentor new faculty parents through the tenure process; (3) assist in finding a second job for dual-career couples; (4) establish and maintain a more family-responsive climate through small changes such as ending faculty meetings by 5 PM; and (5) ensure that stopping the clock or taking family leave does not count against candidates. UC Berkeley has identified increases in hiring rates for new women faculty from 26 percent to nearly 40 percent in the last few years (The Center for WorkLife Law, 2010).

f. Case Western Reserve University developed a toolkit in order to ensure recruitment of women faculty. The university emphasized that "diversity is a process, not an outcome." In addition, the Office of Faculty Diversity provides resources at each stage of the recruitment process, as well as readings and resources to educate its faculty on gender bias (The Center for WorkLife Law, 2010).

Universities who implement such policies report positive ramifications for faculty, including: lower absenteeism, less stress, higher morale, improved work satisfaction, lower turnover rate, staffing over a wide range of hours, child care hours that conform to work hours, and access to quality infant and child care (Frone & Yardley, 1996; Paludi, Vaccariello, Graham, Smith, Allen-Dicker, Kasprzak, & White, 2007). As Chrisler and Johnston-Robledo (2010) concluded:

Given that scholars . . . have concluded that the presence of supportive supervisors may be as important as family-friendly policies, the need for change at the interpersonal level is dire. Human resources personnel could conduct workshops to help supervisors examine their beliefs, stereotypes, biases, and resultant treatment of mothers in the workplace. All managers, supervisors, department chairs, and other leaders should be fully aware of family-responsive policies and other resources that are available to employees in their workplace, and they should make it clear that the resources are there to be used. (pp. 126–27)

These recommendations may be difficult to implement in some universities, considering continued biases toward women in academia and the reluctance of changing tenure and promotion decisions (Halpern, 2004).

We concur with these culture climate changes in the university if women are ever to achieve parity with men in salary, mentoring, and networking opportunities, unbiased evaluations, promotions, and tenure awards and work/life integration. As Chrisler and Johnston-Robledo stated, "Good policies that clearly are supported by top officials eventually will filter down and change organizational culture for the better" (pp. 126–27).

References

Abel, M., & Meltzer, A. (2007). Student ratings of male and female professors' lecture on sex discrimination in the workforce. *Sex Roles, 57,* 173–80.

American Council on Education, Office of Women in Higher Education. (2005). *An agenda for excellence: Creating flexibility in tenure-track faculty careers.* Washington, DC: American Council on Education.

American Psychological Association Center for Workforce Studies. (2008). *2008–09 APA survey of graduate departments of psychology.* Washington, DC: American Psychological Association.

American Psychological Association. (2009). *Faculty salaries in graduate departments of psychology survey, NSF/NIH Survey of doctorate recipients.* Washington, DC: American Psychological Association.

Andersson, L., & Pearson, C. (1999). Tit for tat? The spiraling effect of incivility in the workplace. *Academy of Management Review, 24,* 452–71.

Armenti, C. (2004). May babies and posttenure babies: Maternal decisions of women professors. *Review of Higher Education: Journal of the Association for the Study of Higher Education, 27,* 211–31.

Banerji, S. (2006). AAUP: Women professors lag in tenure, salary. *Diverse.* Retrieved June 21, 2010, from: http://diverseeducation.com/article/6571/.

Basow, S. (2010). Women in education: Students and professors worldwide. In M. Paludi (Ed.), *Feminism and women's rights worldwide. Vol. 1: Heritage, roles and issues* (pp. 43–62). Westport, CT: Praeger.

Beale, F. (1970). *Double jeopardy: To be black and female.* Detroit, MI: Radical Education Project.

Bernstein, B., & Russo, N. F. (2007). Career paths and family in the academy: Progress and challenges. In M. Paludi & P. Niedermeyer (Eds.), *Work, life and family imbalance: How to level the playing field* (pp. 89–119). Westport, CT: Praeger.

Bernstein, B., & Russo, N. F. (2008). Explaining too few women in STEM careers: A psychosocial perspective. In M. Paludi (Ed.), *The psychology of women at work: Challenges and solutions for our female workforce. Vol. 2: Obstacles and the identity juggle* (pp. 1–33). Westport, CT: Praeger.

Betz, N., & Schifano, R. (2000). Evaluation of an intervention to increase realistic self-efficacy and interests in college women. *Journal of Vocational Behavior, 56,* 35–52.

Bilimoria, D., Joy, S., & Liang, X. (2008). Breaking barriers and creating inclusiveness: Lessons of organizational transformation to advance women faculty in academic science and engineering. *Human Resource Management, 47,* 423–41.

Bronstein, P., Rothblum, E., & Solomon, S. (1993). Ivy halls and glass walls: Barriers to academic careers for women and ethnic minorities. In R. Boice & J. Gainen (Eds.), *New directions for teaching and learning, No. 53.* San Francisco: Jossey-Bass.

Brown, A., Swinyard, W., & Ogle, J. (2003). Women in academic medicine: A report of focus groups and questionnaires with conjoint analysis. *Journal of Women's Health, 12,* 999–1008.

Casto, C., Caldwell, C., & Salazar, C. (2005). Creating mentoring relationships between female faculty and students in counselor education: Guidelines for potential mentees and mentors. *Journal of Counseling and Development, 83,* 331–36.

Center for WorkLife Law (2010). *Control bias.* Retrieved June 23, 2010, from http://www.worklifelaw.org/EffectivePracticesToRetainWomen/controlBias.html.

Chrisler, J., & Johnson-Robledo, I. (2010). Pregnancy discrimination. In M. Paludi, C. Paludi, & E. DeSouza (Eds.), *Praeger handbook on understanding and preventing workplace discrimination* (pp. 105–32). Westport, CT: Praeger.

Clifford, V. (2003, May). *Group mentoring: An alternative way of working.* Paper presented at the Second National Conference on Women in Science, Technology, and Engineering, Sydney, Australia.

Collins, A. (2009). *African American women face serious challenges in climb up the corporate ladder.* Retrieved May 19, 2010, from: http://www.theglasshammer.com/news/2009/02/12/african-american-women-face-serious-challenges-in-climb-up-the-corporate-ladder/.

Collins, L., Chrisler, J., & Quina, K. (Eds.). (1998). *Career strategies for women in academe: Arming Athena.* Thousand Oaks, CA: Sage.

Cooper, C., Cartwright, S., & Earley, C. (2001). *The international handbook of organizational culture and climate.* New York: Wiley.

Cross, A. (1986). *Death in a tenured position.* New York: Ballantine.

de Janasz, S. (2006). Alternative approaches to mentoring in the new millennium. In M. Karsten (Ed.), *Gender, race and ethnicity in the workplace* (pp. 131–47). Westport, CT: Praeger.

DeFour, D. C. (1991). Issues in mentoring ethnic minority students. *Focus, 5,* 1–2.

De la Luz Reyes, M., & Halcon, J. (1988). Racism in academia: The old wolf revisited. *Harvard Education Review, 58,* 299–314.

Denmark, F. L., & Klara, M. D. (2010). Women mentors and their effect on educational and professional career development. In C. A. Rayburn, F. L. Denmark, M. E. Reuder, & A. M. Austria (Eds.), *A handbook for women mentors: Transcending barriers of stereotype, race and ethnicity* (pp. 3–20). Westport, CT: Praeger.

Denmark, F. L., & Paludi, M. A. (2010). History of women and feminism. In R. Rieber (Ed.), *Encyclopedia of the history of psychological theories.* New York: Springer.

DeSouza, E., & Fansler, A. (2003). Contrapower sexual harassment: A survey of students and faculty members. *Sex Roles, 48,* 529–42.

Dineen, M., & Bartlett, R. (2002). *Six steps to root cause analysis.* Oxford: Consequence.

Driskill, G., & Benton, A. (2005). *Organizational culture in action: A cultural analysis workbook.* New York: Sage.

Eagly, A., & Karau, S. (2002). Role congruity theory of prejudice toward female leaders. *Psychological Bulletin, 108,* 233–56.

Ely, R., & Rhode, D. (2008). *Women and leadership: Defining the challenges.* Retrieved May 6, 2010, from: http://www.hbs.edu/leadership/docs/ElyRhodepaper.pdf.

Frone, M., & Yardley, J. (1996). Workplace family-supportive programmes: Predictors of employed parents' importance ratings. *Journal of Occupational and Organizational Psychology, 69,* 351–66.

Furumoto, L., & Scarborough, E. (1986). Placing women in the history of psychology: The first American woman psychologists. *American Psychologist, 41,* 35–42.

Gee, M. (2006). Double jeopardy survival: Insights and lessons learned in organizational battlefields. In M. F. Karsten (Ed.), *Gender, race and ethnicity in the workplace: Issues and challenges for today's organizations* (pp. 185–97). Westport, CT: Praeger.

Gibson, S. K. (2006). Mentoring of women faculty: The role of organizational politics and culture. *Innovative Higher Education, 31,* 63–79.

Gonzales-Morales, M., Peiro, J., & Greenglass, E. (2006). Coping and distress in organizations: The role of gender in work stress. *International Journal of Stress Management, 13,* 228–48.

Hall, R. M., & Sandler, B. R. (1982). *The campus climate: A chilly one for women?* Washington, DC: Association of American Colleges (Report of the Project on the Status and Education of Women).

Halpern, D. (2004). President's column: Obstacles to female full professorship: Another civil-rights issue. *APA Monitor, 35,* 5.

Hammer, L., Neal, M., Newsom, J., Brockwood, K., & Collton, C. (2006). A longitudinal study of the effects of dual-earner couples' utilization of family workplace supports on work and family outcomes. *Journal of Applied Psychology, 90,* 799–810.

Han, W., Waldfogel, J., & Brooks-Gunn, J. (2001). The effects of early maternal employment on later cognitive and behavioral outcomes. *Journal of Marriage and the Family, 63,* 336–54.

Hanisch, C. (1969). The personal is political. In K. Sarachild (Ed.), *Feminist revolution: Redstockings of the women's liberation movement.* New York: Random House.

Heilman, M., Wallen, A., Fuchs, D., & Tamkins, M. (2004). Penalties for success: Reactions to women who succeed at male gender-typed tasks. *Journal of Applied Psychology, 89,* 416–27.

Hernandez, A. (2010). Scholar says research universities not serious about faculty diversity. *Diverse.* Retrieved June 21, 2010 from: http://diverseeducation.com/article/13868/scholar-says-research-universities-not-serious.

Hochschild, A. (1989). *The second shift.* New York: Viking.

Hune, S. (1998). Asian Pacific American women in higher education: Claiming visibility and voice. Washington, DC: Association of American Colleges and Universities.

Inside Higher Ed. (2008). *The teaching paradox.* Retrieved June 19, 2010, from http://www.insidehighered.com/news/2008/12/29/gender.

Inside Higher Ed. (2010). *The B-school glass ceiling.* Retrieved June 19, 2010, from www.insidehighered.com/layout/set/print/news/2010/02/23/business.

Jandeska, K. E., & Kraimer, M. L. (2005). Women's perceptions of organizational culture, work attitudes, and role-modeling behaviors. *Journal of Managerial Issues, 18,* 461–78.

Jaschik, S. (2005). New rights for pregnant grad students. *Inside Higher Education.* Retrieved December 9, 2009, from http://www.insidehighered.com/news/2005/11/15/stanford.

Kanter, R. M. (1977). *Work and family in the United States: A critical review and agenda for research and policy.* New York: Russell Sage Foundation.

Karsten, M. (2006). Managerial women, minorities and stress: Causes and consequences. In M. Karsten (Ed.), *Gender, race and ethnicity in the workplace* (pp. 238–72). Westport, CT: Praeger.

Kaschak, E. (2006). Another look at sex bias in students' evaluations of professors. *Psychology of Women Quarterly, 5,* 767–72.

Kim, J. (2006). Gender inequality in the U.S. labor market: Evidence from the 2000 census. In M. F. Karsten (Ed.). *Gender, race and ethnicity in the workplace: Issues and challenges for today's organizations* (pp. 270–90). Westport, CT: Praeger.

Kierstead, D., D'Agostino, P., & Dill, H. (1988). Sex role stereotyping of college professors: Bias in students' ratings of instructors. *Journal of Educational Psychology, 80,* 342–44.

LaFrance, M. (1987, July). *Paradoxes in mentoring.* Paper presented at the International Interdisciplinary Congress on Women, Dublin, Ireland.

Lockwood, N. (2003, June). Work/life balance: Challenges and solutions. *Society for Human Resource Management Research Quarterly,* 1–10

Martin, J. (2008). Shifting the load: Personality factors and women in the workplace. In M. Paludi (Ed.), *The psychology of women at work: Challenges and solutions for our female workforce* (pp. 153–200). Westport, CT: Praeger.

Mason, G. (2010). Sorry, professor, but women do still face hiring discrimination. *The Globe and mail.* Retrieved June 20, 2010, from http://www.theglobeandmail.com/news/national/british-columbia/gary_mason/sorry-professor-but-women-do-still-face-hiring-discrimination/article1589954/.

Mason, M., & Goulden, M. (2004). Do babies matter? The effect of family formation on the lifelong careers of academic men and women. *Academe, 88,* 21–23.

Mason, M., & Goulden, M. (2006). *UC Doctoral Student Career Life Survey.* Retrieved June 21, 2010, from http://ucfamilyedge.berkeley.edu.

Mason, M., Goulden, M., & Wolfinger, N. (2004). Redefining gender equity in the academy. *Annals of the American Academy of Political and Social Science, 596*, 86–193.

Merrigan, T., & White, W. (2010). *Harvard business school grapples with gender imbalance.* Retrieved June 22, 2010, from http://www.the crimson.com/article/2010/4/14/faculty-school-business-women/.

Miles-Cohen, S., Keita, G., Twose, G., & Houston, S. (2010). Beyond mentoring: Opening doors and systems. In C. A. Rayburn, F. L. Denmark, M. E. Reuder, & A. M. Austria (Eds.), *A handbook for women mentors: Transcending barriers of stereotype, race and ethnicity* (pp. 233–48). Westport, CT: Praeger.

Moses, Y. (1988). *Black women in the academy.* Washington, DC: Project on the Status and Education of Women.

Nadal, K. L. (2010). Gender microaggressions: Implications for mental health. In M. Paludi (Ed.), *Feminism and women's rights worldwide. Vol. 2: Mental and physical health* (pp. 155–75). Westport, CT: Praeger.

National Academies. (2009). *Women faring well in hiring and tenure processes for science and engineer jobs at research universities, but still underrepresented in applicant pools.* Retrieved June 24, 2010, from http://www8.nationalacademies.org/onpinews/newsitem.aspx ?RecordID=12062.

Nelson, D. (2007). *A national analysis of minorities in science and engineering faculties at research universities.* Retrieved June 20, 2010, from http://cheminfo.chem.ou.edu/faculty/djn/diversity/Faculty_Tables _FY07/FinalReport07.html.

Paludi, M., Martin, J. L., Paludi, C., Boggess, S., Hicks, K., & Speech, L. (2010). Pay equity as justice: United States and international perspectives. In M. Paludi (Ed.), *Feminism and women's rights worldwide* (vol. 3, pp. 147–76). Westport, CT: Praeger.

Paludi, M., Martin, J., Stern, T., & DeFour, D. (2010). *Mentoring women in academia and business.* In C. A. Rayburn, F. L. Denmark, M. E. Reuder, & A. M. Austria (Eds.), *Handbook for women mentors: Transcending barriers of stereotype, race, and ethnicity* (pp. 80–108). Westport, CT: Praeger.

Paludi, M., & Neidermeyer, P. (Eds.). (2007). *Work, life and family imbalance: How to level the playing field.* Westport, CT: Praeger.

Paludi, M., Vaccariello, R., Graham, T., Smith, M., Allen-Dicker, K., Kasprzak, H., & White, C. (2007). Work/life integration: Impact on women's careers, employment, and family. In M. A. Paludi & P. E. Neidermeyer (Eds.), *Work, life and family imbalance: How to level the playing field* (pp. 21–36). Westport, CT: Praeger.

PhysOrg.com. (2010). *Even highly qualified women in academic medicine paid less than equally qualified men.* Retrieved on June 24, 2010, from http://www.physorg.com/news189233838.html.

Porter, S., Toutkoushian, R., & Moore, J. (2008). Pay inequities for recently hired faculty, 1988–2004. *Review of Higher Education: Journal of the Association for the Study of Higher Education, 31*, 465–87.

Preston, A. (2004). *Leaving science: Occupational exit from science careers.* New York: Russell Sage Foundation.

Quinlan, K. M. (1999). Enhancing mentoring and networking of junior academic women: What, why, and how? *Journal of Higher Education Policy and Management, 21,* 31–42.

Ragins, B. (1989). Barriers to mentoring: The female manager's dilemma. *Human Relations, 42,* 1–22.

Renzulli, L., Aldrich, H. E., & Moody, J. (2000). Family matters: Consequences of personal networks for business startup and survival. Social Forces, *79*, 523–46.

Rospenda, K., Richman, J., & Nawyn, S. (1988). Doing power: The confluence of gender, race, and class in contrapower sexual harassment. *Gender and Society, 12,* 40–60.

Rossiter, M. (1982). *Women scientists in America: Struggles and strategies to 1940.* Baltimore: Johns Hopkins University Press.

Sanders, K., Willemsen, T., & Millar, C. (2009). Views from above the glass ceiling: Does the academic environment influence women professors' careers and experiences? *Sex Roles, 60,* 301–12.

Schmidt, P. (2010, May 4). Chief targets of student incivility are female and young professors. *Chronicle of Higher Education.* Retrieved

June 23, 2010, from http://chronicle.com/article/Chief-Targets-of-Student/ 65396/.

Shakeshaft, C., Brown, G., Irby, B., Grogan, M., & Ballenger, J. (2007). Increasing gender equity in educational leadership. In S. Klein (Ed.), *Handbook for achieving gender equity through education* (2nd ed., pp. 103–29). Mahwah, NJ: Erlbaum.

Sinclair, L., & Kunda, Z. (2000). Motivated stereotyping of women: She's fine if she praised me but incompetent if she criticized me. *Personality and Social Psychology Bulletin, 26,* 1329–42.

Smith, G., & Anderson, K. (2005). Students' ratings of professors: The teaching style contingency for Latino/a professors. *Journal of Latinos and Education, 4,* 115–36.

Smith, S., & Mazin, R. (2004). *The HR answer book.* New York: AMACOM.

Sonnert, G., & Holton, G. (1995). *Gender differences in science careers.* New Brunswick, NJ: Rutgers University Press.

Storm, C., & Gurevich, M. (2001). Looking forward, looking back. Women in psychology. *Canadian Psychology, 42,* 245–48.

Sue, S., Capodilupo, C., Torino, G., Bucceri, J., Holder, A., & Nadal, K. L. (2007). Racial microaggressions in everyday life: Implications for counseling. *The American Psychologist, 62,* 271–86.

Swoboda, M., & Millar, S. (1986). Networking mentoring: Career strategy of women in academic administration. *Journal of the NAWDAC, 49,* 8–13.

Turner, C. (2002). Women of color in academe: Living with multiple marginality. *JSTOR: Journal of Higher Education, 73,* 74–93.

van Anders, S. (2004). Why the academic pipeline leaks: Fewer men than women perceive barriers to becoming professors. *Sex Roles, 51,* 511–21.

Vasquez, M., & Daniel, J. (2010). Women of color as mentors. In C. A. Rayburn, F. L. Denmark, M. E. Reuder, & A. M. Austria (Eds.), *A handbook for women mentors: Transcending barriers of stereotype, race and ethnicity* (pp. 173–86). Westport, CT: Praeger.

Ward, L. (2008). Female faculty in male-dominated fields: Law, medicine and engineering. *New Directions in Higher Education, 2008,* 63–72.

Wiley, M. G., & Eskilson, A. (1985). Speech style, gender stereotypes, and corporate success: What if women talk more like men? *Sex Roles, 12,* 993–1007

Williamson, D., Cooke, P., Jenkins, W., & Moreton, K. (2003). *Strategic management and business analysis.* Burlington, MA: Butterworth-Heinemann.

4

Glass Ceilings and Sticky Floors: Women and Advancement in Higher Education

Susan V. Iverson

An ever-growing body of research exists on women and advancement in higher education, articulating challenges and delineating strategies for women as they seek promotion and enter leadership roles (e.g., professional development, leadership training, mentoring). However, as Harlan and Berheide (1994) observed in their analysis of the advancement of women who work in low-paying jobs, the vast majority of employed women will never advance high enough to encounter the "glass ceiling"—the invisible barrier that keeps women from advancing because they are women. Rather, they are trapped on what Berheide (1992) termed the "sticky floor"—low-wage, low-mobility jobs. Further, as some scholars observe, certain jobs, such as clerical positions, may actually constrain advancement (Gale & Cartwright, 1995; Johnsrud, 1991). This chapter shares findings from a study designed to understand the experiences of those women who occupied clerical positions and then advanced into professional positions.

The concerns of professional women—those occupying faculty, administrative, and managerial ranks—largely remain the focus of most scholarship on women's employment experiences in higher education. Little scholarly attention has been given to women in classified and clerical roles (Bonk, Crouch, Kilian, & Lowell, 2006; Johnsrud & Banaria, 2005), and in particular there is a lack of information on the experiences of women in such roles who move into professional positions (Hite & McDonald,

2003; Pilgrim, 1997; Ransel, Fitzpatrick, & Hinds, 2001). This study of women's advancement from clerical to professional positions serves to contribute to that gap.

Drawing upon a feminist lens, this chapter critically analyzes how this investigation of women crossing the boundary between clerical and professional ranks can expand our understanding of the effect of gendered organization on the careers of women; the ways in which existing practices (may) limit women's advancement; and the ways in which structurally embedded sexism and classism operate to sustain organizational hierarchies that marginalize and restrict women's movement within the educational system.

A Feminist Perspective

A feminist perspective informs this analysis of women's advancement from clerical to professional roles. A feminist approach to research "consists of no single set of agreed upon research guidelines" (Maguire, 1987, p. 74); rather, it attends to the "basic significance of gender . . . accounting for the everyday experiences of women which have been neglected" (Cook & Fonow, 1986, p. 22). This perspective posits that traditional ways of knowing and experiencing the world have excluded women as "agents of knowledge" (Harding, 1986). As a framework for research, feminism aims to give voice to women's experiences; seeks to reveal and overcome androcentric biases; and uses research as a tool for emancipation and social change (McHugh & Cosgrove, 1998; Reinharz, 1992).

The study of organizations, leadership, and power has typically focused on men, maleness, and masculinity, even though we rarely acknowledged it as such (Duerst-Lahti & Kelly, 1995). A feminist perspective serves to challenge the "ungendered innocence" that much of the workplace scholarship claims (Duerst-Lahti & Kelly, 1995, p. 26). Feminist approaches to the study of workplaces situate women as the point of analysis; they recognize "male dominance in social arrangements and [assert] a desire for changes from this form of dominance" (Calas & Smircich, 1996, p. 219). A feminist perspective views organizations, such as work and education, as socially constructed, serving particular (white male) interests, and re/producing a gendered hierarchy with sex-segregated occupations (Acker, 1990; Tierney & Bensimon, 2000). Such an analysis often extends the focus beyond the organization or job or worker (a potentially decontextualized individual or phenomenon) to an analysis of gender and power: it is a "critique of the status quo" (Calas & Smircich, 1996, p. 219).

Review of Relevant Literature

The Gendered Organization

An organizational bureaucracy is traditionally described in the literature as a managerial culture where the leader represents a hero figure at the top of a power hierarchy (Baldridge, Curtis, Ecker, & Riley, 1977). These perspectives focused on the "heroic" or "great" man (Freeman, Bourque, & Shelton, 2001, p. 7) directing an organization by retaining power in a top-down system creating a structure of positional leadership (Kezar, Carducci, & Contraras-McGavin, 2006). Such perspectives on leadership, power, and organizational hierarchy have typically focused on men, maleness, and masculinity (Duerst-Lahti & Kelly, 1995); that is until Acker (1990) and others (Ferguson, 1984; Kanter, 1977; MacKinnon, 1979) began to make explicit—and problematic—that power and leadership were, and remain, male dominated. In the decades since, scholars have continued to illuminate the link between masculinity and organizational power and the production (and maintenance) of the gendered organization and the "ideal worker" (Acker, 1990, 2006; Britton, 2000; Eddy & Cox, 2008).

Acker (1990) defined a gendered organization as a place where "meaning and identity, exploitation and control, and advantage and disadvantage are patterned through and in terms of a distinction between male and female" (p. 146). Kanter (1977) argued that the problems women have in the organization "are consequences of their structural placement, crowded in dead-end jobs at the bottom and exposed as tokens at the top" (in Acker, 1990, p. 143). Yet Kanter's analysis centers on the seemingly gender-neutral organizational structure and not on how these structures—the organization itself—are gendered, producing differential effects for men and women, inextricably linked to other identity dimensions as well (i.e., race, sexuality, class) in the organization. As Acker (2006) observed, gendered practices within the organization, such as hiring practices, wages, supervision, and informal interactions, all "produce class, gender and racial inequalities" (p. 447). These practices, policies, and procedures—the structure of the organization—re/produce the standard of the "ideal worker."

The Ideal Worker

The ideal worker is a masculine notion; someone who works full time, perhaps overtime, and without family responsibilities (Acker, 1990; Tiernari, Quack, & Theobald, 2002; Williams, 2000). Although jobs and workers appear abstract, ungendered, and disembodied, the ideal worker typically corresponds to a man's body. Acker (1992) noted that this worker "turns out to be a man whose work is his life and whose wife takes care of everything else" (p. 257). Williams (2002) too observed, "if employers define the ideal worker as someone who takes no time off for childbearing or childrearing, they are framing their ideal worker as someone with the body and traditional life patterns of a [heterosexual] male" (p. 828). Women, then, should they choose to work outside the home, are consequently situated in a double bind—a situation in which a person cannot win, no matter what she does; they must perform the (masculine) ideal worker role, while then working a "second shift" as the "good" wife and mother (Allan, 2003; Appelbaum, Audet, & Miller, 2003; Hochschild & Machung, 1989).

This definition of the ideal worker is not static or universal. Tiernari et al. (2002) posited that different models of work organization and varied societal contexts yield different albeit "equally gendered notions" of the ideal worker (p. 251). But, as Acker (2006) noted, the gendered organization and gendered notions of work remain resistant to change in spite of efforts to erase inequalities. Williams (2000) argued that instead of simply allowing women to work on the same terms traditionally available to men, we need to restructure the work conditions under which both men and women work and eliminate the masculinist norm of the ideal worker.

Another feature of the gendered organization is "an organizational logic that assumes a congruence between responsibility, job complexity, and hierarchical position" (Acker, 1990, p. 148). The more senior a position in the organization, the more a "skilled" worker (or "professional") is assumed to manage professional tasks that involve complexity. By contrast, lower-level positions in an organizational hierarchy, those jobs disproportionately filled by women, are assumed to have low levels of complexity and responsibility ("unskilled work"). Women seeking advancement in an organization frequently encounter barriers or the "glass ceiling" (Hede & Ralston, 1993; Reichman & Sterling, 2004).

The Glass Ceiling

The glass ceiling is the invisible barrier that prevents a qualified person from advancing. The term, coined in the 1980s (see Carnes, Morrissey, & Geller, 2008; Falk & Grizard, 2005), has many variations to reflect the intersection of gender with other dimensions of identity, such as Latina administrators' encounter with the adobe ceiling (Ramos, 2008), lesbian administrators' bump into the lavender ceiling (Swan, 1995), women administrators in Catholic schools reaching the stained glass ceiling (Adams, 2007; Wood, 2009), the concrete ceiling that will not break for women of color (Davidson, 1997), and the Plexiglas room in which female tenured faculty are placed (Glazer-Raymo, 2008), among other related adaptations (Hesse-Biber & Carter, 2005).

The most tangible evidence of a glass ceiling is unequal pay for comparable work (Booth, Francesconi, & Frank, 2003). A study conducted by the American Association of University Women (AAUW, 2007) found that one year after graduation from college, women earn 5 percent less than men. After ten years, the gap increased to 12 percent. AAUW explained the gap as a clear example of gender discrimination. But explanations for the ceiling continue to be elusive. Some studies have examined the impact of very specific factors on women's advancement, such as the role of mentoring (Anderson, 2005). For instance, Mattis (2004), in her analysis of women entrepreneurs who left corporate careers to start their own businesses, illuminated the lack of role models and mentoring as one of several factors associated with corporate "glass ceilings." Other studies have investigated a range of variables that may serve as determinants of advancement (Giscombe & Mattis, 2002; Ivarsson & Ekehammar, 2001; Tharenou, Latimer, & Conroy, 1994). For example, Marongiu and Ekehammar (1999), in their study of the influence of individual and situational factors on the career advancement of women and men, found that instrumentality/masculinity is positively linked (and the major predictive factor) to managerial advancement.

Sticky Floors

Many women do not ascend high enough to reach the glass ceiling; rather, they are stuck on the "sticky floor" of low-ranking jobs (Reskin & Padavic, 2006). Reichman and Sterling (2004) observed that "simply being female" continues to be a factor in advancement decisions and that "women continue to be systematically disadvantaged" (p. 29), yielding compensation and promotion disparities that "result in 'sticky floors' on which women get stuck, 'broken steps' on which women fall into traps, and 'concrete ceilings' against which women's advancement rebounds" (p. 30). Arguing that individual and interpersonal explanations blame the workers for their failures to advance, Rainbird (2007) further called attention to the structural problems facing low-paid workers: occupational sex segregation, pay inequality, and shallow career progression masked as advancement, but gluing women to low-status, low-wage occupations.

Myerson and Fletcher (2000) observed, "it's not the glass ceiling that's holding women back; it's the whole structure of the organizations in which we work" (p. 136). Numerous researchers agree that structural barriers are pervasive and women (and racial minorities) have less opportunity to advance and less access to power than men do (Anderson, 2005; Gale & Cartwright, 1995; Newman, 1993; Rainbird, 2007; Rasmussen, 2001; Worts, Fox, & McDonough, 2007). The implications of a masculinist organizational culture are often most directly felt by women (and racial minorities), since the dominant culture determines the criteria for distribution of rewards and availability of advancement opportunities (Johnsrud, 1991). For instance, women tend to be clustered in entry-level positions and are rewarded for "long-term loyalty and single-job stability," whereas men tend to enter positions that "foster opportunity because they provide incumbents with exposure, visibility, information, and connections" (Johnsrud, 1991, p. 130). Nearly fifteen years later, Johnsrud and Banaria (2005) document the same gendered distribution in occupations, with women vastly outnumbering men in the clerical and secretarial groups, and men vastly outnumbering women in skilled professions (p. 88). Thus, a feminist analysis holds potential to illuminate how gendered organizational practices hinder women's advancement.

Methods

The data presented here are from an analysis of transcripts from interviews with twenty-two women from one public research university in New England. The qualitative study was informed by phenomenology, an approach that "seeks to make explicit the implicit structure and meaning of human experience" (Sanders, 1982, p. 354), and "focuses on people living experiences" (Davis, 1991, p. 9); through rich and descriptive data, it elicits how people "construct the world through descriptions of perceptions" (p. 11). Central to this approach is the "temporary suspension of all existing personal biases, beliefs, preconceptions, or assumptions" in order to be more open to the phenomenon (Sanders, p. 355); this suspension process is called bracketing. As a university employee, committed to women's equity within higher education, it was necessary for me to acknowledge and attempt to bracket those experiences.

In seeking to understand their women's experiences, I explored:

- What personal and professional needs and interests motivated one's move into a new position?
- What institutional factors enhanced or impeded each woman's job transition?
- What level of educational attainment preceded a woman's advancement?
- What formal and informal systems of support do women take advantage of?

The twenty-two women who comprised the sample for this investigation were employed at the university from seven to forty-five years; they had entered the university workforce from 1961 to 1999. The women ranged in ages from early thirties to mid sixties. All but two women spoke of marriages, divorces, and/or remarriages and rearing one to four children. All participants are white, and two self-identified as Franco-American. This racial profile was reflective of the university's predominantly white demographic; of the 580 female classified employees and 290 female professional employees, nearly 98 percent are Caucasian (per 2007 institutional data).

At the time of their interviews, the women in this sample held a variety of professional positions with the university, such as Director of Human

Resources, Assistant Director for Equal Opportunity and Diversity, Assistant Director for Financial Aid, Computer and Network Specialist, and Senior Assistant to the Provost. Yet all started their careers at the university in part-time and full-time clerical positions, such as secretaries, stenographers, receptionists, clerk typists, and records technicians.

Each participated in one in-depth semistructured interview that explored the following: description of current position, first position, and career trajectory; what personal and organizational factors contributed to advancement (i.e., length of service, skill development, further education); what are differences in perceptions (by self and others) of roles as "classified" and "professional"; what systems of support (i.e., professional organizations, unions, mentoring) were sought or used; what was significant to the career journey about being a woman.

Each audiotaped interview was transcribed and the transcripts were imported into NVivo, computer software designed for qualitative data analysis. Meanings were then formulated from significant statements and phrases; these were clustered, allowing for the emergence of an "essential structure" common to all the participants' transcripts (Polkinghorne, 1989; also Giorgi, 1994; Sanders, 1982). All transcripts were then reanalyzed inductively, listening for silences, exploring how gender shapes workplace experiences, and focusing on how power and knowledge operate through organizational practices (Bloom, 1998; Reinharz, 1992), with the hope that through this feminist exploration, administrators and policy makers can rethink the construction of personnel policies and advancement practices. Methodological rigor, contributing to the trustworthiness and soundness of the findings, was achieved through bracketing past experiences, using an adequate sample, and maintaining an audit trail.

Findings and Interpretation

Several key findings were identified in women's descriptions of their experiences moving from classified to professional ranks (see Iverson, 2009). Drawing on a feminist lens, I illuminate how the boundaries between classified and professional positions are defined and inscribed, the realities for women crossing these boundaries, the organizational practices that (re)produce the boundaries, and the significance of gender to these women's workplace experiences.

Defining the Boundaries

Before hearing women's descriptions of their experiences moving from classified to professional ranks, it was important to understand the "organizational logic" (Acker, 1990) that defined the boundaries between these two groups—professional and classified employees. When I initiated this project, I posed a query to the director of human resources to discern the edges of these abstract job categories. She described one only difference—professionals are exempt from both minimum wage and overtime pay, whereas classified employees are not exempt. Professional employees, thus, are typically paid on a salaried basis and classified employees are generally paid hourly wages,[1] and separate collective bargaining units represent each group.

A review of U.S. Department of Labor definitions gave further meaning to these two groups. Professionals (salaried employees) are distinguished by a key qualification: advanced knowledge, "customarily acquired by a prolonged course of specialized intellectual instruction."[2] The U.S. Fair Labor Standards Act (FLSA) elaborates on the significance of advanced knowledge to the identification of a professional:

> "Work requiring advanced knowledge" means work which is predominantly intellectual in character, and which includes work requiring the consistent exercise of discretion and judgment. *Professional work is therefore distinguished from work involving routine mental, manual, mechanical or physical work.... Advanced knowledge cannot be attained at the high school level.*[3] (italics added)

The classified employee category is often without definition, or rather, it is defined by that which it is not. The labor relations act in the home state of the institution in this study defines "classified" as "any employee not engaged in professional work."[4] Thus, if professional work is

---

[1]More detailed definitions are set forth by U.S. Department of Labor.

[2]See U.S. Department of Labor's definition of a professional. Retrieved March 24, 2007, from http://www.dol.gov/whd/regs/compliance/fairpay/preamble_final.htm.

[3]Retrieved March 24, 2007, from http://www.dol.gov/whd/regs/compliance/fairpay/preamble_final.htm.

[4]The state to which this passage refers is not cited in order to protect the identity of the home campus at which participants are employed.

"distinguished from work involving routine mental, manual, mechanical or physical work," then one can infer that the work of a classified employee involves "routine mental, manual, mechanical or physical work"—what Rasmussen (2001) referred to as "dirty work" and what Berheide (1992) observed as less valued and less rewarded. All the participants in this study started their university employment designated as "classified" employees, and they all later advanced into positions that were designated "professional."

In my interviews I asked participants, "What defines one position as clerical and makes another professional?" One respondent replied, "I haven't seen anything that is a clear indicator. We have [classified employees] on this campus who are truly making independent decisions, have jobs that require a very special knowledge and skill base. . . . I think there are a lot of [classified] people here who are professionals and at the same time, we have professionals who are glorified clericals" (Brenda). Another respondent, reflecting on when she was in a classified position, identified her job as "one of those quasiprofessional positions." Describing her experience in the international student office, Kate noted, "I would get telephone calls in the middle of the night from the airport . . . 'so-and-so has arrived.' [My job] probably should have been a professional position. I guess, it depends on what one's definition of a job is and what role one is willing to fulfill. . . . I have been very willing to go the extra mile. It also means that I don't say often enough 'excuse me, but that is not my job.' Probably a lot of women who try to do it all fall into that role."

There is this status thing . . . and a gender thing, and a class thing.

Most participants were quick to note the clear demarcation between classified and professional employees. Jamie observed, "when somebody goes from classified to professional, *there is this status thing*." Claudia recalled thinking, " 'Oh, I'll become a professional.' That means everything; it means you have made it." But she added, "It was very hard to break into a professional position. It felt so beyond my reach. I guess I felt like I wouldn't fit in to what would be considered a professional position. . . . I felt that the expectations would be way beyond my reach. . . . I guess I still feel that I'm not quite here, that I am not in that professional position. I still very much feel like I'm in a classified position and that I don't always fit in. . . . I feel pretty powerless . . . [and] I think it has been harder for women to break into some of the professional positions. I still feel like there is a lot of *male privilege*."

Serena also observed status, and gender and class, shaping one's experience as a classified and professional employee: "Gender plays in tremendously in both the move from the classified to the professional, and also in the class issues that are going on. I think it is really interplayed a lot with gender." She continued, "I think class is a real issue here, on campus. Even the labeling, from a professional to the classified staff, and I think once you've been in the classified staff, that is how it is always viewed and I think that it is very hard, to make the move" (Serena). By example, when she assumed her professional position in an academic administration office, "I had one faculty person who said to me, 'what, will you be [an administrator's] secretary?' and I just thought, wow." She added, "I have been on search committees and, as I am walking into a room with faculty or deans or whoever, they expect that you are going to be there to take the minutes" (Serena). Wendy too noted that her treatment by faculty and other professionals "just almost feels subservient in some ways." The participants' experiences amplify Acker's (1990) argument that "class is constructed through gender and that class relations are always gendered," and further that organizational processes "powerfully support the reproduction of the class structure" (pp. 145–46).

Feeling Like an Imposter

Brenda shared, "when you get to the upper-level people, it may not be an intentional bias, but they always remember that you were the [classified employee]. 'How the heck could *you* be the Director?' I know some high-level [professionals] still feel like imposters, like AAs or secretaries. . . . I have seen some classified employees apply five or six times for professional positions and not be able to reel one in. Repeatedly, they stay in the number two position. . . . And if you are promoted to professional, you'll always be looked down on as clerical." Janet noted that "those terms [classified and professional] are awkward. . . . [They] create class divisions."

Dorian also observed "There's a negative class connotation to being a classified employee . . . being in these ranks where you're not quite as good; there are haves and have nots; [classified] employees have to account for every minute, and when you go into the professional ranks, you feel like, 'Am I really worthy?' " Having been at the university for thirty years, Dorian observed, however, that perceptions can change; the memory of her former days as a classified employee diminished: "Every time there was a transition to a new Vice President, the further away I got from that classified identity. . . . It would always amaze me that it wasn't kind of written on my forehead. . . . Usually, once classified always a classified kind of thing. . . . So it amazed me that they [professionals] didn't know the difference; I was like any other professional to them." Yet participants noted that crossing the boundary between classified and professional ranks involved challenges and struggles.

Crossing the Boundary

Participants, reflecting on their move from a classified position into professional ranks, described external messages, explicit and implicit, they received about their place and internal struggles in defining who they were within the organization. One woman offered a blatant example of such messages. After her promotion to a professional position, she noted that "if [her supervisor] didn't think I looked professional enough, the way I was dressed, she would say so. . . . It was painful at times; it was very odd to be pulled into the office and told, 'you are not professional looking; I expect you not to wear shoes like that' " (Brenda).

Risky Business

Many identified the move from classified to professional as risky. Kate observed, "There are some classified women that are doing incredible work that they have no business doing, because they don't get the credit for it. They are incredibly bright, they are probably bored out of their minds, and so they take on [extra work]. But I think they are afraid to take a risk. When I took that step [to a professional position], you find yourself with your head spinning and you say 'Oh my God, what did I do? I thought I was capable.' " Brenda also noted that "to apply for a [professional] position takes a risk and is also incredibly painful." Referring to the "desk audit," when someone from Human Resources evaluates the existing job duties to discern if a reclassification is warranted, Brenda shared that people "ask you a lot of questions and then say you are not doing it, you are not worthy of it. . . . By the time it is done, you feel like you don't know anything; maybe you really should be [a classified employee], no one supports you, you have no value."

There is also risk of making little more or even less money. One participant shared that she had been at the top of her pay scale as a classified employee, and when promoted to professional, she was at the bottom of the pay scale, earning only $500 more per year. Another participant, after her desk audit, was informed that she would be "demoted immediately with a cut in pay" (Jamie). Claudia, after her move to a professional— salaried—position, observed "You are not really compensated for extra hours. . . . I know somebody that is in a professional position now, but she was classified, and she worked a lot of hours as a classified and got pretty good [overtime] money. It's almost like they [supervisors] caught on to that, [and thought] 'let's move her into a professional position and then she will have to get it done.' There seems something sneaky about that."

Finding One's Voice

Women described their shifting identities and constituting a new identity; and claiming knowledge and (the struggle of) finding one's voice. Karen reflected, "I should have spoken up and said, 'this is really uncomfortable for me.' I was given the [professional] role and I assumed I had the ability to do that and I don't believe that I did. I should've said, 'Can you help me to get a better grip on what it is I need to do and how to follow through with it?' but I didn't ask those questions" (Karen). Another participant recalled her awareness that people wanted to hear from her, something that had not been sought when she was a classified employee: "I thought, 'oh my, I am really here in a different role [as a professional].' It is very hard to still be able to speak up and to add voice to it. I think of the search committee that I was on and there were a couple deans and faculty and it was really hard to find my voice. I still felt like maybe what I had to say, would it be valued or did I even have legitimacy to put it forth and so I still, you know, it's hard for me when [my supervisor] will say, "what do you think?" and it is kind of like, whoa, it took me a long time to be able to know it. I think that is part of being in that classified secretarial role, is that *people don't think you think*, and so for them to say what do you think or what do you bring? I have to stop and say oh, I don't know" (Serena).

A frustration for several participants was that they were never asked to contribute as a classified employee, whereas now, as a professional, their views are sought. Claudia, for example, noted, "I had a voice before [being a professional employee] . . . my voice was the same but suddenly it became more heard. And even with some departments that I worked with before, I didn't feel that I was taken as seriously as maybe I am now. . . . Why did respect for me change when I became a professional?" MaryAnn too observed: "I had so much more credibility [as a professional]. I remember going to staff meetings and saying things as a classified employee and it was just like the air moving. [Becoming a professional] was like night and day; as soon as I said something, because I was a professional, people listened—it made me really upset. I was angry. A lot of times I would go into silence because I thought, 'you didn't want to listen to me before, now suddenly I'm credible?' It made me pissed off."

Some participants noted that, over time, they were gaining confidence in self and their voice. Wendy, for example, reflected, "I never used to be confident but over the years you just get to the point where it's like you have to say to [your supervisor], this is my opinion, whether you take it or not, I need to say it out loud." Stacy, who advanced from clerical to professional, and after a brief leave from the university, returned in a clerical position and again advanced to another professional position, observed, "I found that actually if I don't shut my mouth when I ought to, I think I'm for the better for it. I know in my last professional position I think I got more respect out of saying, 'No, I'm sorry I can't do that because I don't feel comfortable with that,' or 'You don't need to speak me that way,' or 'You don't need to treat people that way.' And they're like 'Oh, ok, all right,' and at least, if not for nobody else but myself, I'm treated a little bit differently, respectfully." Another woman noted, "I had to work hard to prove I deserved the [professional] position. [My supervisor] came from that old-fashioned idea that women are good secretaries but they don't think. . . . I think he'd prefer to be told what he wants to hear. But I told him what I thought. . . . I think sometimes he went home and told his wife that I was insubordinate" (Janet). The stories shared by these women illustrate "systemic disparities" (Acker, 2006) between their clerical roles and their professional roles, but also how as women and as former classified staff they existed in a liminal space—nomadic and fragmented—once they'd moved into a professional position.

Maintaining Boundaries

Another finding from this study was the organizational factors that (re) produced and maintained structural barriers. Some of these barriers were made apparent when I asked each woman "what changed?" once she entered professional ranks. Perhaps obvious, changing jobs from classified to professional results in a jump in wages and benefits. Classified employees receive two weeks of vacation, whereas professionals earn four weeks of vacation. Retirement packages were also different: Stacy noted a 4 percent contribution to retirement for classified employees where there is a 6 percent contribution for professionals.

Other organizational practices and policies also produce and sustain an organizational hierarchy. For instance, several women recalled a parking policy that has since changed. Carey shared, "Back then, the parking lots were green for classified staff and blue for professional. The blue were closer [to one's building], the green were further out, and then the students were way out. . . . When [promoted to professional], I went to get my blue decal, [thinking] 'Oh boy, big classist distinction'!" Another participant, Brenda, noted a library policy (still in effect) that distinguishes employee type: "If you go to the library and you take out a book as a graduate student, you get it for the semester. If I go to the library . . . I can have it for the semester because I am a professional. If you are hourly-paid [classified] . . . you can have it for two weeks. I asked why and they told me, because the library wanted to promote the academic pursuit of professionals and graduate students. Are we saying that hourly-paid have no academic pursuits? They said, 'it's not really that, it's about circulation.' I see it as a class issue." The participants' examples amplify Acker's (2006) identification of how class inequalities are produced and perpetuated in organizational practices.

Jamie illustrated how general-information meetings on campus are held specific for employee groups. "If there is a candidate for president, classified employees have to come at one time and professionals at another. Why? Are they afraid that somebody is going to ask a stupid question? Anybody can ask a stupid question!" Serena noted that professional development days were separate and the schedule of topics was markedly different: "If you look at the topics, between the two groups, it's like, oh my! I might be at yoga. And I am not downplaying yoga, but let's offer some variety or something, and even be able to cross, have some sessions that were opened up to both." She added that when a new strategic plan was published, informational sessions were held by senior administrators: "Faculty had their session. Professionals had their sessions. Classified had theirs, and God, don't mix them up. Gosh, it would be horrible if you had people that were actually sitting together." Further, Claudia, observing the same, considered "There's got to be some way that something could be done to make it more equitable." The participants' examples illustrate how classified employees were (are) systematically kept out of workplace decision making and learning, reinforcing their low value to the organization and the lack of organizational interest in hearing their contribution. Yet Rainbird (2007) noted that equitable access to meaningful, employer-provided training, development, and other forms of learning plays a role in demonstrating that employees are valued members of the organization and contributes to job mobility for low-paid workers.

Pereira (2009) identified "social rules, economic structures, political battles, religious ideologies, dress codes, gender socialization and the policing of gender and sex orders" (p. 18) as explicit and implicit guidelines to which workers (citizens) are required to adhere. Organizational policies and procedures left these women frustrated, demoralized, and isolated (e.g., desk audit process), and organizational practices created exclusive boundaries between classified and professional positions (i.e., separate meetings and professional development, different benefits). Further, the resources one would access to negotiate or resolve personnel matters are also hierarchically structured, and for personnel crossing categorical boundaries, they are left betwixt and between. By example, almost all participants did not view the unions as useful for them. One woman, venting about the lack of support when a request for promotion failed, illustrated, "who do you go to? You can't go to the union, because how can a classified person go to their union and complain they want to be professional. [The classified union is] not going to represent you to get you [into the professional union]. . . . There is a disconnect" (Brenda). The participants' experiences provide powerful examples of inequality in organizations, what Acker (2006) termed inequality regimes: "systematic

disparities between participants in power and control over goals, resources, and outcomes" (p. 443).

Advanced Knowledge

As noted previously, the U.S. Department of Labor defines professional as
"work requiring advanced knowledge," and further elaborates that this
"advanced knowledge cannot be attained at the high school level."[5] Thus,
promotion and (re)classification of a professional position typically requires
obtaining a college degree. As Dorian, who sought reclassification as a professional with a few classified colleagues, explained, "The deal [was] that
we would have to have a degree or be working towards a degree if we were
going to [be promoted]." While the university offers tuition benefits, it does
not mean an employee can (easily) utilize them. For (hourly wage) classified employees, enrolling in courses must be done at night or time off during
the day must be approved by a supervisor. In the latter instance, women
employed creative strategies in order to complete coursework. For example,
an hourly employee who typically gets two 15-minutes breaks in the day
(one in the morning and one in the afternoon) and a 30-minute lunch break,
with approval from her supervisor, would bundle that time together in order
to leave the office for a 50-minute class (and would thus have no breaks and
would work through lunch). Other women were told to use their vacation
time if they left the office for class. Still others had to "jump through a lot
of hoops." Serena illustrated:

> It was frustrating. . . . My supervisor put a lot of emphasis on the degree.
> . . . I was in the last leg of my bachelor's degree was when [I had to take
> a required course] that met once a week at 2 PM . . . I had to write a let-
> ter to the Dean to get permission to take it, and it was this big deal and I
> had to account for every second and how I was going to make up the
> time and post my schedule. . . . I had to jump through a lot of hoops.

While most tried to complete (as much as possible of) their coursework
after office hours, they noted the stress of juggling coursework with family

---

[5]Retrieved March 24, 2007, from http://www.dol.gov/whd/regs/compliance/fairpay/
preamble_final.htm..

obligations. For some, this delayed or prevented the completion of their degree. Corrin, who advanced with a stipulation that she would complete her degree, stated "I've chosen to wait until after the kids get out of school. . . . So for now, I have this piece of glass sitting right over my head. . . . Whenever raises are talked about, it comes up. [My supervisor will say] 'It's hard to justify it when you don't have a degree.' "

Several participants also raised the question "what counts?" as advanced knowledge. A defining characteristic of being a professional is having a credential. But many participants—those who had earned their degrees and those who were working toward them—felt "advanced knowledge" could or should be defined as work experience. For instance, Colleen considered,

> A professional position probably should have the 4-year degree, but . . . you might have the experience required for that position and, lots of times in life, common sense prevails over all education. Yes, technically the professional world signifies a degree, but is it really necessary? I think some people could do the professional work without the degree but the degree is what typecasts them as a professional.

The struggle, noted above, of balancing (course)work and family was cited by many, and not only in relation to securing a degree. Most spoke of the challenges of working and having a family, of straddling two worlds, uncertain if one is making the right choices and doing anything well (enough). These struggles are one illustration of the significance of being female in the gendered organization.

Significance of Being Female

For many participants, their work life was blurred with their family life. For instance, when Corrin was asked about her first position on campus, she replied, "I came to [university] in August of 1993. I had a 4-year-old and a 6-month-old." She then elaborated on her employment, interweaving stories about her parents, siblings, and spouse. For some, they believed "family comes first" and did not self-identify as "a career person," whereas for others, they felt shame for putting their job first and their children in daycare. For all, though, who expressed these struggles, they felt,

"We all muddle our way through and never feel that we're doing it right!" (Kate). One woman situated this personal struggle in the larger context, noting as she was "maneuvering the home front, the kids, the work responsibilities and some private time, it is very difficult and you have to make priorities and your priorities shift as time goes on. In the late 1970s, early 80s, I thought I could do it all. You know, we were taught that you could have it all, that you could be the best mom, the best wife, the best worker, and have time for yourself. Bull shit! I failed. . . . I had good daycare, lost daycare, got better daycare, you know? It was difficult" (Chloe).

On the job, participants also identified their experiences as tied to their identity as a woman. When asked "what, if anything, do you think is significant to your journey about being a woman?" most participants noted: "It's about office work and I think the majority of people who are in support positions are women. . . . [Men] usually are either in a more blue-collared-type job or management" (Karen). Further illustrating the gendered nature of work, Serena remarked: "Men have more of a trade. . . . I got married young. . . . I was 18 when I had my daughter and, you know, it wasn't until I got to this environment [the university] that I guess I thought about what I could do as a woman."

Several women noted that their experience would have been different if they were men. For instance, Paula stated, "I cannot help but think they [men] would be treated completely differently. I notice it—I see other male professionals and they aren't treated the same way." Carey also remarked that she and a colleague who were promoted to professional positions had "two desks facing each other behind a partition, cubicle, little half-walls . . . I just always felt that if we'd been men, we would not be in this kind of office space." Sarah, who worked in Athletics, observed, "I was a woman coming in and changing things. . . . I was a threat to the good old boys. . . . I think if this position had a man in it, there probably wouldn't have been the same issues."

Claudia provided another example. When she was in her clerical role, she requested a review of her position that led to a HR recommendation that her job should be reclassified as a professional position. But her supervisor instead said, "well, we'll just take away some of your responsibilities." Claudia later secured a professional position in another office, and her former, classified position was filled by a man and reclassified as professional. "I remember resenting that as a prime example of male privilege." Another participant observed that her prior experience as a secretary hindered her from getting administrative support when she advanced into a professional position: "People knew me as a secretary and that I could do all those [clerical] things. And I think some of it is *a woman thing.* . . . If I had been a man [taking the professional position] and I said 'I need a secretary,' it would have been 'of course you need a secretary.' But nobody was ever assigned to me" (Janet). Acker (2006) observed that "gendered and sexualized attitudes and assumptions" remain present in organizations and shape the employment situations for women and men in different ways (p. 444; also Williams, 2000).

Concluding Thoughts

Some of the findings from this investigation resonate with explanations found in previous research on women and advancement; however, these participants' experiences make a unique contribution as they are expressed from a perspective of (previously) classified employees, more likely to be trapped on the "sticky floor" of their low-mobility jobs, yet they advanced into professional roles. Moreover, while they share many of the challenges faced by professional women navigating a male-dominated organizational culture, these women also negotiated the positional boundaries that define (and can constrain) what it means to be classified and professional. Consequently, most of the women in this study felt as if they occupied neither category once promoted—no longer a member of the classified ranks, and never feeling fully admitted or welcomed into the professional ranks. As classified employees, they might express rancor for the boss, only to then become the professional, sometimes supervising those with whom one commiserated. This led to struggles with one's sense of identity, finding voice, and understanding one's place in the organization. It also illuminates how these women occupied liminal spaces, a state of "in-betweenness" (Heilbrun, 1999, p. 98), "never designed for permanent occupation" (pp. 101–2). Some scholars identify this space between what was and what might be as a "place of possibility" (Barbatsis, Fegan, & Hansen, 1999). Kennedy (2001) writes that "Its apparent lack of structure is both its strength and its weakness, a strength because of what it offers to those who engage with it and its weakness because in the structured society in which we live, there is a fear of the chaotic" (in Huber, Murphy, & Clandinin, 2003, p. 351). We have an opportunity in these spaces to "participate in the creation of new ways of being" (Huber et al., 2003, p. 351); to engage dialogue about the socio-political-cultural contexts surrounding "classified" and "professional" statuses, how they produce constraining categories and demarcate real and perceived boundaries that women must cross, and the ways in which organizational practices, institutional cultural structure, and employment policies can systematically work against women in higher education.

In closing, I leave the reader with a question that intruded on me throughout this project: Why is advancement important, and in what ways does our (over)emphasis on advancement contribute to the class hierarchy in the workplace? Rainbird (2007) noted that "not all workers want career advancement" (p. 570). Many workers are committed to their place in the organization and identify their jobs as socially useful work. Thus, equivalent to efforts we might engage in to "crack the glass ceiling" and establish bridges into professional ranks and better-paid work, we must also tackle the structural barriers to learning, the problem of low pay on the "sticky floor," and the undervaluing of the work, voices, and contributions of low-wage workers.

References

Acker, J. (1990). Hierarchies, jobs bodies: A theory of gendered organizations. *Gender and Society, 4*(2), 139–58.

Acker, J. (1992). Gendering organizational theory. In A. J. Mills & P. Tancred (Eds.), *Gendering organizational theory* (pp. 248–60). Thousand Oaks, CA: Sage.

Acker, J. (2006). Inequality regimes: Gender, class and race in organizations. *Gender and Society, 20*(4), 441–64.

Adams, J. (2007). Stained glass makes the ceiling visible: Organizational opposition to women in congregational leadership. Gender and Society, *21*(1), 80–105.

Allan, E. J. (2003). Constructing women's status: Policy discourses of university women's commission reports. *Harvard Educational Review, 73*(1), 44–72.

American Association of University Women. (2007). *Bridging the pay gap.* AAUW Educational Foundation.

Anderson, D. (2005). The importance of mentoring programs to women's career advancement in biotechnology. *Journal of Career Advancement, 32*(1), 60–73.

Appelbaum, S. H., Audet, L., & Miller, J. C. (2003). Gender and leadership? Leadership and gender? A journey through the landscape of theories. *Leadership & Organization Development Journal, 24*(1), 43–51.

Baldridge, V. J., Curtis, D. V., Ecker, G. P., & Riley G. L. (1977/2000). Alternative models of governance in higher education. *Governing academic organizations*. McCutcham Publishing. [Reprinted in Brown, M.C. (Ed.). (2000). *Organization and governance in higher education* (5th ed., pp. 128–42). ASHE Reader Series, Boston, MA: Pearson Custom Publishing.]

Barbatsis, G., Fegan, M., & Hansen, K. (1999). The performance of cyberspace: An exploration into computer-mediated reality. *Journal of Computer-Mediated Communication* [Online Journal], *5*(1). Retrieved December 10, 2004, from http://jcmc.indiana.edu/vol5/issue1/barbatsis.html.

Berheide, C. W. (1992). Women still "stuck" in low-level jobs. *Women in Public Service: A Bulletin of the Center for Women in Government,* 3 (Fall).

Bloom, L. (1998). *Under the sign of hope: Feminist methodology and narrative interpretation*. New York: State University of New York Press.

Bonk, J., Crouch, J., Kilian, M., & Lowell, L. (2006, Fall). Higher ed staff personal economies: We can't eat prestige. *Thought & Action, 22,* 111–20.

Booth, A. L., Francesconi, M., & Frank, J. (2003). A sticky floors model of promotion, pay, and gender. *European Economic Review, 47,* 295–22.

Britton, D. (2000). The epistemology of the gendered organization. *Gender and Society, 14*(3), 418–34.

Calas, M., & Smircich, L. (1996). From "the woman's" point of view: Feminist approaches to organization studies. In S. R. Clegg, C. Hardy, & W. R. Nord (Eds.), *Handbook of organization studies* (pp. 218–57). Thousand Oaks, CA: Sage.

Carnes, M., Morrissey, C., & Geller, S. (2008). Women's health and women's leadership in academic medicine: Hitting the same glass ceiling? *Journal of Women's Health, 17*(9), 1453–62.

Cook, J., & Fonow, M. M. (1986). Knowledge and women's interests: Issues of epistemology and methodology in feminist sociological research. *Sociological Inquiry, 56*(4), 2–29.

Davidson, M. J. (1997). *The black and ethnic minority woman manager.* London: Paul Chapman Publishing.

Davis, K. (1991). *The phenomenology of research: The construction of meaning in data analysis.* Paper presented at the Annual Meeting of the Conference on College Composition and Communication, Boston, MA.

Duerst-Lahti, G., & Kelly, R. M. (Eds.). (1995). *Gender power, leadership, and governance.* Ann Arbor: University of Michigan Press.

Eddy, P. L., & Cox, E. (2008). Gendered leadership: An organizational perspective. In J. Lester (Ed.), *Gendered perspectives on community colleges. New directions in community colleges* (pp. 69–80). San Francisco: Jossey-Bass.

Falk, E., & Grizard, E. (2005). The "glass ceiling" persists: Women leaders in communication companies. *Journal of Media Business Studies, 2*(1), 23–49.

Ferguson, K. E. (1984). *The feminist case against bureaucracy.* Philadelphia: Temple University Press.

Freeman, S. J. M., Bourque, S. C., & Shelton, C. M. (2001). *Women on power: Leadership redefined.* Boston: Northeastern University Press.

Gale, A., & Cartwright, S. (1995). Women in project management: Entry into a male domain? A discussion on gender and organizational culture. *Leadership & Organization Development Journal, 16*(2), 3–8.

Giorgi, A. (1994). A phenomenological perspective on certain qualitative research methods. *Journal of Phenomenological Psychology, 25*(2), 190–220.

Giscombe, K., & Mattis, M. C. (2002). Leveling the playing field for women of color in corporate management: Is the business case enough? *Journal of Business Ethics, 37*(1), 103–19.

Glazer-Raymo, J. (Ed.). (2008). *Unfinished agendas: New and continuing challenges in higher education.* Baltimore: Johns Hopkins University Press.

Harding, S. (1986). *The science question in feminism.* Ithaca, NY: Cornell University Press.

Harlan, S. L., & Berheide, C. W. (1994). *Barriers to workplace advancement experienced by women in low-paying occupations.* Cornell University. Retrieved March 16, 2006, from http://digitalcommons .ilr.cornell.edu/cgi/viewcontent.cgi?article=1123&context=key_work place.

Hede, A., & Ralston, D. (1993). Managerial career progression and aspiration: Evidence of a "glass ceiling"? *International Journal of Employment Studies, 1*(2), 253–82.

Heilbrun, C. (1999). *Women's lives: A view from the threshold.* Toronto: University of Toronto Press.

Hesse-Biber, S. N., & Carter, G. L. (2005). *Working women in America: Split dreams* (2nd ed.). New York: Oxford University Press.

Hite, L. M., & McDonald, K. S. (2003). Career aspirations of non-managerial women: Adjustment and adaptation. *Journal of Career Development, 29*(4), 221–35.

Hochschild, A. R., & Machung, A. (1989). *The second shift: Working parents and the revolution at home.* New York: Viking Penguin.

Huber, J., Murphy, M. S., & Clendenin, D. J. (2003). Creating communities of cultural imagination: Negotiating a curriculum of diversity. *Curriculum Inquiry, 33*(4), 343–62.

Ivarsson, S. M., & Ekehammar, B. (2001). Women's entry into management: Comparing women managers and non-managers. *Journal of Managerial Psychology, 16*(4), 301–14.

Iverson, S. (2009). Crossing boundaries: Understanding women's advancement from clerical to professional positions. *Journal About Women in Higher Education, 2,* 140–66.

Johnsrud, L. K. (1991). Administrative promotion: The power of gender. *Journal of Higher Education, 62*(2), 119–49.

Johnsrud, L. K., & Banaria, J. S. (2005). Higher education support personnel: Trends in demographics and worklife perceptions. In *The NEA 2005 Almanac of Higher Education* (pp. 85–105). Washington, DC: National Education Association.

Kanter, R. M. (1977). *Men and women of the corporation*. New York: Basic Books.

Kezar, A., Carducci, R., & Contraras-McGavin, M. (2006). Rethinking the "L" word in higher education: The revolution of research on leadership. *ASHE Higher Education Report, 31*(6). San Francisco: Jossey-Bass.

MacKinnon, C. A. (1979). *Sexual harassment of working women*. New Haven, CT: Yale University Press.

Maguire, P. (1987). *Doing participatory research: A feminist approach*. Amherst, MA: University of Massachusetts.

McHugh, M. C., & Cosgrove, L. (1998). Research for women: Feminist methods. In D. Ashcraft (Ed.), *Women's work: A survey of scholarship by and about women* (19–43). New York: Hadworth Press.

Marongiu, S., & Ekehammar, B. (1999). Internal and external influences on women's and men's entry into management. *Journal of Managerial Psychology, 14*(5), 421–33.

Mattis, M. C. (2004). Women entrepreneurs: Out from under the glass ceiling. *Women in Management Review, 19*(3), 154–63.

Myerson, D. E., & Fletcher, J. K. (2000). A modest manifesto for shattering the glass ceiling. *Harvard Business Review, 78*(1), 127–36.

Newman, M. A. (1993). Career advancement: Does gender make a difference? *American Review of Public Administration, 23*(4), 361–84.

Pereira, C. (2009). Interrogating norms: Feminists theorizing sexuality, gender, and heterosexuality. *Development, 52*(1), 18–24.

Pilgrim, J. (1997). Secretarial and clerical staff career progression: Some organizational perspectives. *Librarian Career Development, 5*(3), 105–12.

Polkinghorne, D. E. (1989). Phenomenological research methods. In R. S. Valle & S. Halling (Eds.), *Existential-phenomenological perspectives in psychology* (pp. 3–16). New York: Plenum.

Rainbird, H. (2007). Can training remove the glue from the "sticky floor" of low-paid work for women? *Equal Opportunities International, 26* (6), 555–72.

Ramos, S. M. (2008). *Latina presidents of four-year institutions, penetrating the adobe ceiling: A critical view*. Unpublished dissertation, University of Arizona.

Ransel, K. A., Fitzpatrick, J. D., & Hinds, S. L. (2001). Advancement at last: Career-ladder opportunities for library support staff. *Technical Services Quarterly, 19*(2), 17–26.

Rasmussen, B. (2001). Corporate strategy and gendered professional identities: Reorganization and the struggle for recognition and positions. *Gender, Work and Organization, 8*(3), 291–310.

Reichman, N. J., & Sterling, J. S. (2004). Sticky floors, broken steps, and concrete ceilings in legal careers. *Texas Journal of Women and the Law, 14*(27), 27–76.

Reinharz, S. (1992). *Feminist methods in social research.* New York: Oxford University Press.

Reskin, B. F., & Padavic, I. (2006). Sex, race, and ethnic inequality in United States workplaces. In J. S. Chafetz (Ed.), *Handbook of the sociology of gender* (pp. 343–74). New York: Kluwer Academic/Plenum.

Sanders, P. (1982). Phenomenology: A new way of viewing organizational research. *Academy of Management Review, 7*(3), 353–60.

Swan, W. (1995). *Breaking the silence: Gay, lesbian and bisexual issues in public administration.* Washington, DC: American Society for Public Administration.

Tharenou, P., Latimer, S., & Conroy, D. (1994). How do you make it to the top? An examination of influences on women's and men's managerial advancement. *Academy of Management Journal, 37*(4), 899–931.

Tiernari, J., Quack, S., & Theobald, H. (2002). Organizational reforms, "ideal workers" and gender orders: A cross-societal comparison. *Organization Studies, 23*(2), 249–79.

Tierney, W. G., & Bensimon, E. M. (2000). (En)gender(ing) socialization. In J. Glazer-Raymo, B. K. Townsend, & B. Ropers-Huilman, (Eds.), *Women in higher education: A feminist perspective* (pp. 309–25). Pearson.

Williams, J. (2000). *Unbending gender: Why family and work conflict and what to do about it.* New York: Oxford University Press.

Williams, J. (2002). "It's snowing down south": How to help mothers and avoid recycling the sameness/difference debate. *Columbia Law Review, 102*(3), 812–33.

Wood, D. F. (2009). Barriers to women's leadership in faith-based colleges and universities. In D. R. Dean, S. J. Bracken, & J. K. Allen (Eds.), *Women in academic leadership: Professional strategies, personal choices.* Sterling, VA: Stylus.

Worts, D., Fox, B., & McDonough, P. (2007). "Doing something meaningful": Gender and public service during municipal government restructuring. *Gender, Work and Organization, 14*(2), 162–84.

5

Toxic to the Heart: Barriers to Tenure and Leadership for Women Faculty of Color

Heipua Kaopua and Joanne Cooper

I must after thirty-odd years, we must, after centuries, say the obvious to and about the engines of power, knowledge, and politics that our great universities represent in this nation and in the world: This is dreadful.

Right now, I'm tired. I say, "Get me out of here."
I quit.

—Paula Gunn Allen, 2000

Referring to centuries of institutionalized patriarchy, Dr. Paula Gunn Allen, a well-known Native American scholar with thirty years in the academy, describes herself as "discouraged, disengaged, and . . . disenchanted" (2000, p. 147). Dr. Judith Dorney, also a seasoned academic, describes educational institutions as "often toxic to the heart" (2000, p. 238). Why? What has happened to these women that would bring them to such points of despair? While more women, including women of color, are finding their way into the academy, they continue to feel alienated and marginalized. For women faculty of color, the road through the tenure process toward a successful academic career and to positions of leadership remains a fraught and painful path. This chapter explores the literature regarding barriers that are facing women faculty of color in their pursuit of promotion, tenure, and leadership posts in academe, with a particular focus on the case of Native Hawaiian women. While our larger concern is on the barriers—social, institutional, and cultural—that women faculty of color experience, we cannot pursue such a question without a deeper understanding of the status and position of all women within American higher education. Thus, we begin this chapter by providing a brief history of women's education and the role of gender in higher education.

The Role of Gender in Higher Education

From its inception, higher education has served as a citadel of patriarchy that continues to be a major barrier to women in higher education. Ideologies of male supremacy are so ingrained in the American psyche that they are taken as the natural order of things, while suggestions to establish new definitions are rejected as ludicrous, illogical, or an attack on cultural norms (Stromquist, 2006). In the past, men were deemed as central to the purpose of academe as creators of knowledge, while women were relegated to more supportive private roles as wives and mothers centered on the home and family. The dominant group in American higher education consists of white, middle-class males. Minority groups, by default, consist of those groups without power—namely, people of color and women. Historically, women have been marginalized—garnering perhaps a few paragraphs in scholarly texts. The effects of gender bias have often been neglected when describing patriarchal institutions, practices, and norms (Rury, 1986). According to historical texts, the few women who did experience power, prestige, and intellectual freedom were generally white and from privileged aristocratic classes (Women's International Center, 1995). In most scholarly publications, the term *women* was used to refer to white women. Women of color—largely invisible in the literature—are generally included under the general category of "women" or "people of color" (Rains, 1999, p. 151). Conflating women of color under these general categories causes their issues, challenges, and experiences to remain invisible.

It is our assertion that gender is not a peripheral issue but a central story shaping the development of higher education. Gender has shaped American society and serves as a useful category for analyses of power relationships within educational institutions (Dzuback, 2003). Gendered roles continue to influence the policies, practices, and beliefs in academe largely through established narratives and ideologies.

American higher education has also been influenced by the Western ideology of "whiteness" as evidenced by the fact that white middle-class standards have often been considered the academic norm (Maher & Tetreault, 1993; Walker, 1993). Western cultural norms of individuality, rationality, masculinity, and whiteness are promulgated at the expense of communal, intuitive, and feminine values in American institutions (Butler, 1997). The dominant culture has maintained this privileged status despite demographic projections toward a browner America (Maher & Tetreault, 1993; U.S. Census, 2009). White women maintain a position of privilege by virtue of their race and tend to view race and gender as separate entities. For women of color, however, race and gender are intricately linked and cannot be viewed separately (Maher & Tetreault, 1993).

The first wave of feminist activism began in the mid-1800s with the publication of the *Declaration of Sentiments*, a document declaring the legal rights of women, and ended with the passage of suffrage in 1920. Unfortunately, suffrage applied only to white women. Despite the efforts of Anna Julia Cooper, who wanted the issue of racism addressed, white women did not consider racism relative to the right to vote (Carby, 1985). African American women were excluded from this "first wave" of the women's movement. During the 1890s, African American women intellectuals began to insert women into cultural and historical narratives. Through these narratives, African American writers exposed issues of imperialism, unrestrained patriarchal power, and racial and gender oppression. Anna Julia Cooper, for example, attacked the racist attitude of white women and the exclusionary practices of white women's organizations that presumed to speak for all women (Carby, 1985).

The second wave of feminism originated as World War II drew to a close and gained momentum amidst the turbulence of the 1960s (Eisenberg & Ruthsdotter, 1998). Civil unrest resulted in landmark legislation advancing civil rights, with particular significance for women and people of color. As a result of this new legislation, increasing numbers of women of color began to enter university classrooms (Rains, 1999). Whereas white middle-class women generated the first wave of feminism, the second stage attracted women of color from various social classes (Rampton,

2008). Stressing sisterhood and solidarity, these feminists emphasized that issues of race, class, and gender are interrelated.

The third wave of feminism, informed by postcolonial and postmodern thought, began in the 1990s and attacked previous feminist writings as being too white, too middle-class, and too universalizing of all women's experiences (Rampton, 2008). Known as the reform era, it is characterized by an increased demand for access and equality of opportunity for all. Third-wave feminists, also known as "grrls," appear as empowered, global, and multicultural women who are rejecting victimization and redefining femininity (Rampton, 2008).

Whereas nineteenth-century women struggled to gain admission to colleges and universities, women today constitute the majority of students in higher education and represent more than half of those in the United States with bachelor's, master's, or doctoral degrees (NCES, 2009). Despite these advances, women of color still experience disadvantages as faculty members and senior administrators that impede career advancement and pursuit of tenure (Amey & Eddy, 2002; Turner, 2002).

Barriers to Women Faculty of Color

Despite the rhetoric within academe to embrace and encourage diversity, colleges and universities have been reluctant to welcome women scholars of color. In addition to challenges experienced by all women faculty, women of color continue to face institutional, socio-cultural, and personal barriers (ASHE, 2009). Native Hawaiian women faculty further encounter issues of colonialism along with gender, race, and class discrimination. According to *The Chronicle of Higher Education Almanac* (2007), the total number of full-time faculty members, including instructors and lecturers, is 703,463, of which 294,348 are women. Of the total women, only 14 percent are women of color. While overt gender discrimination is no longer as prevalent in women's faculty careers, it is being replaced by more subtle forms of institutional discrimination in the form of (1) institutional practices, (2) structural arrangements, and (3) gendered roles that recreate patriarchal ideologies that are oppressive to women (Jaschik, 2006; Pincus, 1996).

Institutional discrimination refers to the policies, practices, norms, and traditions of the dominant racial, ethnic, or gender group and the implementation of policies that disadvantage one social group for the benefit of another group (Baumgartner & Johnson-Bailey, 2010; Pincus, 1996). In higher education, discriminatory institutional practices begin with recruiting students and hiring faculty and include all efforts that maintain white privilege. While access to higher education has allowed white middle-class women to challenge traditional institutional practices, the pathway for women of color remains obstructed by institutionalized racism and sexism (Stromquist, 2006; Walker, 1993).

Most of the work by feminist historians centers on white middle-class women. Few historians have explored the educational experiences of women of color or women in lower socioeconomic groups (Rains, 1999). A historiography of American women in higher education reveals the intersection of race, gender, and class as social constructs reflected in the policies and practices of educational institutions (Walker, 1993). Maher and Tetreault (1993) assert that our perspective on higher education is framed by our positionality—our particular identity with regard to race, gender, and class. Examining higher education through a lens of positionality reveals certain privileges extended to whites that are withheld from nonwhites. By virtue of their race, whites are empowered and entitled in multiple ways and are considered the norm against which underrepresented, nonwhite groups are compared (Andersen, 2001; Walker, 1993). White women experience oppression from white men and share similar experiences with women of color, yet white women also function as oppressors of women of color (Butler, 1997) and maintain an undeniable racial dominance over women faculty of color.

A second form of institutional discrimination, known as structural discrimination, involves policies and actions that are neutral in intent yet disadvantage minority groups (Pincus, 2003). Originating from privilege and oppression, structural discrimination negatively affects members of racial, gender, and ethnic minority groups. One example is the consistent disparities in salary, rank, and tenure of underrepresented faculty groups, particularly women of color (NCES, 2007). Women of color are more likely to work in teaching-centered institutions than at research universities and thus receive lower compensation (Armenti, 2004; Cooper et al., 2007). Another example of structural discrimination is the faculty evaluation system that exists in most research-intensive institutions. In her study, *Women Faculty Seeking Tenure and Parenthood*, Armenti (2004) points out that the faculty evaluation system at four-year universities undervalues teaching and service and overvalues scholarly research and publication. This disparity is evidenced in the higher compensation allocated to faculty involved in research and publication as compared to teaching and service (Cooper et al., 2007).

A third form of institutional discrimination involves gendered roles, a practice that marginalizes women in less appreciated professional activities, such as teaching lower-level courses in humanities, and taking on a disproportionate share of advising graduate students and committee work (Armenti, 2004; Cooper et al., 2007). Women of color, in particular, are often expected to advise students of color regardless of the presenting issue. Women tend to hold the lower ranks in the professoriate and spend more time teaching than their male colleagues (Dzuback, 2003; Stromquist, 2006). This results in fewer opportunities for these women to conduct research and publish scholarly work, further reducing their likelihood of receiving tenure (Armenti, 2004; Cooper et al., 2007). Simply put, women faculty teach and advise while men research and lead. With fewer courses to teach, male faculty in the higher ranks tend to publish more frequently. For example, Armenti (2004) points out that the natural sciences have the highest publication rate but the lowest number of female faculty while the more "feminized disciplines" such as English, education, and anthropology tend to employ larger numbers of women faculty (Cooper et al., 2007, p. 639). Unfortunately, these departments receive fewer resources, resulting in less support for women to participate in research activities (Armenti, 2004). As research becomes increasingly more specialized, the salary gap for women and men is likely to widen. Additional subtle forms of gender bias are evidenced in decisions over raises, assignments, office space, and promotions to department chair and key committees.

Socio-cultural Barriers

The culture of academe, with its emphasis on individuality, rationality, masculinity, and whiteness is antithetical to the culture of many women of color that emphasizes the communal, intuitive, and feminine (Butler, 1997). Gatta and Roos (2007) discovered feelings of invisibility and marginalization among women faculty of color that grew worse as they moved into the tenure ranks. Women of color feel they must constantly prove themselves in the white, patriarchal world of higher education. Many choose not to assimilate but strive to live in a bicultural world in which they selectively silence their native voices in their journeys through academe (Sadao, 2003). In addition, faculty women of color struggle with an unfamiliar elitist culture, a lack of mentors and role models, and tensions between work, family, and community (Armenti, 2004; Cooper et al., 2007; Wolfinger, Mason, & Goulden, 2009).

Many women faculty of color face the triple threat of being female, of color, and of lower social class. Class discrimination is closely linked with gender and race discrimination as many women of color in lower socio-economic groups lack the power, competence, and academic capital to navigate through the system of higher education. This race/class dynamic is particularly evident in African American and Hispanic populations (ASHE, 2009).

Personal Barriers

Women often strive to achieve a *work/life balance*, a term used by Morrissey and Schmidt (2008) to describe the condition of engaging in purposeful careers and the pursuit of tenure while struggling to carve out time to pursue personal goals with family or friends, contribute to their community, or invest in personal development (p. 1400). Morrissey and Schmidt (2008) believe that focusing only on the needs of faculty with children may alienate faculty without children, who may be asked to cover for their colleagues.

Female faculty with children encounter numerous dilemmas as parents and professors. Armenti (2004) describes the irony women face as their childbearing years parallel with their journey toward tenure. Family care issues have a more negative impact on salary, promotion, and tenure for women than for men since women have a disproportionate share of domestic duties (Cooper et al., 2007), resulting in less time for research than their male counterparts (Armenti, 2004). For example, Schiebinger and Gilmartin (2010) discovered that gifted women scientists are trading research time for domestic chores. Research indicates that women faculty frequently subordinate their academic careers to support those of their partners or assume childrearing responsibilities by accepting contingent positions or by interrupting their careers altogether (McElrath, 1992; Wolfinger et al., 2009). Both of these actions have a deleterious effect on the achievement of tenure. Such interruptions in the academic cycle can serve as indications to the tenure committee that the female academic is not serious or committed to her career. In addition to interruptions, women are more likely to leave the academy because of childcare issues (McElrath, 1992) and less likely to achieve tenure if they have pretenure babies (Armenti, 2004). In short, academic communities are often unsupportive of motherhood when combined with an academic career (Leonard & Malina, 1994). For women of color, who tend to be concentrated in the lower ranks of the professoriate and who place a strong emphasis on the extended family and community, domestic and family care responsibilities create serious barriers to their quest for tenure.

The Case of Native Hawaiian Women Faculty

In *Métis and Feminist*, Emma LaRoque (2007) asserts that indigenous women are victims of oppression, colonization, and patriarchy yet manage to serve as social activists and agents in their own lives. She argues that although these women are among the most "stereotyped, dehumanized and objectified," they continue to fight for their rights as strong and determined women (LaRoque, 2007, p. 53). As women of color, Native Hawaiian faculty experience additional layers of oppression resulting from imperialism and colonialism. Native Hawaiians are the direct descendants of the "aboriginal, indigenous, native people of the Hawaiian islands who resided in the islands prior to January 1, 1893" (The Native Hawaiian Government Reorganization Act of 2005). Before the arrival of white explorers and missionaries, Native Hawaiians maintained their own political and economic systems, culture, language, and traditions (Louis, 2007). The indigenous people of Hawai'i held land in common and had no concept of private land ownership. Imperialism dramatically altered the destiny of this indigenous population.

The American government took control of the Hawaiian monarchy in 1893 and later annexed Hawai'i in 1898 (Silva, 2004). American imperialism has had significant political, economical, social, and cultural effects on Native Hawaiians who have struggled to maintain a sense of political and cultural identity. Colonization has resulted in outmigration, loss of land and natural resources, commercialization of Native Hawaiian culture, and years of substance abuse, mental illness, and language loss (Marshall, 2011).

Today, Native Hawaiians have the highest rate of poverty, homelessness, diabetes, heart disease, and suicide and the lowest education scores (Boyd & Braun, 2007). These problems stem from the loss of land, resources, culture, and self-identity as a result of their colonized status. In 2005, Native Hawaiians comprised about 22 percent of the population of Hawai'i (State of Hawai'i Data Book, 2005). Yet less than 10 percent of students enrolled in Hawai'i colleges and universities are of Native Hawaiian ancestry (Makuakane-Drechsel & Hagedorn, 2000), and fewer than 4 percent of all Native Hawaiians hold a graduate degree (Grieco, 2001). Native Hawaiians comprise less than 4 percent of the University of Hawai'i faculty (Faculty and Staff Report, 2004), which likely is the largest percentage of Native Hawaiian faculty of any college or university in the nation. Little is known about the condition of Native Hawaiian women faculty in the University of Hawai'i system because Native Hawaiians are combined with Asian Pacific Islanders or categorized as "Other Pacific Islander." The need for disaggregated data on Native Hawaiian women is particularly acute in light of the "University of Hawai'i Strategic Plan 2011–2019," which sets forth the success of all Native Hawaiians as its primary objective.

Native Hawaiian women, who have navigated the murky waters of higher education to obtain advanced degrees, have been socialized with a Western pedagogical perspective that may have acculturated them into Western ideology. Western culture advocates individualism and undermines group interdependence, while Native Hawaiian culture is concerned with connecting to other people, emphasizing the group or *'ohana* (family), being of service to the community, and developing meaningful relationships (Meyer, 2001). In a study of Native Hawaiian female elders, Mokuau and Browne (1994) identified three life themes characteristic of Native Hawaiian women—relationships with family, nature, and spiritualism. These values conflict with Western values, creating a need for future research as to how Native Hawaiian women navigate the deep waters of Western pedagogy and academia while remaining on course with their Native Hawaiian values.

Tenure Issues for Women Faculty of Color

The current precarious, eroding state of tenure can be likened to efforts for women to gain a toehold in a sliding landscape. Given that only one-third of women faculty are eligible for tenure and the trend to hire contingent faculty is increasing, the likelihood that women faculty of color will achieve tenure is diminishing (Cooper et al., 2007; Gappa, 2008; Schoening, 2009). As tenure positions decline, the status and security women faculty of color need to hold positions of leadership in academe may also dwindle.

As a pinnacle of academic achievement, tenure brings many benefits to university faculty including institutional status and prestige, freedom to engage in research and teaching without interference, job security, and a sense of community between faculty members and the institution (Perna, 2002). Although women today earn the majority of college degrees, they are less likely than men to experience the benefits associated with tenure and promotion and continue to represent a smaller proportion of tenured faculty (Perna, 2002). Among full-time faculty in 2007–2008, 55 percent of men had tenure, compared with 40 percent of women (NCES, 2009). While women of color have the lowest tenure rate of all faculty groups (Vargas, 2002), their leadership, alternative perspectives, and contributions as role models are sorely needed in the academy. Several factors contribute to the low rate of tenure for these women.

First, a major factor contributing to the tenure challenge for women, especially women of color, is the recent trend to hire increasing numbers of contingent (or adjunct) faculty. Contingent faculty include part-timers and full-time, non-tenure-track lecturers (Gappa, 2008). Although the representation of women faculty has increased over the last three decades, women tend to be concentrated in these part-time and non-tenure-track appointments (Perna, 2002). According to the American Association of University Professors (2005), the percentage of contingent faculty on college and university campuses has expanded from 43 percent in 1975 to nearly 70 percent thirty years later. Today, nearly half of all faculty in higher education serve in part-time appointments, while 68 percent of all new faculty appointments are non-tenure-track positions (AAUP, 2009).

Bousquet (2008) asserts that the precipitous rise in contingent faculty and concomitant lack of tenure-track positions is a race, class, and gender issue as well as an institutional issue. Agathangelou and Ling (2002) add that women of color not only face a glass ceiling when it comes to tenure, they also encounter a subtle yet toxic form of resistance that is fraught with issues of race, gender, class, and culture. Women faculty of color and those from lower-income backgrounds are more likely to be nontenure track and underpaid than similarly qualified white males of middle and upper class (Bousquet, 2008). This alarming trend, for both part- and full-time non-tenure-track appointments, continues to grow and poses a formidable barrier to women of color in pursuit of tenure. As the proportion of contingent faculty expands, the opportunities for appointment to tenure-line positions narrow.

Second, unlike the experiences of white women faculty, whose authority is less challenged, women of color often find themselves at the crossroads of race, class, gender, nationality, language, and sexuality as their enter the classroom (Vargas, 2002). The diverse social identities of women of color cause tension in the classroom. White students often challenge their authority and expertise, particularly when a professor's social identity does not align with her course (Vargas, 2002). For example, the expertise of an Indonesian woman teaching a course in Asian Studies goes unchallenged by white students. However, when the same Indonesian woman teaches American history or French, white students are more likely to challenge her professional authority. When evaluating teaching proficiency, tenure and promotion review committees should take into account how the social identities of women of color affect student/teacher interactions in the classroom and students' resistance to course topics as well as students' perceptions of teaching expertise (Vargas, 2002).

Third, an inhospitable climate often forces women to play a "prescripted" supporting role in the academy (Agathangelou & Ling, 2002, p. 370). This is in part due to the lack of collegiality in higher education (Hune, 1998). Feeling isolated and marginalized, women of color must constantly prove themselves to their senior colleagues while simultaneously trying to establish credibility in the classroom. Institutional structures, policies, and practices, intended to be gender neutral, can often serve to create an unwelcoming environment that is denigrating and unsupportive (Perna, 2002). This is particularly true with the recruitment process. Job postings have a limited circulation. An applicant must not only meet the minimum qualifications but also be compatible with the institutional image and able to fit in with the social group in power. Once hired, the professional lives of women of color are laden with tensions and contradictions in hostile work environments characterized by exclusion from social events and professional collaboration, multiple forms of oppression, and varying degrees of invisibility (Rains, 1999). As described by Rains (1999), *imposed* invisibility is socially constructed, leaving women of color feeling ignored (p. 153). *Selective* invisibility renders a woman of color invisible to white colleagues until they "select" to see her to fill a need (p. 156). Finally, *designated* visibility occurs when women of color are seen as token representatives of their race/ethnicity (p. 157). Rains (1999) likens the pressures and challenges for women of color to having to constantly dance on the sharp edge of a sword.

Fourth, women of color feel pressure to assimilate to Western academic culture both from within their own families and from within the academy (Calhoun, 2003). Assimilation to Western academic culture requires that women of color essentially reject their native culture to adopt the majority culture (Sadao, 2003). These women face a loss of voice and personal identity as they learn to assimilate to the environment of higher education (Calhoun, 2003; Hune, 1998). Commenting on this issue, Anna Ortiz, a professor in educational administration said, "If I remain silent and polite, I get to do the kind of research I want to do, and if I do enough of it, I get tenure" (Cooper & Stevens, 2002, p. 78). In essence, they learn to "play the game" to get what they want (Young, 2006, p. 154). Unfortunately, this sentiment is echoed far too often among women faculty of color who feel they must learn to compromise and bargain to obtain tenure. While assimilation implies the rejection of one's own culture, Sadao (2003) describes the cross-cultural theory of acculturation as requiring one to compromise one's existing beliefs and values to function in the new culture. Sadao (2003) posits a bicultural model as a more effective way of dealing with two distinct cultures. In this model, women faculty of color function both in the academic world and within their ethnic minority communities by successfully learning to code switch between two cultures as the situation requires.

Fifth, women of color may experience feelings of fraudulence as they question their position in the hierarchy of power (Calhoun, 2003; Koch, 2002). With few visible role models, women of color have difficulty visualizing themselves in positions of authority. Their lack of social and cultural capital causes them to feel less entitled to success in the public arena (Cooper & Stevens, 2002), detering their ability to take on leadership roles. Compounding this is the opposing value of community or interdependence in many non-Western cultures. In other words, women of color tend to attribute their success to all those who have supported them rather than take personal credit and draw attention to themselves (Calhoun, 2003). All of these factors contribute to difficulties in achieving promotion and tenure for women of color, who face the combined effects of racism, sexism, and classism (Cooper & Stevens, 2002), which narrows their opportunities for leadership in the academy.

Women of Color as Leaders in Higher Education

Despite their increasing numbers in the academic pipeline, women have only achieved "parity in number but not in positions of power and influence" (Morrissey & Schmidt, p. 1407). In a study of the progress of women of color as administrators from 1991 to 1997, Opp and Gosetti (2000) found that white women experienced the largest increase in proportional representation. The increase in the number of women leaders of color varies by institutional type, with the greatest increases occurring primarily in institutions that serve their respective underrepresented groups. More women leaders of color were found in minority-serving, two-year, and urban institutions.

Unfortunately, power and authority are still dependent on cultural assumptions and gendered understandings (Ideta & Cooper, 1999). To be female is to lack authority, thus a female leader in academe is often construed as an oxymoron (Ideta & Cooper, 1999). Women are disproportionately represented in educational administration as department chairs, academic deans, chancellors, and university presidents. This underrepresentation of women in leadership positions can be attributed to gender biases that inform academic cultural assumptions about women's leadership potential (Dominici, Fried, & Zeger, 2009). In positions of power, gender plays a critical role. In a study of women's and men's effectiveness and leadership behaviors, researchers uncovered perceptions among business managers that women "take care" while men "take charge" (Prime, Carter, & Welbourne, 2009, p. 25). Psychologists have noted that prescriptive gender stereotyping—assumptions about the roles that women play— often conflict with the role of leadership (Prime et al., 2009). Women leaders are often seen as violating their prescribed feminine roles, while men in leadership positions are perceived as acting in compliance with their prescribed masculine roles (Prime et al., 2009). These gender assumptions characterize women as more emotive, participatory, and nurturing and men as more logical, directive, and assertive (Amey & Eddy, 2002).

For women leaders, gender labeling is particularly problematic. For example, men who assert themselves as strong leaders are respectfully addressed as the "boss," whereas a woman with similar traits may be called a disparaging name. A male leader may be viewed as goal oriented, a woman as overly ambitious; a man is described as zealous, a woman as highly emotional; a man is seen as a clever negotiator, a woman as manipulative (Reinarz, 2002). Gender labeling is only one of many problems encountered by women in administrative ranks. Other challenges for women include a negative institutional climate, patriarchal leadership, an absence of peer mentoring and networking, a lack of understanding of the unwritten rules of campus culture, and the need to develop a professional communication style (Reinarz, 2002).

The ascent to academic leadership is often obstructed for women due to a well-defined academic hierarchy in educational administration. Academic administrators generally progress from department chair to dean to university leadership positions. Serving as the department chair enhances a women's credibility within her field, provides her with an opportunity to develop skills and experience in administration, and increases her visibility as a leader (Dominici et al., 2009). Unfortunately, women are not recruited as frequently as men for these positions, resulting in fewer women moving through the leadership pipeline.

Women of color face organizational and institutional barriers, such as policies, procedures, and practices that contribute to their underrepresentation in administrative positions. For example, in a male-dominated institution, there may be no policy in place to actively recruit and retain women of color. Institutional barriers result in a lack of access to informal and professional networks, a lack of mentors, and the absence of suitable role models (ASHE, 2009).

As academic leaders, women of color encounter multiple layers of discrimination. Racism and sexism prevail as the two most significant barriers that they experience (ASHE, 2009). For example, women of color may have their opinions and ideas ignored (only to have someone else credited for their idea) or have their leadership and credibility questioned. The effects of sexism include the prevalence of a patriarchal leadership model that continues to be seen as the norm, less pay for comparable jobs, and less desirable work assignments. In their study of African American and white women business managers, Bell and Nkomo (2003) note that women of color experience daily issues of racism, being held to a higher standard than others, the effects of invisibility, exclusion from informal networks, challenges to their authority, and feeble commitments to the advancement of women of color.

These pervasive and complex barriers to success for women of color have several negative outcomes. First, women of color remain underrepresented in administrative ranks, causing a mismatch with the gender and ethnic profile of the institution's student body (Reinarz, 2002). Second, they are concentrated in low-paying, low-status positions that lack authority, where they are underemployed and overused. Third, women of color experience slower rates of promotion and lower rates of retention. Fourth, women of color struggle for acceptance and equality among colleagues while being used as tokens to represent all persons of color on campus (Dominici et al., 2009). Under these conditions, some women find it necessary to camouflage their color and diversity with a "mask of whiteness" to mirror traditional forms of leadership (Amey & Eddy, 2002, p. 482). In the next section, we discuss more productive ways of coping with the barriers women of color encounter as leaders in academe.

Successful Strategies for Women of Color

We conclude this chapter with a discussion of two categories of strategies: (1) those women of color can employ and (2) those that institutions must take to "fix the system, not the women" (Morrissey & Schmidt, 2008, p. 1399). These efforts include the creation of "sista' networks" of African American women faculty (Cooper, 2006) and the use of peer mentoring and collaborative efforts to create community that combat the isolation women faculty of color often feel (Driscoll, Parkes, Tilley-Lubbs, Brill, & Bannister, 2009; Tierney & Bensimon, 1996).

Tuesday L. Cooper (2006) uses the term *Sista' Network* to describe the relationships between and among African American women faculty

(p. xii). The Sista' Network provides a venue for African American women to learn the formal and informal rules necessary to play the tenure game while gaining access to critical information and social networks. At their roundtable meetings, members of the Sista' Network discuss the tenure process, seek peer mentoring, build collegiality, and strengthen social networks. The benefits of the Sista' Network, which can be applied to all women of color, include establishing strong supportive relationships with other African American women faculty, learning about the tenure process from one another, and providing a means to fight institutional racism and sexism.

Lindsay (1994) argues that mentors are instrumental in the success of academic administrators, particularly for women of color. Peer mentoring and strategic collaboration are effective strategies in helping women of color to navigate the murky waters of the tenure process. In contrast to the dyadic mentoring model of mentor and protégé, peer mentoring, or networking mentoring, involves building a community among several participants at a similar rank and level of decision making who serve as both mentor and mentee, with the common goal of achieving tenure and success in academe. Peer mentoring provides participants with a flexible mentoring model emphasizing mutual interdependence among the members (Driscoll et al., 2009) and an opportunity to share advice, experiences, opinions, and perspectives as well as provide social support (Wasburn, 2007). This form of mentoring enhances an understanding of self, others, and the university environment (Driscoll et al., 2009) while enabling women of color to overcome isolation and become self-reliant and confident tenure-track scholars.

On a similar note, Vargas (2002) recommends that women faculty of color have multiple mentors. One mentor can advise a woman of color about her research, while another can help her with pedagogical challenges common to all instructors and those specific to women of color. Agathangelou and Ling (2002) advocate the need for women of color to construct coalitions to share their mutual struggles in the academy and build a critical mass. In support of such collaborative efforts, Amey and Eddy (2002) propose adopting new models of collaborative, servant-style leadership that promote collegiality, strong interpersonal skills, and consensus building.

As institutions endeavor to increase workforce diversity, they have a responsibility to implement and sustain leadership and mentoring programs and activities that promote the recruitment, retention, and advancement of administrators of color (ASHE, 2009). In their study of women academics in medicine, Morrissey and Schmidt (2008) describe the importance of creating an institution whose faculty, deans, and department and administrative leaders reflect the gender and ethnic profile of the college's student population. Department chairs and academic deans play a critical role in efforts to diversify the academy by encouraging innovative approaches to recruitment and equity in promotion and tenure (Dominici et al., 2009). Morrissey and Schmidt (2008) advocate "fixing the system" through "data gathering, constituency building, department transformation, policy reform, and advocacy" (p. 1399). Leadership seminars can be effective in exposing administrative leaders to strategies for recruiting and retaining women faculty of color. Leadership programs also play an important role in the career development of female administrators of color who often feel overworked, underpaid, isolated, and unappreciated. Continuing professional education and development programs are essential to prepare women of color to assume both faculty and administrative leadership roles (Lindsay, 1994). Institutional support is critical in creating, implementing, and evaluating leadership training.

Conclusion

It has been years since Hall and Sandler (1982) first documented the chilly climate for women in academe. More recent investigations have found that this climate has persisted into the twenty-first century (Allen, 2000; Sandler, Silverberg, & Hall, 1996). Thus, while women who were once barred from institutions of higher education now outnumber male students at all levels, women faculty and administrators, especially women of color, still face many barriers to their success as leaders. Indigenous women, such as Native Hawaiian women, suffer from the effects of colonialism as well as racism and sexism and thus have an even greater need for powerful role models as the next generation of women students make their way into academic positions. The first step is awareness. Beyond that is the need for mentoring programs, collaborative efforts, and more explicit guidelines to help these women successfully navigate the troubled and sometime dangerous waters of academe.

Work must continue to change the current structures of higher education; we believe it is important to focus on the strategies women of color can employ to create a more hospitable environment and to combat current inequities. Hopefully, their leadership can remove the barriers that women such as Paula Gunn Allen have so long struggled with, creating a climate that welcomes their talents and invites them into the heart of academic discourse and scholarly research. It is our sincere hope that the next generation of women scholars will emerge less battered than Paula Gunn Allen, finding a warm climate rather than the hostile environment that causes women to say, "Get me out of here. I quit."

References

Agathangelou, A. M., & Ling, L. H. M. (2002). An unten(ur)able position: The politics of teaching for women of color in the U.S. *International Feminist Journal of Politics, 4*(3), 368–98.

Allen, P. G. (2000). Rant for old teachers. In P. R. Freeman & J. Z. Schmidt (Eds.), *Wise women: Reflections of teachers at midlife* (pp. 147–56). New York: Routledge.

American Association of University Professors [AAUP]. (2005). Inequities persist for women and non-tenure-track faculty: The annual report on the economic status of the profession 2004–05. *Academe, 91* (2), 20–30. Retrieved March 6, 2011 from http://www.aaup.org/AAUP/comm/rep/Z/ecstatreport2004-05/2004-05report.htm.

Amey, M. J., & Eddy, P. L. (2002). Leadership. In A. M. M. Alemán & K. A. Renn (Eds.), *Women in higher education: An encyclopedia* (pp. 482–86). Santa Barbara, CA: ABC-CLIO, Inc.

Andersen, M. L. (2001). Restructuring for whom? Race, class, gender, and the ideology of invisibility. *Sociological Forum, 16*(2), 181–201.

Armenti, C. (2004). Women faculty seeking tenure and parenthood: Lessons from previous generations. *Cambridge Journal of Education, 34*, 65–83.

ASHE Higher Education Report. (2009). Barriers encountered by administrators of color in higher and postsecondary education. *ASHE Higher Education Report, 35*(3), 31–46.

Baumgartner, L. M., & Johnson-Bailey, J. (2010, Spring). Racism and white privilege in adult education graduate programs: Admissions, retention, and curricula. *New Directions for Adult & Continuing Education, 25,* 27–40.

Bell, E. L. J., & Nkomo, S. M. (2003). Our separate ways: Black and white women and the struggle for professional identity. *The Diversity Factor. Women in the Workplace: A Status Report, Winter, 11*(1), 11–15.

Bousquet, M. (2008). *How the university works: Higher education and the low-wage nation.* New York: New York University Press.

Boyd, J. K., & Braun, K. L. (2007). Supports for and barriers to healthy living for Native Hawaiian young adults enrolled in community colleges. *Preventing Chronic Disease (4)*4. Retrieved June 6, 2010, from http://www.cdc.gov/pcd/issues/2007/oct/07_0012.htm.

Butler, J. E. (1997). Transforming the curriculum: Teaching about women of color. In L. R. Lattuca, J. G. Haworth, & C. F. Conrad (Eds.), *College and university curriculum: Developing and cultivating programs of study that enhance student learning* (pp. 615–27). Boston: Pearson Custom.

Calhoun, J. (2003). "It's just a social obligation. You could say 'No'!": Cultural and religious barriers of American Indian faculty in the academy. *American Indian Quarterly, 27,* 132–54.

Carby, H. V. (1985). On the threshold of woman's era: Lynching, empire, and sexuality in black feminist theory. *Critical Inquiry, 12*(1), 262–77.

Cooper, T. L. (2006). *The Sista' Network: African-American women faculty successfully negotiating the road to tenure.* Bolton, MA: Anker.

Cooper, J., Eddy, P., Hart, J., Lester, J., Lukas, S., Eudey, B., et al. (2007). Improving gender equity in postsecondary education. In S. Klein (Ed.), *Handbook for achieving gender equity through education* (2nd ed., pp. 631–54). Mahwah, NJ: Lawrence Erlbaum Associates.

Cooper, J. E., & Stevens, D. D. (Eds.). (2002). *Tenure in the sacred grove: Issues and strategies for women and minority faculty.* Albany: State University of New York Press.

Dominici, F., Fried, L. P., & Zeger, S. L. (2009). So few women leaders. *Academe, 95*(4), 25–27.

Dorney, J. A. (2000). Thinking back through [my] mother. In P. R. Freeman & J. Z. Schmidt (Eds.), *Wise women: Reflections of teachers at midlife* (pp. 231–39). New York: Routledge.

Driscoll, L. G., Parkes, K., Tilley-Lubbs, G. A., Brill, J., & Pitts-Bannister, V. R. (2009). Navigating the lonely sea: Peer mentoring and collaboration among aspiring women scholars. *Mentoring & Tutoring: Partnership in Learning, 17*(1), 5–21.

Dzuback, M. A. (2003). Gender and the politics of knowledge. *History of Education Quarterly, 43*(2), 171–95.

Eisenberg, B., & Ruthsdotter, M. (1998). Living the legacy: The women's rights movement 1848–1998. *The National Women's History Project, 1998*. Retrieved April 15, 2010, from http://www.legacy98.org/move-hist.html.

Faculty and Staff Report University of Hawaii Fall 2003. (2004). Retrieved July 15, 2010, from http://www.hawaii.edu/cgi-bin/iro/maps?fsuhf03.pdf.

Gappa, J. (2008, July). Today's majority: Faculty outside the tenure system. *Change, 40*, 50–54.

Gatta, M. L., & Roos, P. A. (2007). Gender (in)equity in the academy: Subtle mechanisms and the reproduction of inequality. Retrieved July 15, 2010 from http://www.yale.edu/ciqle/INAUGURAL%20PAPERS/genderequity507entire.pdf.

Grieco, E. M. (2001). The Native Hawaiian and Other Pacific Islander population: 2000, U.S. Census Bureau, Census 2000 Brief, C2KBR/01-14. This report is available on the U.S. Census Bureau's Internet site at www.census.gov/prod/2001pubs/c2kbr01-14.pdf.

Hall, R. M., & Sandler, B. R. (1982). *The campus climate: A chilly one for women?* Washington, DC: Association of American Colleges.

Hune, S. (1998). *Asian Pacific American women in higher education: Claiming visibility and voice*. Washington, DC: Association of American Colleges and Universities.

Ideta, L., & Cooper, J. (1999). Asian women leaders of higher education: Stories of strength and self-discovery. In L. K. Christian-Smith & K. Kellor (Eds.), *Everyday knowledge and uncommon truths: Life writings and women's experiences in and outside of the academy* (pp. 129–46). Boulder, CO: Westview Press.

Jaschik, S. (2006, August 14). Sociology, gender and higher ed. *Inside Higher Ed*. Retrieved June 16, 2010, from http://www.insidehighered .com/news/2006/08/14/soc.

Koch, J. (2002). Coping with feelings of fraudulence. In J. Cooper & D. Stevens (Eds.), *Tenure in the sacred grove: Issues and strategies for women and minority faculty* (pp. 107–15). Albany: State University of New York.

LaRoque, E. (2007). Métis and feminist: Ethical reflections on feminism, human rights and decolonization. In J. Green (Ed.), *Making space for indigenous feminism* (pp. 53–71). Canada: Fernwood.

Leonard, P., & Malina, D. (1994). Caught between two worlds: Mothers as academics. In S. Davies, C. Lubelska, & J. Quinn, *Changing the subject: Women in higher education.* (pp. 29–41). London: Taylor & Francis.

Lindsay, B. (1994). African American women and Brown: A lingering twilight or emerging dawn? *Journal of Negro Education, 63*(3), 430–42.

Louis, R. (2007). Can you hear us now? Voices from the margin: Using indigenous methodologies in geographic research. *Geographical Research, 45*, 130–39.

Maher, F. A., & Tetreault, M. K. (1993). Frames of positionality: Constructing meaningful dialogues about gender and race. *Anthropological Quarterly, 66*(3), 118–26.

Makuakane-Drechsel, T., & Hagedorn, L. (2000). Correlates of retention among Asian Pacific Islanders in community colleges: The case for Native Hawaiian students. *Community College Journal of Research Practice, 24*, 639–55.

Marshall, W. E. (2011). *Potent mana: Lessons in healing and power.* Albany, NY: State University of New York Press.

McElrath, K. (1992). Gender, career disruption and academic rewards. *Journal of Higher Education, 63*, 269–81.

Meyer, M. (2001). Our own liberation: Reflections on Hawaiian epistemology. *The Contemporary Pacific*, 124–48.

Mokuau, N., & Browne, C. (1994). Life themes of Native Hawaiian female elders: Resources for cultural preservation. *Social Work, 39*(1), 43–49.

Morrissey, C. S., & Schmidt, M. L. (2008). Fixing the system, not the women: An innovative approach to faculty advancement. *Journal of Women's Health, 17*(8), 1399–408.

National Center for Education Statistics [NCES]. (2007). Retrieved June 16, 2010, from http://www.mnyscherc.org/site/672/doc_library/2007%20Digest%20of%20Education%20Statistics.pdf.

Opp, R., & Gosetti, P. (2000). *Promoting equity for women administrators of color.* Paper presented at the Association for the Study of Higher Education, Sacramento, CA.

Perna, L. (2002). Tenure and promotion. In A. M. M. Alemán & K. A. Renn (Eds.), *Women in higher education: An encyclopedia* (pp. 440–45). Santa Barbara, CA: ABC-CLIO, Inc.

Pincus, F. L. (1996). Discrimination comes in many forms. *American Behavioral Scientist, 40*(2), 186–94. DOI: 10.1177/000276429604 0002009.

Pincus, F. L. (2003). *Reverse discrimination: Dismantling the myth.* Boulder, CO: Lynne Rienner.

Prime, J. L., Carter, N. M., & Welbourne, T. M. (2009). Women "take care," men "take charge": Managers' stereotypic perceptions of women and men leaders. *Psychologist-Manager Journal, 12*, 25–49.

Rains, F. V. (1999). Dancing on the sharp edge of the sword: Women faculty of color in white academe. In L. K. Christian-Smith & K. S. Kellor (Eds.), *Everyday knowledge and uncommon truths: Women of the academy* (pp.147–74). Boulder, CO: Westview Press.

Rampton, M. (2008). The three waves of feminism. *Magazine of Pacific University, 41*(2). Retrieved June 14, 2010, from http://www.pacificu.edu/magazine_archives/2008/fall/echoes/feminism.cfm.

Reinarz, A. G. (2002, December). Issues for women in higher education administration. *Academic Advising News, 25*(4). Retrieved June 20, 2010, from http://www.nacada.ksu.edu/Clearinghouse/AdvisingIssues/women.htm.

Rury, J. (1986). Education in the new women's history. *Educational Studies: A Journal of the American Educational Studies Association, 17*(1), 1–15.

Sadao, K. (2003). Living in two worlds: Success and the bicultural faculty of color. *Review of Higher Education, 26,* 397–418.

Sandler, B. R., Silverberg, L. A., & Hall, R. M. (1996). *The chilly classroom climate: A guide to improve the education of women.* Washington, DC: National Association for Women in Education.

Schiebinger, L., & Gilmartin, S. K. (2010, January/February). Housework is an academic issue. *Academe,* 39–44.

Schoening, A. M. (2009). Women and tenure: Closing the gap. *Journal of Women in Educational Leadership, 7*(2), 77–92.

Silva, N. K. (2004). *Aloha betrayed: Native Hawaiian resistance to American colonialism.* Durham: Duke University Press.

State of Hawai'i Data Book. (2005). Honolulu: Hawaii Department of Business, Economic Development & Tourism. Retrieved June 7, 2010, from http://hawaii.gov/dbedt/info/economic/databook/db2005/.

Stromquist, N. P. (2006). Gender, education and the possibility of transformative knowledge. *Compare, 36*(2), 145–61.

The Chronicle of Higher Education Almanac. (2007). Retrieved June 25, 2010, from http://system4.lib.hawaii.edu:2224/article/Number-of-Full-Time-Faculty/47992/.

The Native Hawaiian Government Reorganization Act of 2005. (2005). Retrieved July 15, 2010, from http://www.usccr.gov/pubs/060531 NatHawBriefReport.pdf.

Tierney, W. G., & Bensimon, E. M. (1996). Promotion and tenure: Community and socialization in academe. New York: State University of New York Press.

Turner, C. S. V. (2002). Women of color in academe: Living with multiple marginality. *Journal of Higher Education, 73*(1), 74–93.

U.S. Census Bureau (2009). Retrieved April 24, 2010, from http://factfinder.census.gov/jsp/saff/SAFFInfo.jsp?_pageId=tp9_race_ethnicity.

Vargas, L. (2002). *Women faculty of color in the white classroom.* New York: Peter Lang.

Walker, A. J. (1993). Teaching about race, gender, and class diversity in United States families. *Family Relations, 42*, 342–50.

Wasburn, M. (2007). Mentoring women faculty: An instrumental case study of strategic collaboration. *Mentoring & Tutoring: Partnership in Learning, 15*(1), 57–72.

Wolfinger, N. H., Mason, M. A., & Goulden, M. (2009). "Stay in the game": Gender, family formation, and alternative trajectories in the academic life course. *Social Forces. 87*, 1591–621.

Women's International Center [WIC]. (1995). Women's history in America. Retrieved June 10, 2010, from http://www.wic.org/misc/history.htm.

Young, L. (2006). *The journey toward the Ph.D.: Native Hawaiian experiences*. Unpublished doctoral dissertation, University of Hawai'i at Mānoa. AAT 3216100, 173, ProQuest 1158525701.

6

Joining Forces: Collaborative Resistance to Privilege and Patriarchal Forms of Leadership

Patricia M. Amburgy, Wanda B. Knight, and Karen Keifer-Boyd

This is a true co-authored work with equal contributions from all of us and no first author. The order in which we list authors is based on a rotation we use in our collaborations on publications.

We are three female professors, at a major university, drawn together by issues that fuel our passion for equity and social justice in our workplace. However, within the patriarchal culture of our university, we each have been silenced and marginalized. We have experienced not only our own marginalization; we also have witnessed the silencing of others. We have been ignored, demeaned, and punished when we spoke out against unfair treatment of others. Through joining forces, we found strategies to change our working conditions. In our chapter, we discuss how we gained strength and enacted change through our collaboration.

By our second year together, we began to work collaboratively on writing projects, presentations, and an online team teaching project. The three of us believe that collaboration is important to share diverse perspectives, to innovatively solve problems, and to deepen reflective practice. Further, we propose that this form of leadership is important for becoming change agents in the pursuit of democratic life. We are strong and passionate advocates for social justice while embracing equity, inclusion, and collective responsibility. Our work, as art educators, is to motivate preservice and practicing teachers to consider the impact that they have on closing achievement gaps, providing genuine opportunities for success, and empowering those who have been disenfranchised or who have been underrepresented in the art world, in classrooms, and in society in general.

For us, collaboration is a critical practice manifested in both content and form. The content of our writing concerns disrupting privilege and antidemocratic forms of power. So does the form of our collaboration. In this chapter, we reflect on the strategies of our resistance to patriarchal systems of academia and how we have created a process and space for empowerment. Examples from our personal experiences inform our feminist perspectives on the larger political issues of work culture in higher education.

We have organized the chapter in four sections: "No Lead Author," "Power Play," "Bending Over or Standing Up," and "Collaborative Resistance." In each section, we address issues that are larger than our individual experiences yet grounded in our particular autoethnographic examples. Autoethnographic texts are written by those who find themselves marginalized within a group, culture, or institution as a response to how they are "othered" and misrepresented (Bochner & Ellis, 2002). Moreover, our purpose is to share how we learned through joining forces that there are several strategies useful to others, as discussed in the final section. Further, we propose that joining forces is an alternative to patriarchal leadership models.

No Lead Author

This section on no lead author stems from our rebellion against the devalued assessment of "tri-authored" work that two of us have received during annual faculty reviews, while others in our academic unit have not been admonished for co-authored publications. We intentionally rotate the listing of our names in publications and presentations. At the beginning of every publication we include the following statement:

> This is a true co-authored work with equal contributions from all of us and no first author. The order in which we list authors is based on a rotation we use in our collaborations on publications.

Resistance to our collaboration in writing has been evident within the institution as well as hierarchical expectations in the field at large. In a review of the existing literature on teacher education in art education, Thurber (2004) notes that researchers have found "many universities do not actually value collaborative or site-based research efforts on the part of their faculty" (p. 515). She includes further studies of collaborative methods as one of six important areas for future research on higher education. Others have recognized the value of our collaborative model. In the 2008 book *InSIGHT, InCITE, InSITE,* on the history of the National Art Education Association's Caucus on Social Theory and Art Education, Dr. jan jagodzinski acknowledges this:

> Although the Caucus for Social Theory might be considered a cogestion model, we have a long way to go. It should be pointed out that three caucus members: Patricia M. Amburgy, Wanda B. Knight, and Karen Keifer-Boyd, have been working cogestively. They have formed a cell attempting to present articles as a force of three, rather than one, not in some scientific model where the head researcher's name appears first, but rather in a round-robin affair—an admirable praxis. (jagodzinski, p. 148)

We rebelled by collaborating to such a high level of publishing that the field of art education took notice.

Having no lead author reflects our reconceptualization of leadership and power. The kind of leadership we practice is different from leadership that coerces people to comply with traditional roles within specific educational contexts (Slater & Ravid, 2010). Leadership is different from management and should be based on principles of participatory democracy. While most intelligent people can manage job-related tasks, not all managers are leaders. Leaders are visionaries who tend to be strategically focused. They develop processes for inclusive decision making and inspire and motivate individuals to be the best that they can be. Moreover, leaders are focused on change. They have the ability to lead people through change, not just manage them through it. Our practice of writing with no lead author is a challenge to patriarchal views of authority and leadership.

As feminists, our sort of collaboration endeavors to create change by "reconceptualizing leadership and power as shared processes" and by joining forces to form "alliances and coalitions that enhance their flow and influence" (Slater & Ravid, 2010, p. 157). Through collaboration, leadership and power are shared processes that value each individual's unique contributions. We have used our "outsider within" position (Collins, 1993) to survive and thrive and to advance our collaborative endeavors.

We view leadership and power as nonhierarchical. Leadership and power are mutually dependent. Power is a concept related to human interaction. Leadership is a collective process of developing empowering relationships through human interactions (Slater & Ravid, 2010). Power and leadership intersect through collaboration. We have strengthened our relationship through collaboration. Through collaboration we have learned to trust one another. We have been able to find common ground by respecting others' interests and values and finding solutions that benefit everyone.

Traditions of academic freedom that pervade institutions of higher education and uncontested rules of conduct within our disciplines have dominated and controlled interactions among our peers and colleagues (Slater & Ravid, 2010). By having no lead author, we seek to collaborate across various educational sectors and within the confines of a large, bureaucratic, patriarchal institution. Through collaboration, we have turned oppressive conditions into sources of critical insight about power and privilege in dominant patriarchal society.

Power Play

Domination power is invisible to those who hold it. In most cases, when people speak of *power play*, they are referring to domination forms of power in which real or perceived threats, coercion, and a sense of obligation are considered a game in which there are winners and losers. Dominating forms of power are part of hierarchical systems, and patriarchy is a hierarchal system. "We need a director who will kick ass," calls out a woman faculty member in a School of Visual Arts faculty meeting. The room is filled with nods and vocal agreements. The *kick ass* model of leadership works well for those individuals who are willing to *kiss ass* to avoid getting their asses kicked.

The long-standing cliché, *what goes around comes around*, can be avoided in the *ass kicking and kissing* approach to leadership if individuals within a group contribute to the decision making that impacts their lives, learn the complexity of making these decisions, and maintain transparency in policies and their rationale. Francis Hesselbaum, CEO of the Girl Scouts in the United States, is effective in a *joining forces* model of leadership regarding girl identity, empowerment, and discrimination in that her leadership style is based on "the power of inclusion, and the power of language, and power of shared interests, and the power of coalition" (Hesselbaum quoted in Collins, 2005, p. 10). For there to be motivation and ambition based on a shared mission, all need to support and help develop each other's strengths. This is joining forces.

Leadership is not synonymous with power over others. Leadership is about the empowerment of others. In joining forces, we are not coerced to come together; we choose to come together. Joining forces involves imagining the situation of others. This not only provides an intelligence of how others are likely to respond, but more importantly, enables multiple perspectives to see a situation from different vantage points. This is "a capacity that is essential for a successful democracy, a necessary cultivation of our 'inner eyes' " (O'Brien, 2010, p. ix). O'Brien is referring to a participatory democracy in which information and insights from a group are pooled to develop decisions on resource allocation and the sharing of work required for a shared vision and mission of the project or program.

Lessons learned from participatory democracy and peaceful activism provide leadership strategies that change the power play game. For faculty members to work together and help each other succeed in academic units, it is essential to develop policy together, to make policy handbooks accessible and official, and to document meetings through recorded minutes. In our unit, we found that simply taking minutes of faculty meetings threatened those in power. Why? Approved minutes provided documentation of discussions, actions, and outcomes of meetings; therefore, they thwarted maverick moves of unilateral decision making that did not take into account the perspectives raised at faculty meetings.

We disrupt the play of patriarchal notions of power by modeling transformative power, which involves community, participation, action to change the current situation, and honest communication. It is developed through the support, encouragement, and team effort of a group of people. Following are several examples of antidemocratic forms of power play that created a hostile environment that one or more of us have experienced. The power play primarily consists of unfounded and inappropriate allegations. Each example presented below includes strategies that successfully changed the power play dynamics by joining forces.

Power Play Example 1: Control through Uniformity

Online courses can be very profit driven and profitable. Clashes between pedagogy and profit and issues of standardization, ownership, and support confront those involved in developing online courses and programs. In developing an online art education program, we have found a clash between economically sound and pedagogically sound perspectives. Issues of standardization confront the need for mutable, scalable, and flexible implementation of online courses. In our development of an online masters program, we have designed each course to create a community view of education with opportunities for course participants to contribute their expertise, to guide course activities and projects in directions relevant to their context and learning goals, and to decenter authority of content in favor of learning that takes place along multiple axes. Further complications to the economic mandates of standardization are our ideas of effective assessment protocols, which we construct through a collaborative educational process with the course participants. It has been our experience that administrators favor profit over pedagogically sound practices and believe that standardization will provide profit, in part because low-salaried adjuncts and instructors can be hired to serve as graders in a standardized approach to teaching, learners, and evaluation.

At an international conference on e-learning, an audience member asked the presenter "What is a live course?" in relation to the "master course." The presenter tried to explain that the "live course" was an offspring of the master course with students participating in the course. The audience member, whose first language was not English, thought for a few moments and said, "I see, then the master is dead." The presenter responded that he did not see that the master is dead. One of us interjected: "Is the live course in the womb in what you refer to as the master?" Personal experiences as a mother living in a world of masters (master narratives, master bedrooms, master authority) reshaped the conversation to a perspective of learning spaces that nourish life (womb) compared to a prototype of excellence intended for duplication (master).

While there have been many attempts to control the work of tenured faculty in the development of an online graduate program, we point out an example in which a contract called a Memorandum of Mutual Understanding was proposed to layer on top of our contract as full-time tenured faculty members. From our perspective, since there was no release time or additional compensation for the preparation and teaching of an online course, this was similar to the preparation and teaching of a resident course and did not warrant an additional contract since we were not contracted for each resident course. By gathering information from a network of colleagues at other universities who teach in or direct both online and resident programs, we were able to utilize the joined forces of our colleagues to change the notions of online teaching as prepackaged knowledge set up for delivery. One administrator, in support of one-size-fits-all, said, "If the wheel works why reinvent it?" Our response is, "If a wheel rolls efficiently it is a wheel." Given the freedom to innovate and to own one's work, the rolling of the wheel can be both efficient and outstanding.

We will not agree to work *under* those that provide the technology support for online programs. Instead, we would like to *collaborate*. Therefore, we asked that the language of expectations in the memorandum of understanding reflect the nature of collaboration. As feminist bell hooks (1994) has argued, dominant and domination language is a way to control people. As long as the language of the memorandum/contract is not that of collaboration and mutual understanding, we will continue to work together to make a case for this change.

Power Play Example 2: Allegations of a "Sharp Edge" in Comments

An e-mail message from an administrator asserted that one of us presented a sharp and angry tone in response to issues raised related to pretenure faculty. The tone and intent were misinterpreted, but even if the tone were sharp and angry, why is a faculty member called to the administrator's office with a sense of urgency? Why did he have the desire to silence her? The intent of her inquiry at the faculty meeting was to seek clarification related to the administrator's process of decision making regarding selecting a semester for release from teaching for those in the tenure track. She asked whether he would encourage dialogue between program heads and tenure-track faculty regarding pretenure release time for research. This would provide an opportunity to provide ideas and information by those impacted by the decision in advance of decisions being made. In response to his e-mail, she restated the question she had asked and joined forces with other faculty so that they too asked this same question.

Power Play Example 3: Overstepping Our "Role" in a Patriarchal System

Creativity is necessary for participatory democracy to function well. Mihaly Csikszentmihalyi's (1997) study of creativity suggests that creativity involves research and deep knowledge, associative and metaphoric thinking for new insights, and perseverance to bring ideas to fruition. Creative people do not place themselves or knowledge into tight roles and compartments. When one of us updated an election ballot in our program, based on the numerous e-mails in which some faculty listed on the ballot did not agree to their nomination and others nominated were not listed, she was told initially that the change would overburden the already overworked office staff. Subsequently, when she responded, "No problem," and made the changes herself to avoid overworking the staff, she was told in an e-mail copied to a large number of our colleagues that she had overstepped her role. In what role was she placed so that she should not correct a ballot that clearly needed to be corrected? This is an example of power play and bullying. She changed the insult to a compliment in her re-envisioning of the idea. Rather than respond to the pettiness of the accusation, she turned to humor with the creation of an image that takes pride in overstepping the roles we are confined to in a patriarchal system of hierarchy.[1] We laughed about the subtle ways that this image could be used on notebooks or other paraphernalia that we brought to meetings or for signs hung on our office doors. However, we did not need to follow through with our initial thought of doing this since the process of creative productivity was all that was needed to avoid taking the accusation seriously, as if there were something wrong with correcting an inaccurate ballot. The three of us used the corrected ballot.

In a patriarchal system, the norm of power play is stereotypical maleness—competition, aggression, and a hierarchical ordering of privileging some over others. Through discussing our personal experiences, we consider how to turn the tables, not for the inverse, but for feminist

---

[1]See Figure 1 at http://tinyurl.com/PMA-WBK-KK-B for this visual play as an example of a strategy of creating images to paint a different picture from the chastised worker position in a fabricated hierarchy to an empowered perspective of scholars working together as colleagues.

goals of collaboration, empowerment, and inclusion. The next section considers one's positionality in relation to overturning power plays.

Bending Over or Standing Up

Like many of our art education colleagues in higher education, we work hard to balance our work lives between professional priorities and institutional expectations in areas of research, teaching, and service. Like others in higher education, we experience tensions between what is personally important to us as art educators and the expectations at our place of work. Like other art educators in higher education, we are concerned with issues of workload, compensation, and promotion and tenure (Galbraith, 2001; Milbrandt & Klein, 2008). But unlike some of our colleagues in higher education—at least, those who have been studied so far in the literature on art educators in higher education institutions—we do not work on level ground. At our institution, some art education faculty are positioned as favorites, people who can do no wrong, while others are positioned as failures, people who do nothing right. We are among the latter, partly because we have stood up for equitable practices.

Michael Bérubé, in the foreword of *Bending Over Backwards* (2002), posits that social constructions of sexuality, gender, and disability are in the margins, a sideshow "of already socially marginal discourses" (p. viii). In the past, each of us has been marginalized by the ways our professional identities were constructed by others at our institution. Two of us were repeatedly stereotyped by the director of our unit and his acolytes among other faculty as being too "practical"; supposedly, we were not sufficiently theoretical in our approaches to art education to warrant respect at a research-oriented institution. One of us was repeatedly characterized as "the wrong kind of feminist," meaning she did not practice an exclusionary form of feminism professed by another, more privileged member of the faculty. Individually, each of us heard these and other derogatory characterizations repeatedly spoken about the other two. Unfortunately, at times, we also heard them spoken by graduate students imitating the destructive attitudes of our colleagues.

The constructed identities imposed on us were not only spoken; they were also manifested in our working conditions of teaching, service, and yearly evaluations. For example, two of us had ever-changing course assignments for years, so that we were constantly in the process of preparing new courses, thus making it more difficult for us than for other more favored faculty to focus on research and writing. Also, two of us were not given graduate courses to teach for more than two years while we were working toward promotion and tenure. This was a way to limit advanced scholarly exchange with graduate students in small classes. Instead we spent time teaching large sections of undergraduate students.

In addition to her regular teaching load, one of us also taught a general education course through the continuing education unit at our university. The course generated extra income for our department and college as well as extra income for her that supplemented her below-average regular salary. She taught the course three semesters per year, year round, for ten years, developing it from a correspondence course with a small enrollment to an online course that was highly enrolled and highly profitable. After the university adopted a policy that regular faculty could not earn more than 20 percent of their base salaries through supplemental online teaching, our director did not propose that a reduction in her supplemental compensation be accomplished through a plan for reducing the number of students or the number of sections she taught, in order to make the workload proportionate to the decrease in compensation. Instead, he offered her an agreement that would have had her teaching the same number of students and sections, thereby continuing to bring in the high levels of income she had generated for the college and the department in previous years, but for one-third of the compensation she had previously received for the same work.

Our constructed identities as disposable people and academic failures were also reflected in our service assignments. As "practical" faculty, we were often assigned to undergraduate service committees with tasks such as compiling a student teaching handbook for undergraduate students. Beudert in her 2006 book, *Work, Pedagogy, and Change*, cites studies of higher education work environments in which "faculty members who work directly with teachers and schools are perceived less highly on college and university campuses" regardless of their published and grant-funded research (p. x). We were seldom appointed to influential service committees such as promotion and tenure committees or search committees in our program. When one of us was appointed to chair a search committee for three new positions in the art education program, which on the surface seemed to be an honor, the director and some of the faculty serving on the search committee undermined her in carrying out the ethical and legal responsibilities of the committee, to the extent that she had to ask a representative from the university's affirmative action office to come in and speak to the director and search committee members. During the search process that year, the director sanctioned a faculty dinner for a favored candidate in one of the searches, to which every faculty member in the art education program was invited except the three of us. The three of us—including the one who was then serving as chair of the search committee—were not informed about the dinner.

As often as not, we were assigned to service committees that were not valued and on which other, more favored faculty did not want to serve. One such committee consisted of representatives from teacher certification programs across the university. One of us represented the art education program on this committee for more than fourteen years, in spite of asking repeatedly to be released from serving on it. The work of the committee was not unimportant. On the contrary, it was of great consequence; it included, for example, preparing our institution's national accreditation reports. The trouble was that the director and other faculty in our program did not value service on this committee. A former head of the art education program used to refer to the committee and its members as "those education people," suggesting that they, along with the art education faculty member who served on the committee, were people with petty and tiresome concerns that were irrelevant to the elevated field of Art. When one of us, as the art education faculty member who served on the committee, spent an exceptional amount of time preparing our program's sections of the institution's National Council for Accreditation of Teacher Education (NCATE) report, the unit director at the time evaluated her accomplishments in the area of service for that year as "Needs Improvement," the lowest of the ratings on the evaluation scale. In contrast, another more privileged faculty member was given release from teaching for a year to prepare the National Association for Schools of Art and Design (NASAD) report, and she was publicly praised for this work.

The ways our professional identities were constructed by others were also reflected in our yearly evaluations. For example, in a year when one of us with a "practical" orientation had six publications, all in peer-reviewed journals and prestigious books in our field, the director did not acknowledge the achievement above the expected two publications per year. Instead, he evaluated her accomplishments in the area of research for that year as "Very Good," a step down from "Outstanding," which was the highest rating on the college's scale. In the second-year review of another of us with a "practical" orientation, the director recommended her pretenure probationary period should be ended and she should be dismissed from the university. The director defined her work toward establishing a charter school in the local community, which had been funded by a substantial grant, and included extensive research on charter schools across the United States, as service rather than research, and thus devalued it. The director cautioned one of us against associating with the other two, when she met with him, regarding her accomplishments one year. He told her that if she disassociated herself from us, he would make her "a star" at our institution.

The incidents described above are not an exhaustive list. There were many other ways that the three of us, individually and collectively, were positioned as expendable failures at our institution. None of the pejorative constructions of our professional identities was based on fact; as often as not, factual evidence suggested precisely the opposite of the ways that others constructed us. Nonetheless, the false constructions of our professional identities were so extensively embedded in our work life, they formed a kind of illusionary world that Wright (2006) compares to the simulated reality in the movie *The Matrix* (Silver, Wachowski, & Wachowski, 1999). What Wright calls "the matrix of privilege" in higher education is difficult for marginalized faculty to overcome, not only because of the pervasiveness of the constructed reality, but also because it is so seductive and effective in controlling the lives of faculty. For those who are willing to go along with the constructed reality, the duality of insiders versus outsiders, favorites versus failures seem normal within "the matrix of privilege." The constructed reality makes institutional privileges for the insider favorites and disadvantages for the outsiders appear to be the inherent nature of things.

At our institution, each of us has stood up to challenge discriminatory working conditions, misrepresentations of others, and other aspects of the constructed reality that positions some people as successful and others as failures. As a result of standing up against unfair treatment of others, we have all experienced retaliation. Standing up for change requires courage. It is not an easy position to take, but all three of us believe that when there is injustice anywhere, there is injustice everywhere, for everyone—including oneself (see Dr. Martin Luther King, Jr.'s "Letter from Birmingham Jail, 16 April 1963" in Shapiro, 2006).

Regardless of how successful we may be, as indicated by the factual record of our accomplishments, we have been positioned at our institution as people who fail. We know that our failure is constructed, not something real. We know it is an illusion that has been created and maintained by an exploitive gatekeeper and his acolytes who reap accolades at the expense of others. But real or not, the construction of us as failures has been a significant obstacle in our professional lives. In the concluding section of the paper, we turn to ways we have resisted this construction and continue to work toward a vision of professional achievement that is grounded in respect and collaboration, not a duality of insiders versus outsiders, favorites versus failures.

Collaborative Resistance

Over the years, we have changed many of the conditions we describe in this chapter. Although we have not always been completely successful in altering the matrix of privilege, we have improved working conditions at our institution. How? Our strategies include communication, humor, and network building.

We have found that communication is especially powerful in changing oppressive working conditions. During periods of adversity, there are times when one of us may be sad; there are times when one may be angry; and times when yet another may feel more driven to action than ever before. Because we are human beings, we have human emotions. There is no one right way to feel when a person is being treated unfairly, as everyone has a unique means for dealing with the situation at hand. Whatever the emotion or challenge, we listen to each other, and we acknowledge each other's feelings. We make sure that we are available when one or the other needs us, and we keep our lines of communication open. For example, two of us found in our annual review the same paragraph that chastised us for service to a new journal in our field, while the other one was praised for her service on the same journal. Such open communication has provided information that could have been damaging to our careers, if left unaddressed.

We go to each other to ask advice and to examine our reaction to adversity. We have asked each other, "Am I crazy?" concerning our experiences, including (mis)representations and interpretations of events. We communicate and value critique from each other, and this helps us to see a situation differently. The open communication helps to build each other's confidence and supplies the fortitude to persevere with working toward change of the patriarchal system that perpetuates injustice and privilege.

We all need an outlet to vent our frustrations and emotions. When we discuss our feelings and express our emotions, we are in a better position to move forward with increased productivity. One of the tools of our resistance has been humor. Whatever our oppressors may imagine, we do not get together and wring our hands or cry. Instead, we laugh. We laugh at their foolishness, the transparency of their lies, and their lame manipulations. Our laughter started one evening when the three of us had gone to dinner at a local restaurant to strategize over whatever the latest insult had been. Referring to one of our oppressors, one of us said, "Oh, he's just a dickhead." The other two started laughing, and one of them said, "So this is what it has come to—juvenile name-calling." At that point, we all started laughing—with big belly laughs—until we literally rolled on the floor. From that day forward, we have had a private language of laughter. In times of aggravation, one of us can say "dh" (meaning dickhead) and make the others chuckle. This is a strategy that helps us keep our sense of purpose, composure, and effectiveness as leaders.

The overstepping role image introduced in the "Power Play" section is another example of using humor to deal with bullying. The created image is a strategy to visualize what is wrong with a scenario, so that we go from feeling bad for being publicly chastised to restating the situation in a powerful visual form that brings laughter and inner power.

Some of the strategies that proved beneficial in helping us achieve promotion and tenure involved developing a support network, both at our institution and beyond, to help get through difficult times. The other strategies outlined here are from our experiences that may provide inspiration and examples for others to follow.

Have open lines of communication. Do not isolate yourself. Make sure that you have a support system. Start by identifying individuals with whom you can openly and honestly communicate. They could be family, friends, and/or colleagues. Share your concerns in confidence with an ombudsperson, and ask for advice. When necessary, have the ombudsperson accompany you to key meetings to serve as witness. If the ombudspersons for your college or unit are too close to the situation, then contact the university-level ombudspersons for other options. Carefully document what transpired at meetings, and seek confirmation from those in attendance that what you witnessed and wrote is accurate. Maintain all meeting records, decisions, and policies in written and digital forms.

Unsubstantiated charges against faculty who are in the promotion and tenure process may seem unrelated to promotion and tenure, and may even seem minor, but they can be trumped up and verbally repeated or included in annual reviews to the extent that the allegations are assumed to be true, and used against the faculty member. Documentation to prove otherwise is essential. Contest untrue statements in annual reviews, and make sure that statements are deleted from the review letter, with the reviewer's signature that an error was corrected in the newly revised review letter. Further, make sure your publication, service, and teaching record is outstanding. Ask to see dossiers and vitas of those who recently received promotion and tenure. If you know someone successful at promotion and tenure, you could ask to see his or her dossier as an example. At this stage, the dossier does not include evaluation letters. Some programs keep exemplars, with approval of the specific faculty members, to share with new faculty members.

We are not victims. We have successfully resisted the patriarchal culture of our university through communication, humor, network building, and when necessary, challenging corrupt practices of those in power. Through collaboration, we have gained new knowledge and devised new strategies to navigate bureaucratic patriarchal structures to initiate change in various educational sectors. "Collaboration challenges existing practices of power, wealth, and control that substantially contribute to growing class, race, gender, and other inequities in many societies" (Himmelman quoted in Slater & Ravid, 2010, p. 159). By joining forces, collaboration becomes a critical leadership strategy to change inequity, discrimination, and other challenges in the workplace in higher education institutions.

References

Bérubé, M. (2002). Foreword: Side shows and back bends. In L. J. Davis (Author), *Bending over backwards: Disability, dismodernism & other difficult positions* (pp. vii–xii). New York: New York University Press.

Beudert, L. (2006). *Work, pedagogy and change: Foundations for the art teacher educator.* Reston, VA: National Art Education Association.

Bochner, A., & Ellis, C. (Eds.). (2002). *Ethnographically speaking: Autoethnography, literature, and aesthetics.* New York: AltaMira.

Csikszentmihalyi, M. (1997). *Creativity: Flow and the psychology of discovery and invention.* New York: Harper Perennial.

Collins, J. (2005). *Good to great and the social sectors.* Boulder, CO: Jim Collins Monograph.

Collins, P. H. (1993). Learning from the outsider within: The sociological significance of black feminists thought. In C. Conrad, A. Neumann, J. G. Haworth, & P. Scott (Eds.), *Qualitative research in higher education: Experiencing alternative perspectives and approaches ASHE reader series* (pp. 111–30). Needham Heights, MA: Ginn.

Galbraith, L. P. (2001). Teachers of teachers: Faculty working lives and art teacher education in the United States. *Studies in Art Education, 42*, 163–81.

hooks, b. (1994). Language; Teaching new worlds/new words. In hooks, b. (Author). *Teaching to transgress: Education as the practice of freedom* (pp. 167–76). New York: Routledge.

jagodzinski, j. (2008). InSITE: The future of pedagogical "hacking": Lines of flight in critical visual art education; or, on the ruin(s) of representation. In K. Keifer-Boyd, M. Emme, & j. jagodzinski (Eds.), *InCITE/InSIGHT/InSITE: Journal of Social Theory in Art Education, The First 25 Years* (pp. 127–54). Reston, VA: National Art Education Association.

Milbrandt, M. K., & Klein, S. R. (2008). Survey of art teacher educators: Qualifications, identity, and practice. *Studies in Art Education, 49*, 343–57.

O'Brien, R. (2010). Foreward. In M. C. Nussbaum, *Not for profit: Why democracy needs the humanities* (pp. ix–xii). Princeton, NJ: Princeton University Press.

Shapiro, F. R. (Ed.). (2006). *Yale book of quotations.* New Haven, CT: Yale University Press.

Silver, J. (Producer), Wachowski, A., & Wachowski, L. (Directors & Writers). (1999). *The matrix* [Motion picture]. United States: Village Roadshow Pictures, Silver Pictures, Warner Bros. Pictures.

Slater, J., & Ravid, R. (Eds.). (2010). *Collaboration in education.* New York: Routledge.

Thurber, F. (2004). Teacher education as a field of study in art education: A comprehensive overview of methodology and methods used in research about art teacher education. In E. W. Eisner & M. D. Day (Eds.), *Handbook of research and policy in art education* (pp. 487–522). Reston, VA: National Art Education Association; Mahwah, NJ: Lawrence Erlbaum.

Wright, S. (2006). Teacher as public art. *Journal of Aesthetic Education, 40*(2), 83–104.

7

Navigating Gender at Thirty Thousand Feet: Women Directors of State Boards of Higher Education

Rosemary F. Powers and Hannah Fisher-Arfer

For students and faculty members at public universities, state higher education governing boards may appear, if they are considered at all, as meddling bureaucracies with little knowledge of the conditions of life "on the ground." Alternatively, they may be imagined as powerful deciders who can, if they choose, intervene to remove an unpopular senior administrator, approve new academic programs, or prevent the implementation of an overreaching increase in tuition. When asked, these trustees, directors, or regents speak of their dedication to the priorities of their state, to affordable quality education for its residents, and to strong stewardship for universities as invaluable engines for democratic citizenship and economic growth. Seldom, if ever, are these groups considered as complex communities that have norms for interacting and carefully constructed processes for decision making. In addition, the continuing discrepancy in gender representation on these boards raises troubling questions about differential power and influence. We argue that what it means to be a board member, within the complex bureaucratic environment of state systems of higher education, involves the muting of some identities, the elevation of others, and virtual silence about the effects of gender and race. We explore the construction of board member identity with a focus on culture and performance and then analyze women's perspectives regarding the effects of gender (and other categorical identities) on their experience as members of public higher education policy boards.

Women and Board Membership

Corporate Boards and the Situation for Women

Corporate boards of *Fortune 500* companies differ markedly from U.S. state boards of higher education, whose members are either appointed by governors or elected by citizens of their states. However, since most research regarding women's participation on policy boards has been conducted on *corporate* boards, these studies offer a general assessment of the current climate for women as members of policy boards and the demonstrated effects of their membership.

When it comes to gender and corporate board membership, numbers matter. Boards with three or more women demonstrate more positive outcomes (Joy & Carter, 2007; Kramer, Konrad, & Erkut, 2008). Companies with greater numbers of women on their boards may show enhanced financial performance (Campbell & Mínguez-Vera, 2007), be more likely to be listed among the "most ethical companies" and "best companies to work for" (Bernardi, Bosco, & Columb, 2009; Bernardi, Bosco, & Vassill, 2006), or show greater corporate responsibility regarding issues such as sexual harassment (Grosser & Moon, 2005). However, while women board members may bring increased board attention to "women's issues," responses to a 1991 survey indicated women members did not want to be seen as bringing a "feminist agenda" but wanted to "be recognized for their expertise rather than their gender" (Catalyst, 1993, p. 40).

In spite of the demonstrated positive effects of increased representation, women's numbers on corporate boards remain low in the United States (Arfken, Bellar, & Helms, 2004; Helms, Arfken, & Bellar, 2008), with women holding only 15.2 percent of *Fortune 500* companies board positions in 2008 (Catalyst, 2009).

While this shows the chilly climate for women in general, numbers show that for women of color on corporate boards, the situation is even cooler. Women of color hold only 3.2 percent of seats for *Fortune 500* boards, and 318 of the companies have no women of color represented (Catalyst,

2009). According to Lisa Fairfax (2005), this failure of representation is a "cause for particular concern" since women of color are appointed less frequently than white women or men of color; those who *are* appointed may be asked to serve on multiple boards and thus be stretched too thin; and stagnation often results (p. 1115).

When considered overall, studies of the characteristics of women corporate board directors do not adequately answer whether the women serving are highly competent or are just token appointments in a male-dominated culture (Burgess & Tharenou, 2002). Additionally, corporations may try to signal a commitment to diversity by showcasing outstanding individuals but not improving the overall participation of underrepresented persons (Gulati & Shin, 2010). Corporate commitment to gender equity also seems weak since women are less often found on more powerful executive, governance, and/or finance committees (Bilimoria & Piderit, 1994; Catalyst, 2008; Kesner, 1988) and more often on public affairs committees (Peterson & Philpot, 2007).

Women and Higher Education Governance Boards

Despite structural and mission differences from corporate boards, private and public university governing boards reflect a similar situation for women. But the numbers are better. According to Ehrenberg and Main (2009), progress has been "slow but steady," with women holding 29 percent of the total positions and 18 percent of the board chair positions in 2004 (Schwartz & Akins, 2005). These percentages are still troubling, especially at a time when women are actually graduating college and gaining advanced degrees in greater numbers than men (Catalyst, 2008).

A few studies explore how gender matters on these higher education governing boards. Twale and Burley's 2007 survey of forty-nine women trustees at land grant universities found that women were underrepresented on financially related committees. Also, in seeking to be taken seriously on the board, these women stated that they "must not 'rock the boat' and should maintain a 'balance' so not to show gender favoritism when making board decisions" (Twale & Burley, 2007, p. 8). Encouraging research by Ehrenberg, Jakubson, Martin, Main, and Eisenberg (2009) shows a positive relationship between increased numbers of female trustees and increased numbers of female university faculty. However, based on her qualitative study of women serving on private and public university boards, Glazer-Raymo (2008a) concludes:

> Diversity and equity as basic components of the cultural norms underlying governance structures have been only partially realized with respect to the inclusion of women trustees, including women of color. ... [T]he composite portrait remains ... overwhelmingly white, predominantly male, affluent, business-connected, middle-aged, active in civic affairs, and serving on multiple boards, both corporate and non-profit. (2008a, pp.185, 205)

This sober assessment demands further research to document women's participation on higher education policy boards, women's evaluation of the experience, and what public policy changes may be required to move beyond the rhetoric of a commitment to diversity.

Study Design, Method, and Approach to Analysis

As appointed directors of a U.S. state system of higher education, and at the time of planning this study the only two women serving on a board of twelve, we decided to undertake the research after reading a short article in the governance journal *Trusteeship,* entitled "Women Trustees: An Untapped Resource" (Glazer-Raymo, 2008b). The author summarized her research with women serving on higher education boards, advocating increased gender representation, and we determined that our "insider" status offered a unique position from which to further examine these experiences.

We were especially interested in learning how the public context of board meetings might influence interactions among members and how women from different state systems experienced the structures of their boards (related to leadership, committee work, conduct of meetings, and relations with office staff and external stakeholders). Focusing exclusively on public higher education boards, this exploratory study sought to understand how board member identities were created and performed and what might be the gendered implications of those performances.

Data Collection

Informed by insights from elite methodology (Kezar, 2006; Odendahl & Shaw, 2002; Winkler, 1987), we knew that while our insider status as board members could be beneficial in establishing our legitimacy as researchers, securing commitments from these busy public officials[1] would be difficult. We sent e-mail invitations introducing ourselves as board members of a state university system and requesting brief phone interviews. Given the political nature of these positions, we promised confidentiality in our reporting both to protect our interview subjects and to encourage candid responses.

Sample

Since we were interested in comparing the experiences of women on boards with similar responsibilities and jurisdictions to ours, we began by identifying states with systems of public higher education governed by a single policy board. The majority of the boards we identified were Boards of Regents (Directors or Trustees) with fiduciary responsibility for all four-year public institutions of higher education within their state. From that list of thirty-one states, we identified eighty-six women currently serving as board members. Given the relatively small population, we decided to use a nonrandom sample and sent a consent form and an e-mail invitation asking for a short phone interview to all the women for whom we were able to find contact information.

We interviewed thirteen women from nine state higher education boards. Interviews of between thirty minutes and one hour were conducted over a several-months period in 2009 to 2010, were recorded with subjects' consent, and were transcribed for coding and analysis. To provide the context for the reader, additional data came from our personal notes from board meetings and informal conversations with board members and system staff.

---

[1]Variously titled "regents," "trustees," or "directors." All three terms will be used in the text, since they are all used by one or more of the boards we examine. We sometimes interchange them to protect confidentiality for specific regents.

Justification for inclusion of our own experiences is two-fold. First, there is wide acceptance among social scientists that "(t)here is no such thing as removing the observer from the knowledge acquisition process since to do so would be like trying to see without eyes" (Stivers, 1993, p. 311). Second, in accepting this unavoidable researcher presence, we use some of the conventions of autoethnography (Ellis & Berger, 2002), inserting our own experience explicitly in the text, but in this study only to offer a deeper sense of context. Our actual board member experience was thus a benefit, as it allowed us to relay the often obscure culture of governance boards.

Approach to Analysis

To present our understanding of the ways these women navigated board culture, we draw on critical feminist and sociological theory and insights from narrative studies. Our analysis is grounded in the belief that gender schemas and norms profoundly shape board culture and interactions, though they may not be attended to consciously. While many of our respondents do not confirm this view, their stories, as ours, are constructions that offer rich texts for reflection but are opaque with regard to their status as objective fact. As Catherine Riessman argues in her review of the uses of personal narrative in social science, "storytelling . . . is what we do with narrative . . . and what informants do with us. The approach does not assume objectivity, but instead privileges positionality and subjectivity" (2002, p. 696).

Unlike the well-established life-history tradition in narrative research involving in-depth storytelling over time, our use of narrative analysis is more limited. We coded the semistructured interviews using conventional qualitative techniques and analyzed these narratives inspired by both Adrianna Kezar's (2006) research on high-performing public higher education boards and the use of the concept of "performance" in creating everyday identities from the classic work of sociologist Erving Goffman (1959) and feminist Judith Butler (1990).

In making sense of interview responses, we applied positionality theory, a feminist approach to understanding structure and power that investigates the role of multiple and intersecting identities and thus the effects of *position* within specific social contexts (Alcoff, 1988; Collins,

1990; Haraway, 1991). According to Kezar and Lester (2010), positionality theory helps us understand power, not as emanating from an individual actor with authority to exert influence but "as socially constructed between people" and as likely to change only when "people come together to examine norms or ideologies that are socially constructed and infused with power" (p. 167). Thus this research analyzes both the underlying norms of board culture and the experiences of women members as they cocreate or reinforce board culture.

Limitations

The public role of these board members encourages the telling of "official" stories that can affect the trustworthiness of data. As Stivers (1993) notes with respect to elite studies, even confidential life-history interviews require public figures to present themselves as successfully performing their public roles. Further, promising not to use any identifying information about the interviewees or their state system limited our ability to analyze specific contextual relationships directly, although clearly the politics, structures, and processes within each state affect the board member experience in important ways. Short interviews limited our ability to probe responses more deeply to gain a richer picture of these women's lives. Even with our small sample and the very specific subset of governance boards, the many differences—in organizational forms, routes to board membership, and scope of decision-making responsibility—made comparisons or generalizations problematic. Finally, while we did send invitations to most of the women serving on these state boards, not all systems make board member contact information available. Since we were not able to reach all the women with an invitation, our sample is even less representative. Still, the data we collected offer important evidence about women's experience in these rarified settings, and the patterns we found reveal both women's important contribution and possible reasons for continuing slow progress toward equity.

Findings and Discussion

Through our interviews, we found that board culture exerted powerful influence on shaping what identities were appropriate to perform in this context. Enacting the board member role with its primary commitment to furthering the mission of higher education, these women participated in highly ritualized public meetings and served on major committees. Several were or had been board chairs. Commitment to their primary identity as fiduciaries of complex bureaucracies and large financial enterprises did not encourage a consideration of how other aspects of identity might shape the policy decisions they made. Given our initial research question about how gender might matter and research that concluded differently (Glazer-Raymo, 2008a, 2008b), we were interested to find that most of the respondents did not see gender as a status with much or any relevance in this context. However, their responses provide an opportunity to explore the ways that women's position with regard to age, accomplishment, race, and length of service as a regent may shape their experience of gender on these policy boards.

Culture and Performance: Constructing Board Member Identity

I arrive 15 minutes before the scheduled beginning of the board meeting, and scan the room for people I know will be easy to engage in conversation. The mostly female central support staff move among us quickly, making the orchestration of one of these gatherings look easy but serious. Around the appointed time, our board chair calls the meeting to order. The script is before us, and the chair moves us through the performance. The meeting over, I debrief with colleagues and leave the stage.

—Rosemary

This description of a typical board meeting will sound familiar to anyone who has participated as a member or attended meetings of most kinds of boards. However, in the case of public higher education boards, member identity is enacted in regular board meetings that are highly ritualized and performed on the public stage required by "sunshine" or open meetings laws for state entities.[2] The importance of this goal of successful public performance presents an opportunity to explore the norms and

_____

[2]Several women stated that their state's public meetings laws were the strictest in the nation.

values that guide board action and how these may affect the enactment of other aspects of board members' social identities.

The women we interviewed presented themselves as knowledgeable, competent, and deeply committed to the goals and mission of public higher education. They bring many years of experience in other settings to this context, some identities that are highly valued and others that appear to have little relevance here. Occupation and experience (both in other situations and on this board) appear to carry significant weight. By their accounting, gender played little or no role, and only women of color spoke about the significance of race. We will address these findings later.

The construction of board member identity occurs within a cultural context where successful performance requires the creation of a professional board from a stock of political appointees or elected members. According to Kezar (2006):

> To be effective, boards must adopt a professional culture where civil interactions are the norm. In addition, many individuals who are appointed or elected to public boards do not have experience with board work and must be socialized to its values. The board culture affects overall board performance "by shaping the decision process; by leading toward or away from consensus; by using data to understand or argue, or by not using data at all; by building or not building constructive relationships among members; and by influencing which matters get on to the board agenda." (p. 987)

In this context, board member competence requires the muting of some identities, the elevation of others, and virtual silence about the effects of gender or race. In this professionalized culture, gender or race *shouldn't* matter, and neither should political party or personal priorities. What *should* matter is thoughtful consideration of state priorities for higher education with colleagues in a civil atmosphere, as one respondent stated, "where we can disagree without being disagreeable." For successful performance in public, board members will have prior access to policy options that have been thoroughly vetted and prepared for approval by institutional administrators and central system staff. By the time these policy options reach the board meeting, the decisions will often be ceremonial. As one respondent noted, "The [chief executive] does what all the good people do—which is to make sure there is consensus before he asks for a vote."

Becoming a Board Member

I opened my e-mail to an intriguing subject line—"An offer you can't refuse." The executive director of the American Federation of Teachers—Oregon wrote to remind me that the Legislature had just passed a bill creating a second faculty position on the state board of higher education. My leadership as a founding member and first president of the faculty union at my university made me a logical choice for the union to put forward. As a sociologist, I warmed to the potential for observing high-level policy organization first hand. As a woman with limited public policy or administrative experience, who would be joining a board composed mainly of men with corporate and legal experience, I was daunted.

—Rosemary

Getting on the Board

We began our interviews with the question: How did you get on the board? Most responded without elaboration: "I was appointed by the Governor." (A minority serve in states where members are elected.) They usually added that the legislature confirmed these appointments, and one suggested that her appointment might have been seen as "confirmable" in a state where gubernatorial appointment requests are taken very seriously. We asked if they thought their governor had prioritized appointing a woman to the state board, and two indicated that might have been the case. The rest discounted the idea of a "gender appointment," with eight stressing instead their personal friendships or long professional association with the governor or engagement and support for the governor's election campaign. Others assumed their appointment provided geographic/regional diversity or was evidence of the governor's effort to be even-handed politically (possibly because of statutes requiring clear bipartisan membership). Other explanations included having specific experience needed by the board at this time and prior service on other statewide policy boards.

Beyond the appointment itself, few identified a specific expectation to represent the governor's perspective in their work as a board member, although one trustee said, "Well, they want us to rubber stamp. That's how these things go. But if you oppose and the governor is aware of the opposition, you are not reprimanded, but you might not be reappointed by the governor." One respondent emphasized the importance of ensuring good working relationships with the governor, stating that, "It's not official but we generally run by the governor's office our choice of chair, just to make sure we're not picking somebody they can't stand. . . . They don't legally have the right to chose our chair, but politically we take their views into consideration."

Internalizing Norms of Civility

As Kezar's (2006) respondents asserted, creating a professional public higher education board demands securing a commitment to norms of interaction that will ensure respectful and collegial exchange of views (in contrast to more "political" boards emphasizing priorities of individual powerful members). The regents were explicit in describing their board exchanges as respectful and professional, though one mentioned less respectful exchanges outside of public meetings. According to one regent, "It's very refreshing to serve on this board, because of the non-political nature of the board . . . as opposed to people in other bodies who are trying to advance their political careers." Another noted that, "In five years, I've never heard anyone get ugly at all." In general, trustees pointed to the respectful board exchange as pleasurable and a distinguishing feature from the culture in other boards on which they had served.

Norms of Interaction and Decision Making

One practice that reinforced the norm of civility and respect was the use of honorifics in addressing other members as a preface to comments or questions, and especially when expressing disagreement. As one woman stated, "We tend to be formal, and that works really well. We get a fair amount of testimony from the public and . . . by referring to each other as Regent Jones or President Smith, I think that elevates the discussion because sometimes we are talking about things that people have strong feelings about. . . . The decorum is raised." This use of formal titles was disconcerting at first for one trustee: "I had trouble at first getting used to the formal titles 'Regent Johnson' etc. I made some mistakes early on calling people by first names, and while it seemed to be OK at the time, people would tell me after that I needed to use the title. I told them that they would need to signal me about that, as I am just not that formal as a person."

Enforcing formal address can appear to equalize status within the board and signal to staff and the public the power invested in the role. It is also an effective mechanism for making other identities less relevant or appropriate to display. On these boards, using formal titles was consistently enacted on three, sometimes in eight, and seldom in two. In one case, a trustee explained, "I call everyone by their first name, except I always call the (chief executive) 'Mr.' " And another said, ". . . we start out trying to call everybody 'regent' and we end up calling them Dick and Pat and that sort of thing. It's relaxed."

All but two of the women said there was seldom any real debate at board meetings, though one stated that there should be more, especially when dealing with issues like tuition. However, if "sunshine" laws limit decision making or quorum discussion outside of public meetings, but there is an effort to seek consensus before a public vote, how do people *reach* consensus?

Boards have both standing and ad hoc committees charged with developing and reviewing specific policy options for consideration by the full board. As respondents confirmed, much discussion occurs in these settings, but usually with much less public attention even though meetings are open and agendas are posted on system websites. Thus committee assignments can have strong effects on board decisions, and appointments to major committees carry significant weight.

In addition, senior system staff develop policy options and are expected to provide board members with enough detail to make thoughtful decisions. Their influence cannot be underestimated. This too was emphasized by all of the respondents. One regent was frustrated with the central staff, saying that procedures and systems needed to be changed so that board members could better see how things were working on campuses and in order to avoid past problems. Another had been more frustrated with a chief executive and worked with others in board leadership to keep time-consuming but not very productive items off the public meeting agenda.

The rest spoke only of the board's strong dependence on the chief executive (chancellor, president, or commissioner) and central staff to help frame the issues and provide essential information.

Importantly, informal conversations and lobbying offer a "grey area" for pursuing consensus. Most respondents were emphatic about the need to avoid any semblance of holding private conversations with a group of board members outside the formal meeting structure. Three trustees stated that their state's public meeting law was "the strictest in the country" (underscoring the due diligence they attached to following it). As one woman recounted, "We had a dinner at one of the regent's houses the night before the meeting and the (chief executive) was there for two reasons— the camaraderie and so forth, and the other to make sure we don't talk about board business. We really do not sit down informally and go through a decision-making process at all. It is all done pretty formally and carefully." Smaller boards have to be even more careful in this regard. As one women noted, "We need to be sure no more than one less than a quorum are speaking together at any one time outside the meeting."

Others were aware that there was "probably a lot of low-key lobbying," though one stated that, "No one has ever called me and attempted to secure my vote." Another suspected that some of this kind of conversation was happening, and that it might explain some of the dysfunction the board experienced. Even the regent who was most clear about avoiding violation of the quorum requirement stated that "informal conversation does take place that changes people's minds," and another added, "This is very important. Work is not done in the board room but over coffee." These comments have implications for power dynamics on the board. The carefully scripted equality enforced at the formal meetings can be undercut in important ways by such conversations. While the more experienced white women we interviewed did not mention informal conversations as a barrier to their participation, younger women and women of color indicated that they were less likely to take part in these informal conversations.

Influence

Obviously, some members exert more influence than others on any policy board, but in the case of public higher education boards, the intention of *public* oversight results in situations where multimillionaire CEOs may share equal vote with young student members. Also, when board members are elected, individuals often bring very uneven professional backgrounds and experience. But equal vote, while significant in its formal meaning, does not, of course, translate into equal influence.

All the trustees asserted that they had influence and were respected within their areas of expertise by their colleagues on the board. Those with years of experience in educational policy and practice described with satisfaction their promotion of specific policies and projects—and the respect they had received for their leadership in these efforts. The younger women and women of color (also earlier in their careers), while describing the opportunity to participate on the board as extremely gratifying and challenging and feeling respect from colleagues, expressed less certainty about their effectiveness. Unable to fully enact the "expert" identity, they spoke instead of being hard workers and of their commitment to provide information that more accomplished and seasoned board members needed to hear. Others emphasized the importance of their own areas of expertise, with one noting her continuing efforts to remind the "corporate types" that public university missions are not about "the bottom line."

Those who were or had been chairs, vice chairs, or committee chairs conveyed both a sense of accomplishment and responsibility and had no question about their achieved status as leaders within their boards. All recognized the importance of such leaders and expected them to work closely with system executives and senior staff to keep the board focused on meeting its goals. Of this group, four have had experience as chair of their boards or had declined an invitation to be chair, and two more have had experience as vice-chair. This maps positively to the national numbers for the thirty-one state higher education system boards we identified in which women trustees account for 22 percent of board chairs or presidents. In our small sample, 30 percent of the women have had experience as chair.

Gender and Board Member Identity

In our interviews, we learned that women governors, whatever their party affiliation or ideology, appeared to appoint more women. This parallels the Ehrenberg et al., (2009) study showing a relationship between increased numbers of female trustees and increased numbers of female faculty at universities. Generally, trustees acknowledged it would be good to have more women on the board. One, after saying she did not think gender currently had much effect, responded to a question about possible effects of increased female members by saying, "It would probably change the whole culture of the board." She paused and then noted the contradiction. Either gender matters or it doesn't. However, it is not as simple as that.

How Gender Does(n't) Matter

As one of two women on a twelve-member statewide board of higher education, the absence of my gender is clear. In my mind this lack of female representation is synonymous with gender mattering, if it didn't there would be more women. While diversity and equity may be a platform for any statewide system, the reality is that foundational principles of diversity are not reflected in boardroom demographics.

—Hannah

Because women remain in the numeric minority, their level of comfort in the boardroom is dependent upon their ability to function in a dominant white male environment. The capacity for women regents to feel secure in a male-dominated atmosphere is related to their individual positional perspectives, shaped by life experiences. Thus each regent's perception of the board room is unique, informed not just by her gender but by multiple identities (such as race, social class, age, and occupation). Positionality theory (Kezar & Lester, 2010), which takes these multiple identities seriously in examining different experiences of power and decision making, can help us explain these different interpretations of board dynamics and culture.

To illustrate this, we introduce a seemingly trivial example—interest in and comfort with the world of sports. Long an area of interest for members of predominantly male groups, sports talk and metaphors may serve as a basis for informal conversation and bonding for board members. We asked women trustees if they noticed this kind of talk. Most did not. They were more likely to remember the sometimes overuse of academic acronyms. However, four did identify sports culture as a subset of board conversation and activity. Two were able to actively engage and enjoy the references and sports-related stories common at board meetings and events. Their identity as a "sports person" was informed by sports culture or through familial and personal experiences. Two others did not feel competent or interested in such conversation or activities. As one regent stated, "the board gets taken to the football games and the basketball games and at those games the trustees talk to one another and about special coaches and players, and I'm completely lost. I haven't got a clue what they're talking about." University athletics, especially during football and basketball season, becomes a topic of informal conversation at both board meetings and games that some women are more equipped to discuss than others. For those who do not possess the vocabulary or knowledge to engage in sports banter, the consequences are isolating. For those women who do have the background, who have taken sports as part of their identity, the significance of gender in the boardroom is diminished, thus contributing to their conclusion (albeit in a small way) that the board is neutral with regard to gender.

In her work on public and private boards of trustees, Judith Glazer-Raymo found the women she interviewed "were unanimous in observing that gender matters on boards" (Glazer-Raymo, 2008b, p. 20). In our research, however, most women did not see the saliency of gender on the board despite their numerical disadvantage. Only three of our thirteen respondents acknowledged gender as affecting their board experience.

In our interviews, we found three responses to questions about how gender might have significance in this setting: "gender neutral," with a subset we call "gender accomplished," and "gender matters." Ten respondents assessed the board as "gender neutral," meaning that when we asked how gender might affect their experience on the board, they gave some version of "not at all" or "I don't think it does." These explanations differed by age, occupational prestige, and length of board service. Younger women and women of color, marginalized by even smaller numerical representation, were able to recall instances of gender salience. For them, "gender matters."

Gender Accomplished

One third of the regents who defined their board experience as "gender neutral" were the most prestigious and, in several cases, longest-serving members of their boards. They had been pioneers at a time when gender discrimination was being challenged in legal battles and when gender integration into major policy-making bodies was new. In response to whether gender mattered in her experience as a board member, one woman responded, "It has been irrelevant really. My experience in having a tough time being a woman on the board goes back to 1970s when I was the first woman elected to (a political position). So those days had plenty of issues at that point but I've been at this for a long time now and in community work and political work so at this point it's just not a factor."

Modern consequences of gender seem trivial in comparison to the overt sexism in which these political veterans began their careers. Their assessment of the role of gender may be due to the more covert nature of institutional sexism in boardrooms today. Since accomplished women can be found in all areas of public higher education administration and all committees and leadership positions within policy boards, the issue becomes one of competence and experience rather than gender. The continued reality of being in the numeric minority on boards, gender-traditional committee membership for most women on the boards and ongoing differences in women's and men's abilities to donate to political campaigns and chosen professions indicate continuing effects of gender.

But these women discounted the effects of gender in *the present*. They seemed to have a "been there, done that" attitude and refer to their experiences with gender as an issue in the past. As one trustee stated, "I am not the right person to talk to who is sensitive to gender because I've been in this business so long." This regent acknowledges that some women may be intimidated by the male-dominated environment in which she operates, but with her commitment and accomplishments, she has emerged as a strong and capable leader and her gender is not a factor on the board. "Gender accomplished" women were able to both identify the absence of gender saliency on their boards and recognize the potential implications gender may have for *other women*.

Women who have become leaders in their occupations and communities are more likely to become board chairs and/or chairs of major committees. However, although they have "accomplished gender" and overcome the barrier of gender in the boardroom, their accomplishments may serve to make continuing issues invisible. Some women, in "accomplishing" gender, may "flee any association with even vaguely feminist issues and remain vociferously committed that gender has no bearing on the major issues a trustee considers" (Howard, 1984, p. 32). As a result, gender issues may be raised by less powerful female board members and receive lower priority on a board agenda.

As strong leaders, gender-accomplished women in our study assert gender neutrality for their boards. For them, the boardroom is not a male domain or a gendered domain but a neutral *public* domain. In this setting everyone—women and men—is called upon to offer her or his best talents for achieving the important mission of public higher education.

Gender Neutral

Judith Glazer-Raymo (2008a) found that the women trustees with whom she spoke were clear about the challenges of exerting power and influence as regents and explicit about their commitment to help shape the legacy of female board members to come. Most women in our study, including the gender-accomplished women described above, seemed sincere in concluding that gender had no effect on their board interactions. As noted above, some cited examples of ability to engage in masculine conversation through their own experience with sports or employed masculine language (using *chairman* instead of the more inclusive *chair*), but more commonly, they made straightforward claims that the operations of their boards were gender neutral, with some providing evidence of collegial relationships with male board members. At times the observations about gender neutrality were followed by contrasting statements, using examples that suggest how gender may be affecting board culture.

The contradictions in their comments regarding gender neutrality suggest the ability to believe in two opposing thoughts at one time—or doublethink. For those who described their boards as gender neutral, it did not seem problematic to hold contrasting views. Consequently, while the sincerity of their beliefs is not in question, the fact of gender neutrality is. The claims that gender both does and doesn't matter are mutually exclusive—although of course gender does not always matter in the same ways. Because most respondents discounted the importance of gender in this setting but simultaneously acknowledged its importance, we question the actual meaning of gender impartiality.

"Gender neutral" respondents were diverse in their descriptions of why gender didn't matter on the board. They largely pointed to collegial and productive relationships with male regents, the absence of a gendered board committee structure, and commitment to balanced representation as evidence of a gender-neutral board environment.

When asked whether it is important to achieve a balance of region, gender, and people of color on her board, a senior trustee replied, "I think all of those. All of them. People are very conscious and certainly our governor is very conscious of the balance with those that are on the board and making it as balanced as possible. When I get off the board, there will be no women, unless he appoints a woman." This regent is both confirming the importance of diverse board membership and at the same time emphasizing that she is the only female member on her board. Priorities of representational balance cannot be reflected with only one woman on the board.

When asked if she thought that being the only woman was problematic, her response was "No." Such seemingly contradictory attitudes were common in the responses of most women. For example, while other regents expressed that gender did not affect board interactions, they still had a desire to see more women appointed, with some recognizing the potential impact on policy and board culture. For the majority of regents who claimed gender neutrality, the statements of desire for more women board members were consistently coupled with the sentiment that *gender did not matter* in every day board practice.

Women consistently gave examples of collegial relationships with men on their boards as evidence of a gender-neutral atmosphere. In order to explain her feeling of equality with other board members, one regent stated, "I am actually closer to the men than I am to the women." Whether it was a professional friendship or a story concerning how men on their board were more sensitive to issues of higher education relative to other men or women, regents who claimed their boards were gender neutral pointed to their experience with "good men" to demonstrate it.

This regent went on to say, "I feel like they accept me and we have a positive working relationship. And I don't think it happens all over but like I said right now on our board we have very accepting men." While we do not doubt the genuine experience that their boards are respectful of women and that gender is a "nonissue," a statement alluding to men having the power to "accept" (and therefore potentially reject) their female counterparts illustrates the complexity of gender in the boardroom. Gender as a part of board culture is not necessarily visible. Rather than the influence of gender on public higher education policy boards meaning overt sexism toward female members, many functions of gender simply go unnoticed.

When we asked, "how does it feel for you to be a woman on your board?" we were not looking for examples of discrimination. Yet some women responded to the question by assuring us that the men on their board were not sexist. Gender would matter, in this view, if women were aware of negative experiences with gender. We agree with Judith Glazer-Raymo when she states, "that gender matters even when it is not articulated, that thinking in existential terms, one's gender, whether male or female, is part of and defines our identity" (2008a, p. 185). Thus, to speak about gender is not necessarily to focus on individual sexist behavior. Rather, the issue becomes who feels comfortable speaking at meetings, the networks women have, the committees on which men and women serve, the amount of time regents are able to give, or the amount of money they are able to donate. On the surface, these ideas could seem unaffected by gender. However, these normal functions of public boards tell us a great deal about how gender is constructed and reinforced in our culture.

Regents both choose and receive committee assignments based on personal preference and professional background. In our sample, most women (including some who have or are currently board chair) serve on committees related to academic affairs rather than finance. As one woman stated, "I think there is a little bit of mommy in me that gravitated me toward the Academic Committee." However, being siloed into academic committees (by preference and/or appointment) may decrease their effectiveness overall, especially if decisions about finance and budgets require a major portion of board attention. Regents understand this priority, and when asked if interviewees had recommendations for aspiring female regents, several suggested having a strong familiarity with accounting and finance.

At the same time, many of the women we interviewed see their expertise in higher education policy rather than finance as an asset. A board member in our study summed up her lacking finance ability positively, saying, "I don't have the financial background, but when it comes to a topic that deals with the background that I come from, I probably carry more weight because I've been there, and done that." In reference to her board, one regent claimed that the women's occupational background and presence on academic committees "showed that women know much more about higher ed. than men." While this clearly is a very valuable skill to bring to the board, and essential to responsible oversight of university programs, in an era when state budget shortfalls present financial crises, it seems likely that those with more financial expertise will have increasing power to shape board decisions. One regent with strong business credentials herself stressed the need to recruit both women and men with business backgrounds because of the current financial situation.

According to Kiersh (2009), women are less able than men to contribute significant dollars to political campaigns. Because one's appointment as a regent, trustee, or director is often tied to fundraising ability or personal contributions to political campaigns, fewer women may be appointed. For less affluent women who may be appointed to meet other statewide goals, the board experience can be intimidating. Although highly successful and educated, one regent recalls her feelings when first appointed to the board of higher education in her state: "These people have been in the community and they have made their connections . . . and they sit on many other boards. This is the first board that I was ever appointed to so it was very overwhelming initially." Because navigating a world of affluence is unfamiliar territory for some regents, assimilation into board culture can be hard.

On state university governing boards, regents will not be aware of the many ways gender matters unless they are looking for or have personally experienced them. Importantly, although these examples show how women are affected by the gendered spaces they govern, "they want to be seen as directors first and women second. They want to be known for their competence on board issues rather than feminists" (Burke, 1993, p. 30). A failure to analyze why more men have been appointed to their boards than women allows the primary identity as *board members* to remain unchallenged. In a society that emphasizes independence and an ability to succeed *as an individual*, the notion that one's membership in a category might convey privilege and power (or the lack of it) raises questions about merit as the determinant of success. It is therefore not surprising that many women assert that their boardrooms are, and should be, gender neutral.

Gender Matters
Although the majority of respondents note no difference in treatment between male and female regents, the women of color and younger women we interviewed identified their age, gender, race, and socio-economic

class as barriers to full board participation. The experience of an older, wealthier, white woman on a state board is very different from that of a young woman or woman of color. While often explicitly appointed to the board to bring perspectives valued by stakeholders in higher education, if their contributions are not valued equally to older, white, and affluent members, they will experience greater marginalization.

The youngest woman we interviewed was a student regent on her board. She recounted numerous instances of interactions in the boardroom and at public events that objectified her by gender. Whether it was a passing comment about her undergarments, reference to her beauty as a factor in her board appointment or accusations (by other students) of sleeping with the governor in order to be appointed, it was clear that gender influenced her relationships and position on the board. The power differential that allows older, white, and wealthy male board members to feel comfortable commenting on a younger women regent's appearance reflects the sexual objectification that young women must overcome to be taken seriously in professional arenas. For this young regent, finding commonality with fellow board members was difficult. As she states, "I don't play golf so it's kind of difficult, you know, to find common ground between myself, a twenty-year-old female in college, and a seventy-year-old male millionaire." Unlike older regents, young women's struggle to have successful interactions as *board members* is complicated by differentials in power, age, *and* gender.

Not only do they experience less common ground with the other members of their board, but these regents may also have more restrictive time constraints. Younger women are juggling both the effort to make progress in their careers and, for some, significant family responsibilities. The time they have to spend as board members is limited. These positions are time consuming and voluntary, and several regents noted that they devote sixty hours or more a month to board responsibilities. Women with families and career responsibilities feel the pinch on their boards. One stated, "As an individual, for *me*, with balancing kids and work—sometimes I'm reading the materials the night before, glancing at it in traffic (not very safe), but I just wish I had time to develop myself more to be able to speak publicly about the issues and therefore be a chair of a committee." In order to be powerful board members, women must be at a place in their lives in which they can dedicate significant time each week to board service, including the time-consuming but essential work of networking.

Younger women and women of color are thus more likely to see gender as a factor on their boards but be less able to do anything about it. They state that that they feel responsible to remind other board members of their underrepresented constituencies. For example, one woman acknowledged her presumed status as the only debt-carrying member of her board, "These people (older board members) don't have a concept of academic debt because they make a lot of money and it is not an issue for them. Not everybody has that luxury, so I try to always remind them of that while also trying to keep his or her respect." That she feels the need to be careful in her message about debt offers further evidence about the difficulty of bringing other aspects of one's identity to the board. Her social position, influenced by her unique life experience, differs from that of the more affluent board members.

However, advocating too strongly for actions to address the dilemmas faced by others in her situation risks her expected board member identity and being seen as a crusader for social justice or a single-issue person. Muting her identity as a mother with debt seems important to maintaining her board member identity and other board members' respect. As one regent stated in regard to advancing issues of inclusion, "I also think you approach these things not as an ideologue. You get known as a one-issue person and I think that makes you ineffective when you DO want to be an advocate around an issue that is particularly provocative or relates to gender." Despite the importance of assessing whether university systems are treating all students equally, when compared to capital projects or program reviews, issues of inclusion become special-issue concerns.

For the two women of color we interviewed, the interplay between their race and their role on the board required significant emotional work and produced a double bind. They knew they were expected to bring a "diversity" perspective to the board. However, they could not stress this too much or they would be seen as "biased." As one woman interviewed recalled, she had to "fight against the bias" that she favored underrepresented groups. "Oftentimes if asked questions . . . as a matter of fact someone (from a legislative body) asked a question about grants and opportunities for small business owners in our state. And the representative automatically assumed I was speaking about minority businesses." This assumption that women of color are going to only represent marginalized constituencies, coupled with the political culture of boards that negatively sanctions "rocking the boat," makes navigating board membership more complex for a woman of color than for the white businessman sitting next to her.

This difficult balance between board respect, activism, and perception can be detrimental to the underrepresented constituents of state systems.

> Since trustees are so often male (and white), it is easy for a woman trustee to feel the intense marginality of her position, and to compensate by either assuming a male perspective on every issue, or by ostentatiously separating herself from the kind of activist woman who makes many men in power uncomfortable. (Howard, 1984, p. 31)

Some women counteract their marginalization in an attempt to be seen as "race and gender neutral" at all times and cite specific examples of their conscious attempts to be perceived as impartial to any constituency. Consequently, they do not raise issues of inequity easily. Being a token is analogous to the assumption that you will automatically advocate for groups who share your status. This does not seem to be a judgment made on those in the majority for their advocacy of the status quo—which *overprivileges* certain groups. However, just as white women regents wish to be seen as talented and successful board members rather than as women regents, so do women of color. Whichever route these women choose to navigate, the expectations are clear. They need to choose their words and causes carefully, "Because when you really speak, people do listen to you because they want to know what the Black Woman is saying."

Although there are added pressures to being a female board member for some, the overall experiences of the women we interviewed were unequivocally positive. These women loved higher education, were appreciative of the opportunity to serve their states, and respected their colleagues on the boards. While some wrote letters to their governors and held informal conversations advocating for more women to be appointed to the boards, others were content with the teams on which they served—even if there were few or no other women. Women regents, trustees, directors, or commissioners are not a socially aligned block. They are diverse in their views toward gender and higher-education governance. A board member's willingness and likelihood to be cognizant of the effects of gender or race in this environment depends, as we have argued here, on her social position and life experience. In the end, it is not the gender of the board member that makes a difference in policy making and governance; it is the diversity in history and perspective she or he offers.

Conclusion

> 3:15 p.m. We have concluded the formal business, and the chair announces that we have about 15 minutes for public comment, noting that each speaker will have a maximum of three minutes to address the board. Several students have signed up to urge the board not to raise tuition, including an older white man with bushy hair and beard wearing a T-shirt and ill-fitting jeans. He speaks last, reinforcing the comments of previous speakers. When the board chair reminds him that his time is up and he needs to stop, he reacts by saying loudly: "NO! You have had a long time to speak today and I have listened to you. I will finish what I have to say." He continues, and is again asked by the chair to end his comments. In response to this firm request, the man surveys the assembled board with a hostile glare and proclaims: "Look around this table! You should be ashamed! You have two women here and one man of color? What does that say about your priorities???"
>
> —Rosemary

This public comment violated the board's civility norms and carefully crafted meeting script and likely reinforced for many the reason the board provides a *short* time at the end of meetings for those "on the ground" to speak. This performance was uncomfortable to experience, with a valid message about equity in representation lost in the delivery. Here was a "crazy man," describing a tableau that can be difficult for board members to acknowledge *and* on the public stage. It reminds us that the board member identity is crafted to reinforce a public culture promoting serious and respectful consideration of policies with wide-ranging application, where answers to uncomfortable questions can be sought before meetings and integrated into the formal script. The considerations of these boards *are* weighty, and the women regents with whom we spoke took their responsibilities very seriously.

It is not news that context affects behavior or that women who are using their talents to further higher education goals should expect their skills rather than their gender to be the focus. However, operating always at the general policy level may mean that women who do wish to focus on issues of inclusion will not have a legitimate or regularized venue for doing so. How might the trustee in our sample who repeatedly advocates for more appointments of women to her board become effective? What policy outcome could be a positive consequence of efforts by the regent who tries to help wealthy board members understand the struggle of people, like herself, who are deeply in debt after pursuing their academic or professional degrees? Is their advocacy simply another version of public comment, but at a higher level?

Whether appointed by governors or elected, trustees, directors, or regents have important fiscal and pedagogical prerogatives. As we have argued, the policy decisions of these directors are shaped by their histories, identities, and experiences within the higher education environment. As such, the diversity of governing boards can powerfully influence the university systems' guiding principles and the kind of approaches they take to the policy concerns over which they have control.

This research suggests that without thoughtful action by state, national, and federal decision-making bodies, women will remain in the numerical minority on statewide boards of higher education and both the culture and structure of boards will further marginalize underrepresented women. We believe navigating the restrictive appointment process, environment, and composition of boards will continue to be easier for gender-accomplished women and the dominant white male elite unless some action is taken.

At the state level, public policy boards of higher education are in need of a reflection mechanism that allows for more than ritualized analysis of standard board performance. Thoughtful critiques of all aspects of board culture and leadership will enable their members to see how standard board procedures reinforce the structures of white male dominance.

Instead of relying on established networks of accomplished men, governors should appoint more highly accomplished women, not to tokenize specific demographics but to achieve honest diversity in board governance.

Several countries have recognized the need to mandate movement toward greater gender diversity on corporate boards. In the United States, there are some states that require gender equity on public higher education policy boards. If all boards of higher education are to achieve representational balance, federal legislation may be needed to mandate the appointments and election of qualified women to state boards.

Women have made progress and continue to increase their participation and leadership within state systems of higher education. Their ability to govern effectively, despite the cultural and structural barriers we have identified, is admirable. Although the view from thirty thousand feet is not always clear, what *is* evident is women directors' commitment to carrying out the best interests of their states for those on the ground.

References

Alcoff, L. (1988). Cultural feminism versus post-structuralism: The identity crisis in feminist theory. *Signs, 13*(3), 405–36.

Arfken, D., Bellar, S., & Helms, M. (2004). The ultimate glass ceiling revisited: The presence of women on corporate boards. *Journal of Business Ethics, 50*(2), 177–86.

Bernardi, R. A., Bosco, S. M., & Columb, V. L. (2009). Does female representation on boards of directors associate with "Most Ethical Companies' List?" *Corporate Reputation Review, 12*(3), 270–80.

Bernardi, R. A., Bosco, S. M., & Vassill, K. M. (2006). Does female representation on boards of directors associate with Fortune 100 "Best Companies' List"? *Business & Society, 45*(2), 235–48.

Bilimoria, D., & Piderit, S. K. (1994). Board committee membership: Effects of sex based bias. *Academy of Management Journal, 37*(6), 1453–77.

Burgess, Z., & Tharenou, P. (2002). Women board directors: Characteristics of the few. *Journal of Business Ethics, 37*(1), 39–49.

Burke, R. J. (1993). Women on corporate boards of directors. *Equal Opportunities International, 12*(6), 5–13.

Butler, J. (1990). *Gender trouble: Feminism and the subversion of identity.* New York: Routledge.

Campbell, K., & Mínguez-Vera, A. (2007). Gender diversity in the boardroom and firm financial performance. *Journal of Business Ethics, 83*, 435–51.

Catalyst. (1993). *Women on corporate boards: The challenge of change.* Retrieved July 10, 2010, from http://www.catalyst.org/publication/270/women-on-corporate-boards-the-challenge-of-change.

Catalyst. (2008). *Women in academia*. Retrieved July 25, 2010, from http://catalyst.org/publication/327/women%20in%20academia.

Catalyst. (2009). 2009 *Catalyst census: Fortune 500 women board directors*. Retrieved July 10, 2010, from http://www.catalyst.org/file/320/2009_fortune_500_census_women_board_directors.pdf.

Collins, P. H. (1990). *Black feminist thought: Knowledge, consciousness and the politics of empowerment*. New York: Routledge.

Ehrenberg, R. G., Jakubson, G. H., Martin, M. L., Main, J. B., & Eisenberg, T. (2009). *Do trustees and administrators matter? Diversifying the faculty across gender lines*. Working paper from the National Bureau of Economic Research, Cambridge, MA.

Ehrenberg, R., & Main, J. B. (2009). Females on academic boards of trustees: Slow but steady progress. *Trusteeship, 17*(2), 34–35.

Ellis, C., & Berger, L. (2002). Their story/my story/our story: Including the researcher's experience in the interview research. In J. F. Gubrium & J. A. Holstein (Eds.), *Handbook of interview research: Concept and method,* (pp. 849–75). Thousand Oaks, CA: Sage.

Fairfax, L. M. (2005). Some reflections on the diversity of corporate boards: Women, people of color, and the unique issues associated with women of color. *St. John's Law Review, 79*, 1105–20.

Glazer-Raymo, J. (2008a). Women on governing boards: Why gender matters. In J. Glazer-Raymo (Ed.), *Unfinished agenda: New and continuing gender challenges in higher education* (pp. 185–210). Baltimore, MD: Johns Hopkins University Press.

Glazer-Raymo, J. (2008b). Women trustees: An untapped resource. *Trusteeship 16*(6), 20–24.

Goffman, E. (1959). *The presentation of self in everyday life*. New York: Routledge.

Grosser, K., & Moon, J. (2005). Gender mainstreaming and corporate social responsibility: Reporting workplace issues. *Journal of Business Ethics, 62*, 327–40.

Gulati, M. & Shin, P. S.(2010). Showcasing diversity. Duke Law working papers, Paper 31. http://scholarship.law.duke.edu/.

Haraway, D. (1991). *Simians, cyborgs and women*. New York: Routledge.

Helms, M. M., Arfken, D., & Bellar, S. (2008). Still chilly after all these years: A longitudinal study of corporate board composition in Tennessee. *Business Perspectives,* Winter/Spring. Retrieved July 11, 2010, from http://www.entrepreneur.com/tradejournals/article/179031793_3.html.

Howard, J. E. (1984). Women trustees and educational equity. *Women's Studies Quarterly 12*(1) 12–13.

Joy, L., & Carter, N. (2007). *The bottom line: Corporate performance and women's representation on boards*. Retrieved July 20, 2010, from http://www.catalyst.org/publication/200/the-bottom-line-corporate -performance-and-womens-representation-on-boards.

Kesner, I. (1988). Directors' characteristics and committee membership: An investigation of type, occupation, tenure and gender. *Academy of Management Journal, 31*(1), 66–84.

Kezar, A. (2006). Rethinking public higher education governing boards performance: Results of a national study of governing boards in the United States. *Journal of Higher Education, 77*(6), 968–1008.

Kezar, A., & Lester, J. (2010). Breaking the barriers of essentialism in leadership research: Positionality as a promising approach. *Feminist Formations, 22*(1), 163–85.

Kiersh, A. (2009). *Women still lag behind men in campaign contributions, study says*. Retrieved July 25, 2010, from http://www.opensecrets.org/ news/2009/06/women-still-lag-behind-men-in.html.

Kramer, V., Konrad, A., & Erkut, S. (2008). Critical mass: The impact of three or more women on corporate boards. *Organizational Dynamics, 37*(2), 145–64.

Odendahl, T., & Shaw, A. M. (2002). Interviewing elites. In J. F. Gubrium & J. A. Holstein (Eds.), *Handbook of interview research: Concept and method* (pp. 299–16). Thousand Oaks, CA: Sage.

Peterson, C., & Philpot, J. (2007). Women's roles in U.S. Fortune 500 boards: Director expertise and committee membership. *Journal of Business Ethics, 72*(2), 177–96.

Riessman, C. (2002). Analysis of personal narratives. In J. F. Gubrium & J. A. Holstein (Eds.), *Handbook of interview research: Concept and method* (pp. 675–710). Thousand Oaks, CA: Sage.

Schwartz, M. P., & Akins, L. (2005). *2004 policies, practices, and composition of governing boards of public colleges and universities.* Washington, DC: Association of Governing Boards of Colleges and Universities, Board Basics Series. Retrieved February 21, 2010, from http://www.agb.org/what-governance.

Stivers, C. (1993). Reflections on the role of personal narrative in social science. *Signs, 18*(2), 408–25.

Twale, D. J., & Burley, J. E. (2007). Profile of women trustees at land grant institutions: Roles, responsibilities and reflections. *Academic Leadership: The Online Journal, 1*(3). Retrieved March 21, 2011, from http://www.academicleadership.org/article/print/Profile_of_Women _Trustees_at_Land_Grant_Institutions.

Winkler, J. (1987). The fly on the wall of the inner sanctum: Observing company directors at work. In G. Moyser & M. Wagstaff (Eds.), *Research methods for elite studies,* (pp. 129–65). London: Allen and Unwin.

8

Slaying Two Dragons: For Black Women Leaders in Education, Gender Equity Is Only Half the Battle

M. Cookie Newsom

Being a black woman in academe is not an easy thing. We are double minorities but frequently find ourselves being expected to ignore one of our identities, either our gender or our race. If we involve ourselves in "women's issues," there is rarely any discussion in the room of race and racism; if we involve ourselves in antiracist work, there is rarely any discussion of sexism. In many ways the question asked by Sojourner Truth so many years ago, "Ain't I a woman?" is still very relevant today.

A prime example is the manner in which the existence of women of color is frequently ignored. It has become common usage in many circles, including the media, to use the term "women and minorities" to describe demographic characteristics. What is meant, of course, is white women and minorities, but because for some strange reason it has evidently come to be viewed as impolite to say "white women"; the language is, as usual, adjusted to the detriment of the minority, effectively neutering all women who are not white. Black is one category, woman is another category, and never the twain shall meet in many articles, books, and public media. Frequently we are told what "women" think or who they are inclined to vote for or how their lives are going, when the women they are talking about are almost exclusively white women. As Terhune (2008) says, "Too often the experiences of Black women are homogenized within the race and the nuisances of gender and class are glossed over or diminished" (p. 547).

In addition to the propensity to lump all blacks into an amorphous mass where gender is ignored, black women have to battle to get their white sisters to understand that racism and sexism are two sides of the same coin, and that black women are subject to both and are therefore generally unwilling to address one without addressing the other. This is an old battle that can be traced back a long way to some of the struggles experienced in early attempts to ally white women and black men and women in civil rights efforts. The experiences of white women and the experiences of black women, while we share some things in common, are not identical. Audre Lorde (1984) expresses it this way:

> As white women ignore their built-in privilege of whiteness and define *woman* in terms of their own experience alone, then women of Color become "other," the outsider whose experience and tradition is too "alien" to comprehend. (p. 114)

One would think that since we are all women, our white sisters in the academy could be counted on to understand and offer sympathy and assistance. While there are certainly times that this happens, it is not, sadly, the general pattern. Racism and sexism are both components of our lived experience on college campuses. As Simien and Clawson (2004) state:

> Black feminist consciousness stems from the understanding that black women are discriminated against on the basis of both their race and gender. The recognition of the simultaneity of oppression faced by black women is not captured by the dominant conceptualization of group consciousness. As a result the empirical study of black feminist consciousness has been neglected. (p. 793)

When black women are acknowledged as present in the academy—distinct from their white peers—far too often it is as the stereotypical "angry black woman" (ABW). Strangely, while engaging in this type of categorization, those dubbing black women as angry never seem to delve into the reasons some of us may be justified if we do express anger. The ABW, a mythological creature created partially out of white guilt and fear and partially out of pandering black entertainers, is simply viewed as irrational; anger is part of her personality, not something rooted in justifiable frustration with a system that seems determined to keep her an outsider.

If black women express concern or objection to language, policies, or procedures that they view as racist and/or sexist, they are viewed as not being team players, as difficult, or as not a "good fit" for the institution. Ironically, the leadership of many majority white institutions profess to want diversity and inclusion, all the while frequently marginalizing black women in jobs that actually have no power to truly effect change. In the majority of white institutions, for example, the person in the president's office is almost certain to be a white male. An article by ASHE (2009) reports:

> June (2007) reports on the state of affairs regarding diversity among college presidents, noting that the profile of the typical president has remained the same over the past twenty years. That is, the typical president is a married, older White male with a doctorate. Minority representation in the college presidency has lagged behind White women as well. Prior experience as a president is increasingly becoming a preference, thus calling into question the future for people of color in these positions who are less likely to have that previous experience. (p. 1)

When the frustrations of the black women at this circumstance are expressed, shoulders are shrugged and they are simply labeled as being of the angry ilk. More tractable black women are pointed to as the example that should be followed, those that go along to get along. In other words, just do what we want and we will reward you for it; try to push the envelope and prepare to pay the price. Williams (2001) says in her article "The Angry Black Woman Scholar":

> My experience of feeling privileged, then having the privilege snatched away when I pushed beyond the boundaries, is consistent with institutional practices that welcome diversity as long as it is prepared to assimilate to a mainstream norm. In the current discourse of a diversity-aware academia, women of color are positioned to seek favor with powerful white men who can grant privilege or take it away. (p. 90)

Being a tenure-track or tenured professor or college administrator—the categories that the women in this chapter fall into—is indeed being privileged. Like everything else, however, privilege is a matter of perspective. I can feel privileged and yet resent the fact that some of my white sisters and almost all of my white brothers are much more privileged, often with the same or less education and experience. The myth of the meritocracy is strong in academe; we presume that those who do well and prosper do so because they are more skilled, when in fact many, if not most, times they are simply more privileged. White faculty and administrators also tend to have more financial resources than black faculty and administrators, having benefited both from the inherited wealth historically denied many blacks, higher salaries in some cases, and from less debt upon graduation, student loan, and otherwise (Merchand, 2010).

Add to that the fact that whatever my demeanor, behavior, or tone, I am at risk of being declared an ABW as soon as I open my mouth to express my opinion, and the role of the black woman at white institutions of higher learning becomes a truly daunting experience. You are theoretically there, at least partially, to represent blacks in general and black women in particular, but if you advocate for social justice, equity, and fairness you are "angry." Kretsedemas (2010) says:

> Much of the recent criticism of black media stereotypes has focused on portrayals of women. Some scholars and media critics have argued that these media depictions have become distinctly more negative over the past two decades and that stereotypes of black women have begun to eclipse the more familiar stereotype of the aggressive black male. A common theme of these recent stereotypes is that of the angry black woman. (p. 142)

It is a quietly kept secret in higher education that the more a black woman can "pass" as a white woman, the easier her path will be. This can be accomplished in several ways, or more accurately, in a matrix of ways. Those with light skin have a decided advantage from the beginning. If they are "articulate and clean," chalk up another advantage. The ability to "fit in" includes not being overly assertive, not speaking in a loud voice, not being too opinionated—at least not if you disagree with the white hierarchy—and (most importantly) agreeing as often as possible that there is absolutely nothing wrong with ways in which the leaders of the institution deal with race and racism. Lorde (1984) says:

> Traditionally, in American society, it is the members of oppressed, objectified groups who are expected to stretch out and bridge the gap between the actualities of our lives and the consciousness of our oppressor. For in order to survive, those of us for whom oppression is as American as apple pie have always had to be watchers, to become familiar with the language and manners of the oppressor, even sometimes adopting them for some illusion of protection. Whenever the need for some pretense of communication arises, those who profit from our oppression call upon us to share our knowledge with them. In other words, it is the responsibility of the oppressed to teach the oppressors their mistakes. (p. 114)

Lorde is, as usual, able to express what many, if not most, black women in higher education have felt but been unable to express so eloquently. We do have to adopt the manners and language of white society to have some illusion of protection from their view of us as alien.

So black women in the academy have to face being viewed as "other" in myriad ways—we are women, but not white women, and therefore not mainstream, we are highly educated and skilled, but "difficult." My hope is that this chapter will shed some light on the experiences, insights, and perceptions of black women in the academy. In the book *All the Women Are White, All the Blacks Are Men, But Some of Us Are Brave,* Carroll, (1982) says:

> Four years ago, if anyone had said to me that the Black woman in higher education faces greater risks and problems now than in the past, I doubt I would have taken the remark seriously. I would have marveled at the rhetoric and pointed to federal legislation enacted on the crest of the civil rights movement of the 1950s and1960s, and nodded proudly at the few Blacks in token positions in major institutions. . . . A great deal still needs to be done. I would have said, but Blacks, including women, have come a long way. In 1972, after four years of teaching and working in a university administration, I would nod my head in ready agreement if the same remark were made. My mind was changed . . . Black women in higher education are isolated, underutilized, and often demoralized. (p. 115)

TABLE 8.1
Respondents' information

Pseudonym	Age	Degree	Employment: Institution Type	Job Category/Title
Helena	49	PhD	Public-Research1	Associate Professor
Annette	63	PhD	Public-Research1	Associate Professor
Chantal	46	BS	Public-Research1	Director
Monique	35	MA	Public-Research1	Assistant Professor
Malia	57	PhD	Public-Research1	Vice President
Mary	49	JD	Public- HBCU[a]	Associate Dean
Sarah	59	PhD	Public-Reseach1	Professor
Anna	50	PhD	Public-Research 1	Dean
Athena	62	PhD	Public-Research 1	Director
Carolyn	53	MA	Public-Research 1	Director
Danielle	53	MPH	Public-Research 1	Associate Director

[a]Historically black college or university

Unfortunately, those words, written in 1972, seem to be equally true in 2010.

For this chapter I interviewed ten black women colleagues[1]. Their stories, along with mine, will make up the bulk of the chapter. These are stories that we do not often get a chance to tell for fear of being labeled an ABW, not a team player, or not a good fit. See Table 8.1 for respondents' information.

Reviewing the interviews, several themes emerged quite early. Gathered into broad categories they are:

I. Incidents of gender and/or racial bias in undergraduate and graduate school

II. Incidents of racial and/or gender bias in employment including bias against research interests that have to do with race or other aspects of diversity

---

[1]All of the women were given aliases so that they could feel free to express themselves without fear of retribution, also their job descriptions, although accurate are less specific as to discipline, department, etc. for the same reason.

III. Being the only one or one of a few

IV. Importance of mentoring

The average age of my respondents is 52. This may raise the question of generational differences: Are older black women more likely to have found the academy a hostile place? I might give that question some credence were it not for the continued stream of articles written by younger black women of the academy and my interactions with black women graduate students and postdoctoral students that seem to reflect the existence of the same issues in 2010 that some of us experienced in 1980. The manifestation of those issues may be quite different. One of the respondents, Anna, told me of having to confront Confederate flags at her undergraduate institution and enduring the presence of a fraternity pledge activity called the "Five screaming niggers party." That would not happen on most campuses today. We have driven racism underground, but we have not eradicated it; it is expressed in more subtle but no less demeaning and debilitating ways on campuses every day.

For example, one black woman, an associate vice chancellor, told me of standing in a crowd last fall to watch the university football team march to the stadium on game day. She does quite a bit of work with athletics and many of the players were stopping to greet her, frequently with hugs. An older white woman in the crowd observed this and remarked to her, "They all seem to like you. Are you the cook?" This is the type of microaggression that black women in higher education have to deal with on a regular basis, along with the sexism that our white sisters endure.

Not surprisingly, all of the women I interviewed expressed some degree of frustration with their treatment in the academy. The lone participant from an HBCU had spent most of her career at a majority white institution, transitioning to an HBCU only two years ago; so among all of the women we probably have more than three hundred years of experience on predominantly white campuses as students, faculty, or administrators.

I. Bias, Bigotry, and Disparate Treatment in the Educational Experience

In the first thematic category, incidents of bias during their undergraduate or graduate programs were shared. Several of the respondents reported being excluded from group activities by their white classmates. Study groups, sharing old exams, and so forth were not available to them, impacting their opportunities to interact with white classmates and excluding them from some of the advantages of group preparation.

> **Sarah:** "As far as interactions with classmates, I was never invited to the various campus study groups, I worked alone. My white classmates never sought me out and they never believed that I was doing better than most in our classes. College was, in that respect, a lonely sojourn."

Nor was Sarah the only person to experience this feeling of isolation and difference from her white classmates; Chantal describes a similar situation:

> **Chantal:** I accepted admission to a large majority institution and later was accepted into a professional program that had two African American students, including me, in a student body of approximately one hundred and twenty students. Roughly, eighty percent appeared to be upper-middle to upper-class Caucasian students. This was the typical student demographic. The program was rigorous. There were numerous study groups with people collaborating and sharing information. I was not invited to any of these group learning opportunities; therefore, I would ask my colleagues if I could come and they would occasionally allow me to join them. Also, I was told that I could not make copies of old exams that were being widely circulated via the class, because the exams belonged to someone else.

Unfortunately, many of the respondents reported encountering even more egregious examples of bias and disparate treatment in their own undergraduate and graduate experiences.

> **Athena:** "When I was in my doctoral program I received an A on a paper in a statistics class. I was the only person in the class to receive an A. When we had a break and everyone was comparing grades one of the white women in my cohort looked at my paper and sniffed 'He just gave you an A because you are the only black person in the class.' So, black students are often in an untenable situation on a white campus. If we are good students we are judged to be getting special

treatment, if we struggle it is because we are inherently inferior. If the evidence is clear that we are earning our grades then the escape clause is used 'you are not like most blacks.' "

Anna: When I was in graduate school pursuing a Master's Degree, a faculty member was very interested in meeting me after he read my research interests and my academic record. I was excited too. When I met him, introduced myself, he was in disbelief, and in fact questioned me as if I was some imposter. Eventually, I filed a grievance against him, and I won. He did not pass me on one of my papers. When I took my comprehensive exams, I asked for all of ours to be graded blindly, and to be typed. I received highest honors with basically the same information that I had used in my paper. When that occurred, and he found out it was me, he was gently asked to leave. Of course, no one initially believed me. After this situation came to light, not only did they believe me, they worked hard to make sure he left and it did not get public.

Malia: In graduate school race and gender was a critical factor in admissions, class assignments, work groups, research projects teams, and housing. I remember clearly that my roommate expressly asked to be moved to another room because of the race difference. Housing refused so she ended up leaving school in the early part of the term and moving back to New York. In the classroom I found that my experiences were very different from my white classmates and my view of the world was also. The idea of social justice and inequality was not really brought into any conversations unless I or the one other person of color (a black man) put it there. Then it was there as an appendage to the real discussion—no one ever picked up our line of thinking. Our contributions would just fall to the floor and the discussion went on as if we had not spoken. However, that did not happen in written assignments or research papers; which had the disadvantage of having no impact on the classroom discussion and fueled the concern over why I was making the top grades in the toughest classes or from the toughest professors on the graded assignments.

Helena: When I attended graduate school it was even more obvious the role that race played in acceptance and retention of minority students. During the admissions process, it was understood that only a finite number of black students would be admitted. Once admitted the black males would have the most difficult time throughout our training. I remember an instance where a faculty member (white male) had an opportunity to help me with a patient that was straightforward, but when I presented the patient he began ranting and raving in front of the patient accusing me of not being prepared. The patient was scared to death and asked to be reassigned to another student because he felt that I did not know what I was doing. He was reassigned to a classmate (white female) with the same skill level and the same faculty member who then sat down and performed the procedure for the student and gave her a good grade. I ended up writing a letter to the dean and copying the chancellor about this incident and the dean met with me apologizing profusely and vowed I would never report to that faculty member again during my matriculation and he kept his word. In situations where the grading was subjective, it was very obvious and many times blatant where the faculty member would sit down and then do the work for the student (usually a white female) and the student would receive an A. I sat next to students on many occasions where the faculty member would sit down and help do the work and give the student an A or B and then evaluate my work and give me a C or B—(this happened to all the other black students on many occasions as we talked about it when we would get together).

Sarah: Both my African American ethnicity (sociological race) and female gender played big roles in my education. With my instructors, I was consistently underrated so, in every class, on the first day of class, I would make it a priority to introduce myself to the instructor, sit in the front of the class, and essentially convey to them that I was not going to be their "C" or "D" student. I was going to be their "A" student, so they should discard whatever assumptions they had about my abilities and recognize my intentions to excel. Usually this worked but I feel that I was rarely given the benefit of the doubt with my professors. So when I did receive a compliment or some other gesture of kindness from a professor, I would memorize the words or the event, playing it over and over in my mind to reinforce my sense of self-worth. When I took classes in the social sciences, the prejudice against me as an African American and a woman was more evident than in the life sciences, but the bias against me and my abilities, insights, and perspectives was always there. I can count on one hand the exceptions and to this day (40 years later) I can remember the names of any exceptional professors and the settings within which, for that moment, I felt respected and my intellect valued.

These experiences, some of them decades old, are still fresh in the minds of these black women who are working on our university campuses. It would be disingenuous to presume that memories of these kinds of incidents during our own undergraduate and graduate years do not have any impact on our perceptions, behaviors, and expectations in our current jobs. Nor are they isolated incidents in the lives of many black women on college campuses. One professor describes an incident that made her leave a predominantly white campus. Williams (2008) recounts several racist incidents that happened to her, but it was an affront to one of her students that finally made her leave:

> But I do know that the incident that finally made me leave involved one of my students. She was walking to class one day when a car drove up, and the occupants yelled, "Go back to Africa, n*****" and then used a spray gun to shoot her with paint. She ran to my office in tears, and I immediately called the police. But she refused to file a complaint, afraid of what would happen if she stirred things up on campus and in the community. The police and administration let the matter drop, and there was nothing I could do to convince anyone that such behavior should not be tolerated. On that day in 1999 at the ripe old age of 29, hope for me died. (p. 20)

On many college campuses all over America today, such incidents as those described by my respondents and by the author of the above-cited article are happening regularly. One of the reasons higher education is able to pretend that such incidents, if they come to light, are isolated and rare is the unwillingness of many, like the young woman described above, to file formal complaints or bring public attention to the events. There are several reasons for this, including accounts I have been privy to where students are cautioned against "stirring up trouble" lest it follow them and impact their future academic or professional careers. In other words, they are frequently told to just deal with it and let it go, no one wants to give a job or an internship to a "troublemaker." How many times, one has to wonder, can you just let it go before it changes how you view the world in general and academe in particular?

Perhaps one of the reasons we have so much difficulty convincing black women to consider entering the professorate is that they do not want to revisit a place where they did not feel welcome and valued when they were undergraduates or graduate/professional students.

II. Bias, Bigotry, and Disparate Treatment in Employment

The events of bias and disparate treatment follow black women in the academy into their professional lives as well. Articles are abundant that describe some of the humiliating and debilitating events that happen to African American women on college campuses, yet they are still viewed, like the events experienced in undergraduate and graduate programs, as isolated and rare. The fact is that incidents from microaggressions to overtly racist acts happen on college campuses daily. As the respondents' comments below show, they are all still all too common.

> **Anna:** Race and gender have had a definite role in my career. It has opened the door for my first job in higher education because I was such an "anomaly," as one person said to me. He had never met such an educated, articulate, innovative black woman in his entire life. It has also worked against me. It appears that being a black female, who is articulate and capable also can be a hindrance especially if you talk too much and don't go along to get along (I was told that at my last job as the reason I was not given a promotion). I have also found being single can be a point of contention. I have had my work schedule altered because after all I don't have a spouse or children so I should be the one to attend the late night and weekend functions.

> **Danielle:** I understand clearly the environment in which I work: white males and females with preconceived thoughts and committed opinions about people of other races and origins. What is ironic: gender orientation is widely accepted; however, people of color still remain on the bottom rung of the ladder. Recruitment for African Americans is nil to none. I have been told, just recently that, "there is just no one

who is qualified." As an Associate Director, I have not been allowed to chair or sit on search committees. I have been told that I was "hard to manage," merely because I query that, which I do not understand. I am a consummate team player, however, I speak up when injustice occurs and it occurs very often. I have seen students of color condemned, lied on and even dismissed because "they just did not fit." I have seen professionals who were told to go home and never return, without a reason as to *why*. When I asked about the matter, I was labeled "insubordinate" and "stirring up matters." Subtle inferences were made that it "could have been you." Control by fear is the name of the game. I do not exaggerate. I have seen psychological and political games played like nobody's business. It is the nature of the beast in my unit where there are less than 5% African American professional staff members.

Mary: Race played a large role in my employment experiences. This is as true of my earlier employment as it was for my more recent employment. In my role as recruiter for my universities I think it was important for me to be seen by the public as an example of a minority "friendly" institution. I think that at least initially, my salary was lower than my white co-workers. That had to do with both my race and gender.

Malia: Race and gender have opened the door for me to be considered and it has closed the door for me to be considered further. Race and gender are in full effect during salary decisions because salary decisions are in large measure discretionary and beyond the consideration of merit based on performance. My goal is to be present in every room—gender and race. Bigotry, name calling, regionalism, nationalism, remains a vibrant part of the academy in the classroom, in the work place, in every place and every corner. Political correctness has put a mask on this ever present problem created by and feeding greed.

Monique: As a young Black administrator, I feel that I am challenged by students (Black and White) in a different way than my White colleagues. I currently supervise a White woman that serves as my administrative assistant; when we've attended events together, people have assumed she was in my position and that I was her subordinate. When I taught in our program, I often felt the most resistance from White males in terms of their questioning of course assignments, validity of readings and assigned projects, etc.

Helena: I have many examples of race playing a significant role in my career. I recall when I was completing one of my graduate programs and was interested in pursuing a career in academics. I made an appointment with the dean of the school and told him I was interested in pursuing an academic career. I informed him that I knew about a junior-level position that was open in one of his departments and was interested in applying. He basically told me he was not hiring anyone as junior as I was for the position and that there was a real need for African Americans in my area in the private sector and that is what he would recommend for me. I was later made aware that the dean was interviewing my classmate for the position I had inquired about. The person was a white female with no graduate education and identical other experience to mine. In fact at that time she was going back for a second interview. I confronted the dean and he denied it of course, but after the confrontation and exchange of letters between myself and the dean, the position was instantly frozen and my classmate was hired into a visiting position (which can be appointed by the dean) for a year and then hired permanently after she was allowed to gain the on the job experience. It was not until I received my PhD was I deemed worthy to be hired as a faculty member where a significant number of my white colleagues were deemed worthy right after graduation and to this day have attained no other degrees that what they initially received. They have continued to move up the academic ladder and through the tenure process uneventfully.

Annette: The university setting is not friendly toward African American females. I believe we are marginalized as we look at salaries, opportunities available to others as they move through the tenure process. For example, the younger white junior faculty have received a semester off to prepare for their 3rd-year review or tenure review. This was not offered to me during that time period.

Athena: My frustration with the role of race in my career is that I am expected to be black, but not too black, strong, but not too strong and to always consider the wishes and desires of the white people on campus first if I want to be successful. No matter what documentation you can provide to support your position on an issue, if it is at odds with what the white majority believes to be true no evidence to the contrary can change their minds. The idea that racism is dead, that only five or six toothless people in Snake's Navel Arkansas or some other backwater, are racist and that all the other documented incidents of racism are either fabricated, blown out of proportion or the result of black women being "too sensitive" is prevalent. On many campuses pointing out racism is deemed more egregiously wrong than committing racist acts or saying overtly racist things.

III. Being the One and Only or One of the Few

It is not surprising that a number of the respondents expressed dismay at being one or only one of a few minority members of the faculty or administration. It is well known that the numbers of historically underrepresented minorities among tenured and tenure-track faculty are dismally low. As one article states, "While the numbers of undergraduate and graduate students of color on college campuses have risen over the years, the growth in the numbers of faculty of color has lagged far behind" (Jayakumar et al., 2009, p. 539). Minorities only account for 16 percent of tenured and tenure-track teaching positions in America's university and college campuses[2]. Blacks only account for 5.3 percent of that 16 percent. If we presume that approximately half of the professors listed in NCES data are female—or we can conjecture that there are more black female professors—that still means black women account for less than or slightly more than 3 percent of all professors in America. Black administrators are hardly present in larger numbers (see Table 8.2).

Being the only one or only one of a few brings specific stressors to your daily existence. Not only are you aware that you are being considered the representative of your entire race, you lack colleagues and peers to share concerns with, bounce ideas off of, or commiserate with when one of the incidents outlined above occurs, as they so frequently do. You are expected to

---

[2]National Center for Education Statistics

TABLE 8.2.
Percentage of full-time administrative positions 1998

Race/ethnicity	%
Black	6.5
Hispanic	2.6
Asian/Pacific Islander	2.7
American Indian	.6
White	87.6

Source: National Association of Student Personnel Administrators Salary Survey, 1999.

give the "black view" in any committee, board, or meeting you are part of and yet expected to reassure your white colleagues that all is well. Failure to agree that things are fine on the campus can get you labeled, once again, as "difficult."

For the women in my study, being the only one, or one of a few, carried certain disadvantages. These ranged from isolation and loneliness to bearing the burden of representing an entire race and gender to feeling invisible.

Chantal: I've been on faculty for thirteen years and I am the first and still the only campus-based African American faculty member in our department in a top-ranked program in the south. Out of fairness, this is typical for most majority schools for my profession. For the first few years, I was not provided with the same opportunities to collaborate and work on scholarly projects. Often, some of my colleagues would try to avoid me. I made them uncomfortable, because they clearly did not interact with very many African American people. This was evident, when I would attend weddings and other events away from work, and I was still the only minority. That was very telling. They simply lacked exposure. I felt sorry for them. They were missing out on amazing perspectives. How can we, in academia be held in such high regard if our perspectives are so narrow . . . hmmm? When I entered in the classroom to teach, some of the students looked surprised to see me. The room fell silent immediately and they would stare. Imagine one hundred and forty students staring. It was amusing.

Helena: As I look around our university, we still have not been able to address the problem of recruitment and retention of African American faculty members period. This is how far behind we are with this issue. It is quite common to see our white female counterparts in leadership positions across campus from department chairs to deans, and chancellors. It appears that only a few black faculty only one or two are tapped to take any leadership positions. I do not believe at all that African American faculty are not qualified, it just does not seem to be a priority for the university and individual units when considering filling such positions. I believe until there is a genuine interest in improving the number of black faculty, the issue of empowering black women in education will be lost in the translation.

Anna: Since I was the only black and female in my masters program, I was often called on by classmates and professors to provide voice to those topics as it related to course materials. I remember one professor in a class on the politics of poverty asking me to share the view of "my people" on a particular subject. Up to that point, I had worked hard to be "invisible" so I could just get through with the program and move on with my career and life. I had spent the last two years of my undergraduate experience fighting and I was tired. However, something exploded inside of me when he asked me that question. My mind was racing, and I decided to ask him to be more specific about what he meant by "my people." I wanted and needed clarification in order to properly answer his question. I probed deeper and deeper with each answer he provided until he finally gave up and asked to speak with me after class. That interaction set the tone for the rest of that class and proved to be a turning point personally and academically. I was no longer asked to be part of study groups, and when it came to prepare for the comprehensive exams (where one typically prepared for in groups because of the nature of the materials) I had to do so on my own. Well, I passed with highest honors, and used research materials from non-traditional sources as well as those from our standard texts (I even quoted Huey[3]).

Athena: Being a black female on a predominantly white campus means having to be constantly vigilant. You are, whether you want to accept it or not, being viewed as a representative for your race and you have to keep in mind constantly that any misstep may have

---

[3]Huey P. Newton, co-founder of the Black Panther Party.

implications not just for yourself, but for future hires or other opportunities for other blacks in the future, particularly for black women.

Monique: I was often the only Black person in my class (I was 1 of 3 Black women in my program; there were no men of color), so I often felt the "pressure" to be the Black representative in the room. I often had White classmates and professors literally turn in my direction for a response to anything that came up in class that related to Black folks! I even had faculty tell me after the first couple weeks of any given semester that they were glad I was in the room "to represent the Black voice."

Carolyn: I have experienced feeling invisible and being ignored in meetings because someone didn't want to hear what I had to say. I felt tremendous pressure to make sure I did everything so there wouldn't be any question about me being less than capable because of my race.

Being one of a few or the only one is very challenging in academe besides the aforementioned tendency of being overwhelmed with the need to represent your gender and/or race on committees, boards, and other groups; there is the sense of isolation that comes along with being "different." Higher education communities operate on relationships. The ability to get something done, to find resources, to establish partnerships is all dependent on knowing people and having at least a collegial relationship with them. If the climate is exclusive, hostile, or unwelcoming to black women, it impacts not only the daily lives and morale of the black woman administrator or faculty member but also her ability to accomplish her duties and goals. The hierarchical nature of higher education is also a barrier. If a dean or chair or other person in authority does not like black people, it is very difficult to get upper-level administration to do anything about it. There is presumption of a meritocratic authority, that the person in charge has to be, as one president told me "trusted to run his/her shop." Yet most institutions do very little to train their supervisors in the areas of either racism or sexism. The idea that EEO and other offices exist to address blatant racism (or sexism, come to that) is great in theory, but in practice filing a formal grievance is a risky business.

IV. Importance of Mentoring

Virtually all of the respondents mentioned the importance of mentoring, particularly by other black women. Mentoring in the framework they mentioned included not only academic and career advice and support but also friendship and commiseration. When you are a double minority on campus, it is too often true that the only person who can truly understand your frustrations, challenges, and barriers is another double minority.

> **Anna:** I think having a greater presence of black women in higher education in a wide array of positions is definitely a big plus. We need the critical mass. However, these women need to be empowered by their other sisters. There should be a connection where stories are told and help provided in problem solving and understanding institutional culture.

> **Mary:** I think it gets easier as more of us get into the field of higher education.It helps significantly to know that there are others out there like you with whom you can share your experiences.

> **Monique:** The most beneficial resource I have found is the informal support networks that have been created with Black women in the academy and connecting with mentors. Much of the empowerment I have experienced has come from Black elders and peers in the academy that have offered their support and guidance.

> **Annette:** Black women have to share information and support each other. Support could include mentoring, writing together, sharing the secrets of the political process of the university. If you don't know the political landscape, there are lots of minefields.

Black women in the academy carry some heavy burdens, from being the representative for all black women, and in some cases all blacks, to having to deal with the stereotypes, xenophobia, and racism that are all endemic in higher education. Two years ago I was on the dissertation committee of a young black woman who wrote her dissertation on black women K–12 administrators. Her position was that they had at least two jobs, that of the administrator and that of being the social justice conscience of the school, the students, and the community. I would suggest that black women in the academy have myriad jobs, most of which one will not find listed in any job description.

So, how do we make the academy a better fit with black women? My suggestions:

- Make certain all members of the campus community understand that being black is not monolithic any more than being white is; that we are not all alike and will not all fit your stereotypes.

- Stop asking black women to be white women by pretending addressing "women's issues" without addressing racism is appropriate.

- Acknowledge the requirements of black women to do more than the jobs they were hired to do; they also have to be mentors, be social justice advocates, and serve on committees and boards to "represent" and educate others about race and gender.

- Investigate reasons that black women are criticized. We are not perfect, some criticism is no doubt valid, but make certain the criticism is not based in something other than ability and performance.

- Take allegations of racism seriously and investigate them aggressively— we are NOT in a postracial society by a long shot.

- Help black women find mentors—they do not have to be other black women, but they do have to have some understanding of race and racism.

- Help the campus community understand that being a team player does not require ignoring racism and sexism when it is observed.

- Hire more black women in decision-making positions.

The academy will continue to be a hard row for most black women to hoe. There is no question that apart from a few chosen (and chosen for reasons that are not always valid) superstars, black women, as shown by the experiences of the respondents, have to work twice as hard to be considered half as good as our white sisters. I look forward to the day when it is possible for a black woman in the academy to be viewed, to paraphrase Martin Luther King, by the content of her character and the level of her scholarship and performance and not by the color of her skin.

As a final note, almost all of the women thanked me for allowing them to tell their stories. They used words like "liberating" and "cathartic" to describe the experience. I hope that more research is done on black women in the academy so that voices too long ignored can finally be heard.

References

ASHE Higher Education Report. (2009). *Special issue: Ethnic and racial administrative diversity: Understanding work life realities and experiences in higher education, 35*(3), 1–95.

Carroll, C. M. (1982). Three's a crowd: The dilemma of the black woman in higher education. In G. T. Hull, P B. Scott, & B. Smith (Eds.), *All the women are white, all the blacks are men, but some of us are brave* (pp. 115–28). Old Westbury, NY: Feminist Press.

Jayakumar, U., Howard, T., Allen, W., & Han, J. C. (2009). Racial privilege in the professoriate: An exploration of campus climate, retention and satisfaction. *Journal of Higher Education, 80*(5), 538–63.

Kretsedemas, P. (2010). But she's not black! *Journal of African American Studies, 14*(2), 149–70.

Lorde, A. (1984). *Sister outsider.* Freedom, CA: Crossing Press.

Merchand, A. (2010). Black graduates owe more debt than white, Asian, or Hispanic graduates. *Chronicle of Higher Education. Com.* Retrieved August 12, 2010 from http://chronicle.com/article/Black-Graduates-Owe-More-Debt/65253/.

Reason, R. (2000). NASPA Salary Survey 1999–2000: Comprehensive report. Retrieved August 12, 2010 from http://www.naspa.org.

Simien, E. M., & Clawson, R. A. (2004). The intersection of race and gender: An examination of black feminist consciousness, race consciousness, and policy attitudes. *Social Science Quarterly, 85*(3), 793–810.

Terhune, C. P. (2008). Coping in isolation: The experiences of black women in white communities. *Journal of Black Studies, 38.* Retrieved from http://jbs.sagepub.com doi: 10.1177/0021934706288144.

Williams, C. (2001). The angry black woman scholar. *NWSA Journal, 13* (2), 87–97.

Williams, T. (2008) Reflections on a personal, historic, movement. The Jepson Blog. Retrieved September 6, 2010, from http://blog.richmond.edu/jepson/2008/11/11/one-week-after-reflections-on-a-personal-historic-moment/.

9

Academic Leaders with Disabilities: How Do We Know If We Are Winning When No One Is Keeping Score?

Rhoda Olkin

This chapter is about women with disabilities as leaders in academia—not specific people, but the issues that arise for any woman with a disability rising through the academic ranks and into leadership and administrative positions. First, I discuss why we might think about people with disabilities categorically when addressing academia. Second, I outline the numerous potential barriers for people with disabilities in leadership roles. Throughout the discussion I use examples from my own life, but only inasmuch as I believe they are not idiosyncratic to me or to my particular disability (polio and mobility limitations). Third, I make ten recommendations for academia to adopt to increase the chances for women with disabilities to participate in leadership roles.

One thing is clear about women with disabilities in academia: there are no data. This is perhaps the most salient point that underscores all that follows. Women with disabilities in academia have not been tabulated, monitored, discussed, or written about. There are programs for advancement of women in academic leadership (Baker, 2009). For example, the percentage of women in senior academic positions in New Zealand, Australia, and Canada has gone from 5 percent in 1960 to 20 percent in 2008. Furthermore, there are efforts to increase the number of people with disabilities in certain fields; more attention has been paid to this issue in the STEM fields (science, technology, engineering, math); there is relatively little being done in social sciences to increase participation by people with disabilities. Yet the confluence of gender, disability, and academic careers has not been subject to any scrutiny. The absence of information about academic leaders with disabilities implies that the questions of proportional representation, affirmative action, and hiring goals are not being asked with regard to people with disabilities in academia. This absence—the failure to see people with disabilities as a minority group about whom we need information for the purpose of greater representation—is rampant in academia. Thus it becomes necessary in this chapter to tread new ground. But readers should be aware that empirical support is scanty at best, and many of the issues I raise here remain ripe for investigation.

Why Talk about Female Academics with Disabilities?

Many discussions of diverse groups start with statistics about the size of the group, as if prevalence is a rationale for inclusion. I could do the same—19 percent of the noninstitutionalized population have a disability (U.S. Census Bureau, 2001), and 50 percent of all families are directly affected by disability. But whether there are few or many women with disabilities in academia is not the point; democracy is protection of the minority from the tyranny of the majority. Furthermore, I do not believe that numbers are the sole or even main rationale for focusing on people with disabilities in academia. If we buy the basic premise that diversity is valuable for institutions that are at the forefront of progressive thought then ostensibly women with disabilities would have much to contribute. But to ensure women with disabilities in leadership positions, there must be women with disabilities early in the pipeline, and that pipeline should not leak. Academic institutions can have subtle ways of being gendered (Kantola, 2008; Saunderson, 2002), and I would posit that they also have ways of being able-ist. In the following sections I explore the many barriers in academia for women with disabilities.

Barriers to Academic Leadership Roles

There are numerous barriers for people with disabilities in academia, at whatever faculty rank or level of administration. I divide these barriers into four areas: (a) logistics directly related to disability; (b) financial

and budgetary constraints; (c) interpersonal, social, attitudinal, and per-
ceptual prejudices; and (d) the confluence of disability and other aspects
of identity.

Logistics

Logistical barriers are in many ways the most salient to outsiders (i.e., persons without disabilities). First is simple access to campus. You might think,
thirty years after the Rehabilitation Act (1975) required accessibility of
institutions receiving federal monies (virtually all universities and colleges),
and twenty years after passage of the Americans with Disabilities Act
(1990), that all campuses would be physically accessible. But accessibility
is a relative term. Take, for example, the University of California at Berkeley,
which was the birthplace of the disability rights movement. Despite ideal
weather, the campus is difficult to access: not all buildings are accessible,
hilly terrain and great distances make going from one place to another difficult, there are historical buildings that cannot be altered, many places on
campus are not reachable by car, and parking is at such a premium that a
parking spot is the gift given to Nobel prize winners. Furthermore, what is
accessible to someone who uses a wheelchair is different than for someone
who is ambulatory but limited by endurance. A person with paraplegia may
be able to open a bathroom door, but a person with limits to hand strength
may not be able to open that same door. The definition of *accessible* might
address the width of the door, but not the ease of opening it or the necessity
of an automatic door opener. Administrators are fond of touting the ADA
compliance of the campus, but this is in many ways a nonsensical notion.
The ADA does not address such specifics (state building codes do). Rather,
it requires reasonable accommodations on the basis of disability, and as
we've seen, what works for one person may not work for another. To give a
concrete example, my university installed an automatic door opener for the
outside door to the main building. There were two problems. First, the button
to activate the door was small and required finger dexterity and strength.
Second, the door opened into the cafeteria, which was accessible when
empty but difficult to navigate and mostly inaccessible when crowded. If it
therefore didn't work for me, then claiming *ADA compliance* is irrelevant.

When I think about what physical accessibility means for me, there are
layers to be dealt with. First priority is where I can park and its proximity

to my office. The route from parking to my office has to have curb cuts and an automatic front door opener to my building. The elevator has to have space for me to turn around in so I can reach the button. The next area to be considered is my office, which needs space for a wheelchair. My desk is a specific nonstandard height. Then I need bathroom access, which necessitated putting in an automatic door. I need a plug to charge my wheelchair. The emergency plans have to include how I would leave my second-floor office and exit the building. I need my classes to be scheduled in such a way that I can use a particular room that has been made accessible for me. These considerations just cover the bare minimum of needs. Suppose, for example, I need to attend a meeting on the first floor. If it is a long meeting, I usually try to get it changed to the second floor, because the first floor bathroom is much less accessible. If I have to meet with people from one of our other campuses, I try to have the meeting on my campus so I don't have to travel and in a room that will be comfortable for a long meeting. Any off-campus meeting has to be scouted for accessibility before it can be booked. Since people without disabilities have trouble really knowing what accessibility entails, I often have to be the one to do the scouting for the parking, the entrance, the slope of the ramp, the size of the bathroom, and other factors; changes to routine require extra work on my part.

Faculty often hold events at different arenas on campus or even away from campus. Off-campus buildings may be less accessible or even completely inaccessible. For example, my first year of teaching a faculty retreat was held at the Chancellor's house; I could not attend because his house was up a flight of steps. Winter holiday lunches were hosted at restaurants, some of which were not accessible (or said they were and then turned out not to be). Whenever an event was held elsewhere, I had to do extra work to assess access. I might call the location or ask a staff person to inquire about access and parking. Sometimes I would even scout a location in advance to see where to park and how to access the building. Even after all this, I might have to enter through the kitchen, past the garbage, and separately from my peers. These extra tasks and attention are particularly stressful for newer faculty. They isolate her and make her disability a more salient feature to others.

Faculty work on average a fifty-five-hour week (O'Laughlin & Bischoff, 2005). Administrators and those in other leadership positions (e.g., program chairs, department heads, union presidents) may work even more hours. The commitment of time, energy, and personal resources expected in academia, especially in leadership positions, is extraordinary. When I began teaching in graduate school, I figured out that for every three-hour class, it took me approximately twenty hours of preparation, and I taught four classes a semester. As any new faculty member can attest, this is probably common. The sheer volume of work is difficult to manage. Later, as one advances in rank, the expectations for research, presentations, and mentoring increase. Thus, even as course preparation gets easier, other aspects of the job increase. This work demand may not be feasible for women with certain types of disabilities. Many physical disabilities incur fatigue and weakness; how might a woman with multiple sclerosis, polio, muscular dystrophy, lupus, rheumatoid arthritis, or a host of other disabilities manage the time demands of work?

In addition to fatigue and weakness, many disabilities incur pain to varying degrees. Pain might not seem like much of a barrier; one can be in pain and work. But if you've ever had a toothache for several days, you know that even relatively small amounts of pain can be distracting. Chronic pain doesn't need to be intense to be debilitating; it's the chronicity that wears one down.

Some disabilities are unpredictable. For example, multiple sclerosis and lupus can be episodic; Crohn's disease can flare up unexpectedly. One way to live with these kinds of disorders is to have a lifestyle that doesn't overtax you and that allows for down time as needed. Travel, meetings, and work demands of leadership positions may dictate a schedule with peaks (e.g., a two-day retreat; travel to another campus; attendance at conferences) from which there is scant time to recover, and these peaks can exacerbate the chronic condition. Aging compounds all of the difficulties of disability, predominantly fatigue, weakness, and pain.

For example, in the past decade there have been several opportunities for me to be considered for program director. I have not put myself up for the position because I didn't think I could physically manage the three-year commitment. There were numerous problems. One was that I would move from a nine-month/year to a twelve-month/year contract. Second, I would be expected to be on campus at least four days a week, which not only made a long work week but added to commute times. Third, I would be working many evenings and weekends. Do I even need a fourth reason? Ironically,

I might have been able to manage this when much younger, but of course then I wouldn't have been experienced enough to take the position. Furthermore, I had young children and would not have wanted that great a job commitment when they lived at home. Now that they are grown, I am older too, and therefore much more fatigued and limited in mobility and stamina.

As seen in this section, the physical aspects alone of leadership positions entail considerable barriers. Do these barriers mean that women with disabilities should not take on leadership roles? Of course not. But leadership positions have many requirements that make them hard for a woman with a disability. The problems are compounded as we look at other types of barriers in the next sections.

Financial and Budgetary Constraints

There is a simple truth, which is that disability often costs money. Even for my relatively minimal needs, my university has spent money to install an automatic door opener on the front door and the women's bathroom, bought a new desk for my office and tailored it to my needs, purchased several tables that are wheelchair accessible for conference rooms, and paid for me to have a monthly parking pass at a privately owned parking lot next door. There are other expenses as well. When I go to a conference, I often have an extra night in the hotel, use valet parking, and sometimes take an assistant. A critical question is where this money comes from. Universities have funds for an office of disability services, but this serves students; where does money for faculty and administrators come from? Unfortunately, it often comes from the general budget rather than a percentage set aside for reasonable accommodations (RA). This means that money for RA directly subtracts from other departmental needs. For example, I wanted to stay overnight in a downtown hotel about an hour from my home because my talk was scheduled for 8:00 AM. First I asked for and got approval from Human Resources, but HR doesn't have a budget, so the request was forwarded to my Dean. Because the RA was approved, he really had no choice but to fund it. A few months later I learned that we had no money to hold our faculty retreat off campus; we needed an amount roughly equivalent to my one night's stay in a hotel.

There are three obvious problems here. One is that the money had not been set aside and thus had to be found from a budget that had already been slashed. In austere times, finding even a few hundred dollars can be difficult. Second, the money spent on RA directly affected the department's ability to pursue other activities. Third, I was made aware (as were others) of the lack of funds and the ostensible reasons for it. This prompted me to call university council to request a line item in the budget for RA. I explained the necessity of insulating faculty with disabilities from any backlash for requesting RA. Fortunately, she agreed with me and about six months later this item was added to the budget for the following year.

A similar issue arises when submitting grants for outside funding. To include researchers with disabilities often requires that some RA are made. Thus it is prudent to include these as a line item in the budget for the grant. To give a ballpark figure, when I submit grants in which I want participants with disabilities, I make the amount for RA 4 percent of the total budget. When researchers with disabilities are included, I make it 1 percent of the budget. This covers not only any accommodations I need to conduct the study but also accommodations when I disseminate results of the study.

Conferences are an area where accommodations are often needed. When considering the cost of attending, I have to include extra expenses. I might rent a scooter that can be delivered to the hotel. I tend to use room service when I'm fatigued. I take taxis when others might take public transportation or walk. I tip the people who push the wheelchair in the airport. These are usually out-of-pocket expenses for me, either adding to the cost of the conference or subtracted from any honorarium I might receive. If administrators travel for the job, these types of expenses must be considered. Is the university willing to pay for these?

Interpersonal, Social, Attitudinal, and Perceptual Prejudices

Most people with disabilities would cite interpersonal interactions as the most problematic, troublesome, and annoying aspect of having a disability (Olkin, 1999; Yuker, 1988, 1994). Physical access allows one in the door but doesn't dictate a welcome environment. One of the first things noticeable would be the absence of other faculty and administrators with disabilities. This absence has several ramifications. When you are in the meetings, it will be up to you to raise disability issues. And since the absence of disability is rarely observed, if you are not in the room, no one else will raise these issues. When advocating for changes that remove barriers or foster a more disability-friendly environment, you may be the lone voice. And you will have to be that voice often. You risk becoming seen as a one-note administrator, the one who keeps bringing up the same issue all the time. This could lead to others viewing you through a narrow lens as the disability person and nothing else. Such pigeonholing could affect your prospects for promotion.

The administrator with a disability needs to be vigilant for activities in the university that could have a differential effect on students, staff, or faculty with disabilities. For example, recently my university established a new grading policy whereby grades of Incomplete would be noted next to a final grade once the incomplete was remediated. This policy was decided by the President, Provost, Deans, and Registrars and did not include anyone from Disability Services. When I heard about the policy, my immediate concern was students who took a leave or extended time due to medical or disability issues. I was told that students could petition for an exception to the policy. However, I saw this as yet another burden placed on students with disabilities, as well as sending the message that once again students with disabilities were exceptions. These kinds of examples can create cognitive dissonance for women with disabilities in academia (Kjeldal, Rindfleish, & Sheridan, 2005). Although written policies cite relevant laws, and there are statements about nondiscrimination on the basis of disability, actual practices and procedures and common microaggressions (Sue, 2010) counter the notion of equity.

There will never be a critical mass of people with disabilities in faculty or administrator roles, and in fact there may not be any academic leaders with disabilities in your institution. The presence of women leaders creates the perception of a more women-friendly environment (Sanders, Willemsen, & Millar, 2009). I surmise that the presence of academic leaders with disabilities would likewise create a more disability-friendly environment. The absence of such leaders can lead to perceptions of stigma.

Being groomed for promotion is one place where mentoring is a valuable advantage. Mentoring of women faculty benefits both the women and the university through retention, more grant income, and promotion (Gardiner, Tiggemann, Kearns, & Marshall, 2007). But you will be lucky to have a female mentor, and very unlikely to have a mentor of either gender with a disability. A sounding board for vetting your ideas and a place for feedback about how you are perceived can be important tools in the ladder up. However, your mentor may likewise see you as being too focused on disability.

There are other interpersonal barriers for women with disabilities in academia. Being the public face of the university and a fundraiser are areas in which stereotypes and stigma can play large roles. Disability is often used as a scare tactic in advertising, the thing to be avoided by safe driving, attending to health, abstaining from drugs. Similarly, disability is used to evoke pity and thus money (e.g., the Muscular Dystrophy Telethon). These images of disability as something to be feared or pitied are legion and can complicate the role of an administrator with a disability. She may have internalized some of these images. Even if she has not, when fundraising or doing other types of public relations for the university, these ubiquitous images can be raised in others' minds. Responses can range from outright dismissal to subtle expressions of pity to exaggerated admiration.

People with disabilities are constrained by affective prescriptions and restrictions. An early work in this area discussed the *requirement of mourning* (Wright, 1983). This requirement stems from the idea that those without disabilities view disability as a tragedy and think that they themselves would not be able to handle having such a burden. They thus infer that the person with the disability feels similarly and is in mourning for the loss disability incurs. If in fact the person with the disability is not demonstrably in mourning, then he or she is seen as having overcome great odds to be not depressed and must have special or super powers of emotion. This creates a dialectic such that persons with disabilities are seen either as appropriately depressed (the requirement of mourning) or as superordinate people (what Olkin, 1999, called the *requirement of pluckiness*); in either case they are not viewed accurately or individually but rather as representatives of a category. If people with disabilities should be either depressed or plucky, they also have a prohibition against anger. When a person with a disability is angry, there is a tendency to label that person as maladjusted or as having failed to accept the disability (whatever that might mean). But the pervasiveness of microaggressions makes anger a probable response.

Microaggressions (Sue, 2010) are subtle acts or slights perpetrated by the dominant culture that make a member of a minority group feel wounded. In the case of disability, there are two differences. First, the act might be by another person of the same minority, that is, a person with a disability. Second, the act might not be by a person. For example, if I encounter a door that I cannot open, there is no specific person who is carrying out a microaggression at the time of the encounter. However, many microaggressions do involve another person. For example, about once a week someone at my school says something to me about the speed of my wheelchair (e.g., "don't run me over," or "you could get a speeding ticket"). A few times a month the sole handicapped stall in the bathroom is taken by an able-bodied person when there are many other empty stalls available. About twice a semester the wheelchair-height table I use when teaching is moved to another classroom. In some cases I can see the perpetrator; in other cases the person is not visible to me. The prohibition against anger coupled with daily microaggressions requires careful affective management by a mature person and is yet another distraction for the woman with a disability in a leadership role.

Disability is rarely included as a topic of diversity in undergraduate or graduate programs (Bluestone, Stokes, & Kuba, 1996; Green, Callands, Radcliffe, Luebbe, & Klonoff, 2009; Hogben & Waterman, 1997; Kemp & Mallinckrodt, 1996; Olkin & Pledger, 2003). This may be because disability is rarely seen as an advantage but rather as an absence or a deficiency. Thus it is relegated to abnormal psychology, special education, or courses about specific so-called special populations (e.g., autism, learning disabilities, intellectual impairment). If this is how undergraduates become exposed to disability, it can discourage students with disabilities from thinking of themselves in leadership roles. The absence of instructors, mentors, and administrators with disabilities, plus the silence about people with disabilities as a minority group, can have a chilling effect on students early in the pipeline. Couple this with the pervasive negative images of disability in the media and we can see how people with disabilities are not groomed for leadership roles.

Most academic leaders start out as assistant professors and are promoted through the ranks and into administrative roles. One portion of retention and promotion decisions comes from teaching evaluations. Results of studies on effects of gender on teaching evaluations are equivocal, but the better-controlled studies suggest that there are no differences (though the questions asked on evaluations are a key variable, inasmuch as these questions are not gender-neutral; Huston, 2005). Studies on effects of being an instructor of color generally show some negative bias in student evaluations if the students believe the evaluations are not going directly to the instructor, though effects vary by ethnicity of the instructor (Huston, 2005). Style of teaching (strict or lenient; warm or cold) and course topic also interacted with instructors' ethnicity. What we see from the results of these studies is that gender, ethnicity, and style can affect teaching evaluations. Unfortunately, we know nothing about the effects of instructors' disabilities on evaluations by students. The interaction among disability, gender, and ethnicity is hard to gauge. But given the results cited above, we might surmise that disability is not neutral, and its effects on student evaluations would vary with other attributes of the instructor as well as with teaching style and discipline.

Because we are not collecting data on women with disabilities in academia, there are many things we don't know. Unfortunately, we probably don't know what we don't know, that is, because the questions have not yet been asked, there is a void regarding what questions are important, what data tell us that leads us to new questions, and what areas we ought to explore further.

Disability and Other Identities

Women with disabilities are, obviously, women, with all the issues well documented for women in academia. Although the issue of balancing roles for women in academia has been well explored, the balancing act has not been eased. The effect of child rearing on women's careers has been documented (Armenti, 2004; van Anders, 2004) and would perhaps be even greater on women who take on leadership roles. How might disability interact with these already conflictual roles? Again, this is an area in which there are scant data, despite the fact of 8 million families with children under 18 who have a parent with a disability, or 11 percent of all families (LaPlante, Miller, & Miller, 1992; Toms-Barker & Maralani, 1997). But several studies indirectly suggest that being a mother with a disability requires more time and attention than can be easily balanced with a career. For example, several studies on mothers with disabilities had participants with master's degrees, all of whom had stopped out of the workforce during the early and preteen years of their children (Cohen, 1998; Conley-Jung & Olkin, 2001; Kirshbaum & Preston, 1998). Another study showed that families with teenagers wherein the mother had a disability had incomes of about $15,000 less per year than friends in their neighborhood, in part because mothers had stopped working (Olkin, Abrams, Preston, & Kirshbaum, 2006). So it would seem that even well-educated mothers with disabilities step out of the workforce as long as there are young children in the home. Parenting with a disability is an area in which there are few structural or emotional supports. Combine this with working with a disability in a time- and energy-demanding career in which there are few role models and many demands, and the sheer volume of demands may be too much to juggle. Thus the forced choice between mothering and academic career may be more salient for women with disabilities.

Women with disabilities may be persons of color, lesbian or bisexual, foreign born, or have other identities that intermingle with being a woman and a person with a disability. Some of those identities may carry privilege (e.g., heterosexual; native born) and others may engender stigma and discrimination. Although there is some literature on lesbians with disabilities, it is neither empirical nor about academia. The confluence of gender, disability, other demographic variables, academia, and leadership roles is an untapped area for research, understanding, and ultimately movement forward toward more equitable institutions of higher learning. Toward that goal, here are some recommendations for institutions to consider to make the environment more hospitable to women with disabilities wherever they are in the pipeline.

Recommendations

1. *Lead, don't follow.* Institutions of higher learning should be leaders in accessibility and disability-friendly environments. At the very least, this requires early adoption of new technologies that allow greater access for people with disabilities, innovation in teaching methods, means of job restructuring, and equitable rubrics for retention, tenure, and promotion.

2. *Make disability part of the dialogue.* All nondiscrimination statements, if they specify protected groups, should include disability. Affirmative action should be specified for women and for people with disabilities, with the express goals of increasing numbers of each. Policies for accommodations should be well delineated and published appropriately and ubiquitously in print and online materials. Diversity training should include gender and disability.

3. *Collect and understand the data.* This is one way to include disability in the dialogue. Having data on the number of women with disabilities at various ranks and in administrative roles makes disability a more salient factor. Data may have to be aggregated to protect individuals' confidentiality; collecting data across campuses and institutions is one way to get greater estimates without jeopardizing identities.

4. *Plan for disability costs.* The institution's budget should have a line item for reasonable accommodations that is a percentage of the overall budget. Those monies should be available to any level of faculty and administration and should not detract from other budgeted items.

5. *Restructure job demands.* Leadership positions may have to be reconfigured. Job sharing is one method. A similar method is job restructuring such that the job is broken into different parts and each part assigned to different people. In job restructuring, the main position would be parsed for those parts that would make it unmanageable for the woman with a disability, and those parts would be parceled out.

6. *Train search committees.* From writing the advertisement to conducting interviews, there are steps that can make the institution more welcoming to women with disabilities. For example, ads could state that reasonable accommodations are available in the application process. If the statement *women and minorities are especially encouraged to apply* is included, this should be changed to *women, people with disabilities, and other minorities are especially encouraged to apply.* Help the search committee with where to place ads to attract women with disabilities and to change wording that might be unintentionally off-putting to potential candidates with disabilities. Make sure the committee knows what questions can and cannot be asked in an interview. Simple points of etiquette should be reviewed (e.g., discuss whether you should shake hands with someone with limb differences; make the interview room readily accessible without having to rearrange the furniture when someone arrives in a wheelchair).

7. *Equity requires consistent efforts.* Develop a multiyear plan to recruit, retain, and promote women with disabilities. Consider all aspects of leadership roles, from mentors to institution president, and how the job descriptions might invite or deter women with disabilities. Be vigilant to include disability when discussing diversity.

8. *Be accountable, starting at the top.* Institutional cultures cannot be more inviting than the top level of administration. Thus from the president on down, every level of administration and leadership role must be on board with not just the talk but also the walk of diversity as a valuable asset for the institution.

9. *Have written, clear, and consistent procedures for exceptions.* Institutional policies are predicated on equality and fairness; reasonable accommodations are predicated on individualization and equity. Discussion of these ideas should be part of the diversity dialogue to avoid having women with disabilities seen as having so-called special treatment. Procedures for women with disabilities to do things differently, be innovative in their job duties, and use assistance as needed should be clearly delineated. Acceptance that one size never fits all should be a part of the corporate culture.

10. *Do debriefing after failures and learn from them.* Rather than hide mistakes, they should be viewed as valuable opportunities to make corrections. This fosters an openness to experimentation and risk taking that is necessary if the institution is to be a pioneer (see recommendation #1).

Conclusions

When discussing women with disabilities in leadership roles in academia, several factors are paramount. First is the relative invisibility of these women, such that there is an almost total lack of data about numbers or characteristics of such women. Second, as outlined in this chapter, there are many barriers for women with disabilities as women and as people with disabilities and in the ways in which these two variables interact. Third, although academia prides itself as a bastion of equality, subtle but pervasive factors have favored those in more privileged positions, namely men and able-bodied persons. Given these facts, we can see that fostering women with disability in leadership positions in academia is not going to spontaneously happen. Rather, it will take concerted efforts on the parts of current leaders, instructors, researchers, mentors, and people with disabilities themselves, bolstered by appropriate policies and procedures, to achieve greater representation.

References

Americans with Disabilities Act of 1990, Public Law 101-336, 42 U.S.C. 12111, 12112.

Armenti, C. (2004). May babies and posttenure babies: Maternal decisions of women professors. *Review of Higher Education, 27*, 211–31.

Baker, M. (2009). Gender, academia and the managerial university. *New Zealand Sociology, 24*(1), 24–48.

Bluestone, H. H., Stokes, A., & Kuba, S. A. (1996). Toward an integrated program design: Evaluating the status of diversity training in graduate school curriculum. *Professional Psychology: Research and Practice, 27*, 394–400.

Cohen, L. J. (1998). *Mothers' perceptions of the influence of their physical disabilities on the developmental tasks of children.* Unpublished doctoral dissertation, California School of Professional Psychology, Alameda.

Conley-Jung, C., & Olkin, R. (2001). Mothers with visual impairments or blindness raising young children. *Journal of Visual Impairment and Blindness, 91*(1), 14–29.

Gardiner, M., Tiggemann, M., Kearns, H., & Marshall, K. (2007). Show me the money! An empirical analysis of mentoring outcomes for women in academia. *Higher Education Research & Development, 26* (4), 425–42.

Green, D., Callands, T., Radcliffe, A., Luebbe, & Klonoff, E. (2009). Clinical psychology students' perceptions of diversity training: A study of exposure and satisfaction. *Journal of Clinical Psychology, 65*(10), 1056–70.

Hogben, M., & Waterman, C. K. (1997). Are all of your students represented in their textbooks? A content analysis of coverage of diversity issues in introductory psychology textbooks. *Teaching of Psychology, 24*, 95–100.

Huston, T. (2005). *Empirical research on the impact of race and gender in the evaluation of teaching.* Seattle: Center for Excellence in Teaching and Learning. Retrieved October 6, 2010, from http://www.seattleu.edu/CETL/resources.aspx.

Kantola, J. (2008). "Why do all the women disappear?" Gendering processes in a political science department. *Gender, Work, and Organization, 15*(2), 202–25.

Kemp, N. T., & Mallinckrodt, B. (1996). Impact of professional training on case conceptualization of clients with disabilities. *Professional Psychology: Research and Practice, 27*, 378–85.

Kirshbaum, M., & Preston, P. (1998). *Keeping our families together: A report of the national task force on parents with disabilities and their families* (National Institute on Disability and Rehabilitation Research grant # H133B30076). Berkeley, CA: Research and Training Center, Through the Looking Glass.

Kjeldal, S. E., Rindfleish, J., & Sheridan, A. (2005). Deal-making and rule-breaking: Behind the façade of equity in academia.*Gender and Education, 17*(4), 431–47.

LaPlante, M., Miller, S., & Miller, K. (1992). People with work disability in the U.S. *Disability Statistics Abstract No. 4*. Washington, DC: National Institute on Disability and Rehabilitation Research.

O'Laughlin, E. M., & Bischoff, L. G. (2005). Balancing parenthood and academia: Work/family stress as influenced by gender and tenure status. *Journal of Family Issues, 26*, 79–106.

Olkin, R. (1999). *What psychotherapists should know about disability*. New York: Guilford.

Olkin, R., Abrams, K., Preston, P., & Kirshbaum, M. (2006). Comparison of parents with and without disabilities raising teens: Information from the NHIS and two national surveys. *Rehabilitation Psychology, 51*(1), 43–49.

Olkin, R., & Pledger, C. (2003). Can disability studies and psychology join hands? *American Psychologist, 58*(4), 296–304.

Rehabilitation Act of 1973, Public Law 93–112.

Sanders, K., Willemsen, T. M., & Millar, C. (2009). Views from above the glass ceiling: Does the academic environment influence women professors' careers and experiences? *Sex Roles, 60*, 301–12.

Saunderson, W. (2002). Women, academia, and identity: Constructions of equal opportunities in the "new managerialism"—A case of lipstick on the gorilla? *Higher Education Quarterly, 56*(4), 376–406.

Sue, D. W. (2010). *Microaggressions in everyday life: Race, gender, and sexual orientation.* Hoboken, NJ: Wiley.

Toms-Barker, L. T., & Maralani, V. (1997). *Challenges and strategies of disabled parents: Findings from a national survey of parents with disabilities.* Oakland, CA: Berkeley Planning Associates.

U.S. Census Bureau. (2001). *U.S. Census 2000, Demographic Profiles.* Retrieved October 6, 2010, from http://www.census.gov/main/weee/cen2000.html.

van Anders, S. M. (2004). Why the academic pipeline leaks: Fewer men than women perceive barriers to becoming professors.*Sex Roles, 51*(9/10), 511–21.

Yuker, H. E. (Ed.). (1988). *Attitudes toward persons with disabilities.* New York: Springer.

Yuker, H. E. (1994). Variables that influence attitudes toward persons with disabilities: Conclusions from the data. *Psychosocial Perspectives on Disability, A Special Issue of the Journal of social Behavior and Personality, 9,* 3–22.

Wright, B. (1983). *Physical disability: A psychosocial approach* (2nd ed.). New York: Harper & Row.

10

Inclusive Leadership: Helping Women Negotiate the Labyrinth of Leadership in Higher Education

Brenda L. Berkelaar, Katie Pope, Beverly Davenport Sypher, and Monica F. Cox

Increasing numbers of women have reached top leadership positions in colleges and universities in the United States. Currently, women occupy 23 percent of academic presidencies (American Council on Education [ACE], 2007) and 38 percent of provost or chief academic officer positions, the most likely position from which institutions find new presidents (King & Gomez, 2008). Despite this progress, women remain significantly underrepresented in upper levels of academic administration, a situation that many argue "places serious limitations on the success of educational institutions themselves" (West & Curtis, 2006, p. 4).

According to large national surveys sponsored by the ACE, the percentage of women in upper administration is substantially less than the percentage of female students, faculty, and staff (King & Gomez, 2008). Also, women are less likely to occupy the key line positions from which educational institutions typically select presidents, provosts, and vice presidents (King & Gomez, 2008). Since the late 1990s, the proportion of women in academic presidencies slowed or stagnated, particularly among large national universities (ACE, 2007). In many ways, this pattern mimics the lower numbers of women in executive-level positions in Fortune 500 companies as opposed to businesses overall (Eagly & Carli,

2007a). Despite projections, continued progress toward equal representation is neither guaranteed nor clearly evident (see Eagly & Carli, 2007a, 2007b). The question becomes: How do we reinvigorate progress toward an inclusive model of academic leadership that better represents the institutional constituents these individuals lead?

In this chapter, we outline the problem of the underrepresentation of women in formal academic leadership positions and describe opportunities and challenges for realizing more inclusive leadership in higher education. The chapter concludes with a case study of Purdue Women Lead, a faculty development program at Purdue University introduced to educate, encourage, and recognize women leaders. Purdue Women Lead provides one model for helping to develop women's leadership capacity through education, collaboration, research, and recognition.

A Brief Primer on Academic Leadership

In describing leadership positions in higher education, we are referring to those employees primarily responsible for advancing a vision, making and implementing decisions, and securing and managing financial resources for colleges and universities. Although there are similarities between formal academic leadership positions and those in corporations, the titles, positions, responsibilities, and structure do differ. Although they may also vary from institution to institution, positions in academic administration typically include the roles and associated responsibilities described below:

The *president* (sometimes called the chancellor) is the chief executive officer of the college or university, typically reporting to the Board of Trustees. A series of *vice presidents* handle areas ranging from finance, research, fundraising, information technology and human resources to physical facilities, compliance, diversity, and marketing and media. The *provost*, (alternatively called the chief academic officer or the vice chancellor or vice president of academic affairs) is second in command and typically responsible for all academic matters relevant to both students and faculty members. In larger institutions particularly, the provost may lead a number of associate and vice provosts who manage different areas (e.g., faculty affairs, student affairs, enrollment management, diversity, engagement, and sometimes global affairs). Below these upper levels of academic administration are academic *deans* who have responsibility for a significant area or academic unit such as a college or school (e.g., Dean of the College of Engineering, Dean of Arts and Sciences, and Dean of the Business School, Medical School, Law School, and others), or a functional area of administration (e.g., Dean of Students, Dean of Libraries). For deans particularly, the division and type of responsibilities varies widely between institutions. In addition, larger institutions may have associate or assistant deans who are responsible for specific administrative areas (e.g., research, undergraduate studies). Finally, *department heads* or *department chairs* administer or lead individual departments. Although some institutions include other academic administration positions (e.g., director or chief of staff), the five described above—president, provost, vice presidents, deans, and department chairs or heads—exist in most institutions of higher education, although the specific division and type of responsibilities may vary to some degree.

The typical and traditional career path for someone pursuing a career in academic administration is fairly linear, most often starting with tenure as a faculty member (ACE, 2007; Birnbaum & Umbach, 2001; King & Gomez, 2008). The tenure process differs between institutions, but typically it requires earning a doctoral degree and six years of successful performance in research, teaching, and service. When tenured, a faculty member is typically promoted to an associate professor. Approximately six years after one is tenured, he or she is considered for promotion to full professor, the highest possible rank for a faculty member. Seldom are faculty appointed to deanships or higher postings before becoming a full professor. Most individuals in upper levels of administration follow career paths that include department head or chair and a deanship or vice presidency. For those who eventually become president, most have previous experience as a provost or vice president, and a growing number of sitting presidents have served as presidents at other schools (ACE, 2007). Although there are exceptions to this pathway (e.g., multiple deanships or provost positions at successively larger schools or even some corporate experience), the consistent profile evidences a fairly significant underrepresentation of women.

Inclusive Leadership in Higher Education

The notion that institutions of higher education should be *inclusive institutions* grows out of a value for diversity and an appreciation of difference:

> Inclusive institutions help people feel connected and sustained as they grow and achieve. These institutions celebrate, promote, recognize, and make visible their efforts to support all stakeholders, including those who have been historically underrepresented. Inclusive institutions ensure that everyone has a voice and an opportunity to speak. Providing women leaders access to opportunities for career success is a key component for strengthening inclusive leadership. (Sypher & Pope, 2009, para. 3)

An *inclusive leadership* perspective is therefore "concerned first and foremost with inclusion, both in its processes and the ends for which it strives" (Ryan, 2006, abstract). Our focus is not simply an increase in numbers of women leaders only, although numbers matter and are certainly a commonly used measure of success. Rather, we want all groups to have an equal opportunity to influence the visioning, decision making, strategic planning, and day-to-day focus of education institutions in particular. Increasing representation for one group and potentially other underrepresented groups benefits the organization at large.

Connecting notions of inclusion to leadership recognizes that organizations benefit from strategically identifying, recruiting, and/or developing women and other underrepresented faculty as leaders, tapping into and developing the full spectrum of leadership capacity and organizational possibility. The implication is that a lack of women in formal positions of authority is an obstacle to fulfilling the potential and promise of higher education for students, faculty, staff, administration, and society (see Touchton, Musli, & Campbell, 2008).

Inclusive leadership as manifested in gender representation affects institutions, society, and individuals' institutional, social, and individual benefits. In effect, colleges and universities may lose access to a larger talent pool from which they can recruit and develop the most qualified leadership talent (Rhode & Kellerman, 2007). A culture of equal opportunity reduces attrition, increases commitment, and decreases the costs of replacing talented personnel (Rhode & Kellerman, 2007). Furthermore, in higher education, recent research suggests that having women in significant leadership positions increases the number of female faculty (Ehrenberg, Jakubson, Martin, Main, & Eisenberg, 2009). This in turn has social implications, since the number of female faculty can help increase the number of female students within a field, a concern of particular importance for many STEM (science, technology, engineering, and math) fields where women remain underrepresented and the shortage of qualified STEM graduates threatens the future economic potential of the United States (Committee on Science, Engineering, and Public Policy, 2007). Individually, women leaders given equal opportunity to develop leadership capacity and to occupy leadership positions receive a number of tangible and intangible benefits including a sense of purpose, intellectual stimulation, positional influence, and power to help shape change and other financial and nonfinancial rewards (Ciulla, 2000). Without opportunities to lead, these are benefits they might otherwise never experience despite leadership capacity and competency.

Despite Challenges: An Opportune Time for Inclusive Leadership

As mentioned previously, diversification in the highest levels of academic administration remains slow or even stagnant. In 1986, 92 percent of academic presidents were white, 91 percent were male, 8 percent were domestic minorities, and 8 percent were female. In 2006, 86 percent were white, 77 percent were male, 14 percent were domestic minorities, and 8 percent were female (ACE, 1986, 2007). Despite this increasing inclusiveness, the percentage of women presidents has not increased in more than two decades. Moreover, they are less likely to hold upper leadership positions in doctorate-granting institutions, or even four-year colleges, as compared to higher education institutions overall. Although the number of women in presidencies at doctorate-granting institutions increased from 4 percent to 13 percent from 1986 to 1996, in 2006 that number remained at 13 percent (ACE, 1986, 1996, 2007), well below the percentages of women graduating with doctoral degrees or represented in the ranks of undergraduate and graduate students and faculty. In addition, the representation of women in mid-level and upper-level administrative positions is not equal to that of men (West & Curtis, 2006). Most presidents come from previous presidencies or provost positions and 50 percent of other senior administrators are promoted from within the ranks of the particular institution (King & Gomez, 2008). Therefore, the presence of a particular group in key line positions at any institution of higher learning is critical to achieving inclusive leadership at all higher education institutions.

Most standing and recent academic presidents and provosts previously held tenure-track faculty positions (King & Gomez, 2008). Yet the growth we see in women leaders in higher education does not parallel the growth of women attaining advanced degrees, presumably the starting point for such a role. At the undergraduate level, women represent more than half of bachelor degrees overall (ACE, 2010), and at the graduate level, women represent 60 percent of the total population (ACE, 2010), even though some disciplines have greater proportions of females than others. For example, in fields such as education, nursing, pharmacy, and veterinary medicine, women are more highly represented, yet as of 2000, women were less represented in fields such as engineering, the physical sciences, and business (see ACE, 2010; Etzkowitz et al., 2000), fields in which many standing presidents in top national universities completed their studies (Sypher & Berkelaar, 2010). Similar to statistics about women in graduate education, women continue to be less represented in faculty ranks than male counterparts, particularly at doctoral-granting universities and particularly in STEM disciplines (Chliwniak, 1997; West & Curtis, 2006). At doctoral universities, women held 34 percent of all faculty positions (41% assistant professor positions and 24% of full professor) in 2006. In terms of evaluating equity, doctoral universities are significant because of their large numbers of faculty members as compared to other colleges and universities (West & Curtis, 2006).

Despite the underrepresentation of women, this is a time of unique opportunity for better realizing inclusive leadership. The academic presidency in the United States is at a point of imminent turnover. Academic presidents are significantly older as a group, with 49 percent of presidents 61 years of age or older (ACE, 2006). Even though the average tenure of the average academic president has increased from an average of 6.3 years in 1986 to 8.5 years in 2006 (ACE, 1986, 2007), the average tenure of provosts (5.2 years) remains among the shortest of all upper administration positions (ACE, 2007). This short tenure may be a result of provosts being tapped for presidential positions since fewer former presidents are available to fill the increasing presidential openings (King & Gomez, 2008). Or it may be a function of provosts' alleged decreasing interest in being a college or university president (Hartley III & Godin, 2010). Nonetheless, the argument remains that more women at every level increases the possibility of more women leaders. Consequently, the growing proportion of women in graduate ranks and among tenured faculty provides an increasing pool of potential leaders insofar as retention and development efforts continue to improve. Nonetheless, a number of visible and less visible barriers challenge women who seek to navigate the labyrinth of leadership.

In asserting that for women, the pathway to leadership positions is not a pipeline, nor limited by a glass ceiling, but a labyrinth, Eagly and Carli (2007a) note that the path is not impossible to navigate but is full of visible and invisible obstacles that undermine leadership ascension. That is,

> A labyrinth is not simple or direct, but requires persistence, awareness of one's progress, and a careful analysis of the puzzles that lie ahead. ... For women who aspire to top leadership, routes exist but are full of twists and turns, both unexpected and expected. Because all labyrinths have a viable route to the center, it is understood that goals are attainable. The metaphor acknowledges obstacles but is not ultimately discouraging. (p. 64)

We find that moving away from the metaphor of a glass ceiling or pipeline to the image of a labyrinth is useful for a number of reasons. The pipeline metaphor, although useful, still assumes that one need only get into or fill the right pipeline to ensure adequate leadership representation or development. The notion of the glass ceiling suggests that the obstacles to career progression are visible. It "give[s] the illusion of opportunity for women" (Buzzanell, 1995, abstract), so long as women break though the barrier. However, thinking about the challenge of underrepresentation as a glass ceiling does not address some of the invisible and visible obstacles and increased challenges that might impede formal leadership progress. Some of these challenges and obstacles for women center on previous experience in key line positions, isolation, and pioneerism, the double bind of leadership, educational experiences, family, and personal issues, and lack of leadership training.

First, women are less likely to hold key line positions like provosts or deans, the positions from which future presidents are often recruited. For example women hold only 38 percent of Provost positions and 36 percent of deanships (King & Gomez, 2008). More typically, women leaders are in positions least likely targeted for provosts and presidents. For example, 55 percent of chief of staff positions are women, and 57 percent of chief diversity officers are women (King & Gomez, 2008). Clearly, there are fewer female candidates in positions targeted for senior-level hires.

Second, women face "pioneerism" and isolation as they attempt to succeed as faculty members, especially in the fields where they are most underrepresented (e.g., STEM), and also when trying to negotiate the labyrinth of leadership. In their roles as pioneers, women might be the first or only woman to enter a field or to represent women professionally in a certain environment. Research demonstrates increased physiological stress associated with being the only or one of few representing a social group within a setting (Murphy, Steele, & Gross, 2007). When part of an underrepresented group, women often need to demonstrate competence in their respective fields at levels much above the expectations set for their peers (Stanley, 2006). Pioneerism is compounded when a women is also a member of an underrepresented racial or other minority group.

Furthermore, women who are pioneers also often experience isolation. As recently as 2010, the National Research Council's survey on *Gender Differences at Critical Transitions in the Careers of Science, Engineering, and Mathematics Faculty* noted that women faculty were less likely to engage with their colleagues in professional conversations than their male counterparts, although the reasons for this difference are not provided in the survey. Similar findings have been reported among women in various disciplines and of different races and ethnicities (e.g., ACE, 2010). Whatever the reason, an unwillingness or inability to engage colleagues in conversations about their work and/or the lack of access to key social networks reduces the potential for successful career and leadership development (Ibarra & Hunter, 2007; see also Kouzes & Posner, 2002). There has long been a gender gap in access to informal leadership networks (Ibarra, 1997; Ragins, 1998). Research suggests that the development of informal networks, whether similar to or different from those of other groups (e.g., men) offers benefits in terms of leadership development and success (Ibarra, 1997; National Research Council, 2010; Ragins, 1998). Given this challenge, women are often encouraged to be proactive about finding out pertinent information and about identifying mentors who can demystify the promotion and tenure or succession process. In addition, policymakers often recommend that administrators become aware of a lack of access by women to such conversations and to the likelihood that they will experience isolation. This model, however, is not as effective for women who are in top-level administrative positions who may lack peers able to offer mentorship, especially in difficult situations. Women administrators can often be the "first" at their institutions, and they too can experience isolation and the stress and lack of support that entails.

Third, women often face a double bind when entering formal leadership positions. A *double bind* occurs in situations where an individual experiences contradictory demands. For women, society's expectations of being a good leader often conflict with being a good woman and certainly a good mother. Society expects women to be communal, self-sacrificing, and helpful, traits typical of traditional roles and desirable in women; yet these same traits undermine the respect of women in leadership positions, since society often expects leaders to be agentic, assertive, directive, and/or dominant (Eagly & Carli, 2007). As a result, women leaders often face criticism and resistance if they demonstrate this masculine leadership style, but they are also deemed less competent if they enact communal rather than agentic behavior. Conversely, men tend to be rewarded for both communal and agentic behavior (Eagly & Carli, 2007). Therefore, resistance to women leaders is common in part because this double bind violates social expectations for success.

Fourth, the lack of women presidents might be linked to the lower proportions of tenured and tenure-track female faculty members despite high numbers of female undergraduate and graduate students. Women may be reinforced by educational and classroom experiences to behave in a way that discourages leadership behavior (Chliwniak, 1997). Additionally, particularly in male-dominated disciplines, women might not even be taught by a woman faculty member or identify a woman who might serve as a role model during their undergraduate or graduate studies (e.g., Etzkowitz et al., 2000). For this and other reasons, women often do not want to pursue faculty careers or the kind of faculty careers that lead to upper-level leadership positions. There are, for example, more women in nontenure-track and part-time positions than men (King & Gomez, 2008), and more women than men choose to "off-ramp" on their way to tenure. This illustrates the complexity of the leadership labyrinth and the need for multiple efforts on different fronts to encourage women to develop the skills and abilities necessary for leadership and to encourage their interest in pursuing leadership positions and the path via which they are obtained. As pointed out earlier, research suggests that increasing the number of female faculty can lead to increased numbers of women in academic leadership; however, research also suggests the increased numbers of women in academic leadership lead to increased numbers of women faculty.

Fifth, family and personal issues inordinately burden female as opposed to male faculty members. Even though men share increasing burdens for home and family, women tend to carry the majority of the responsibility for home life, including household responsibilities, childcare, and aging parental care (Eagly & Carli, 2007b; see also Kellerman & Rhode, 2007). These demands often occur at the same time that faculty face pressures to achieve tenure, potentially interfering with research and teaching success necessary for promotion and tenure. Because of the challenges that many women faculty face in these areas, women in graduate school often report that they are not attracted to tenure-track positions (Mason, 2009). Those that are may face assumptions that they are less committed to their careers because of competing demands. That being said, many institutions continue to improve the institutional culture to better meet the unique challenges of particular groups such as women by improving parental leave policies, adjusting the tenure clock, and working to change assumptions that commitment can be evaluated on the basis of physical presence rather than work products.

A final challenge is a lack of leadership training at all levels of higher education. In the same way that many faculty often do not receive formal pedagogical training as graduate students or early career faculty, many also do not become trained formally for leadership positions (Cox, Cekic, & Adams, 2010). This compounds lack of access to key line positions that provide opportunities for experiential learning, experience, and the social networks important and often necessary for leadership development and promotion. Without such training, faculty may not be selected to serve in leadership positions, or they may not gain access to the relational connections that smooth the career transitions. Plus, with an absence of leadership training, sensitivity to gender issues and deliberate efforts to encourage and to include women in higher education leadership may be missing.

All of these challenges present means of postponing, diverting, complicating, or even ending women's paths through the labyrinth toward leadership in higher education. They highlight the myriad of concerns necessary to develop inclusive leadership in the higher education environment. Although each of these challenges is presented individually, they interact and intersect, forming a complex labyrinth that limits opportunities for women to develop or contribute their leadership capacity in formal positions of authority.

Women at Purdue University

In the last five years, women and minority men have constituted more than half of new faculty hires at Purdue University (Purdue University, 2008a), the result of concerted efforts on the part of university leadership to pursue the inclusive vision laid out in Purdue's recent strategic plans. In fact, a primary goal of the current strategic plan is to create:

> learner-centered, inspiring, and nurturing educational communities marked by human and intellectual diversity, and the promotion of a dynamic culture of equity and inclusion for all people, in a pervasively supportive climate that fosters excellence of students, faculty, and staff. (Purdue University, 2008b, p. 4)

As noted earlier (Sypher & Pope, 2009), Purdue engaged in various converging efforts to encourage and develop an inclusive talent pool, including preparing women and members of other underrepresented groups to engage in formal leadership positions. "Although Purdue has long led the nation and the world in scientific discoveries that are changing lives and solving human problems, we also aspire to be a leader among our peers in terms of inclusive leadership" (Sypher & Pope, 2009, para. 1).

As of 2007, women held a minority of all formal leadership roles, including 12 percent of department heads and 42 percent of deanships, despite representing 42 percent of undergraduate students, 38 percent of graduate students, 31 percent of faculty, and 58 percent of staff (Purdue University, 2008b). Even though women held 43 percent of professional staff positions, which include program, center, and project directors, as well as nonacademic directors and vice presidents, only a few held top leadership roles in their respective units (Purdue University, 2008b).

To increase the numbers of women in leadership positions, we must make institutional changes, including but not limited to providing opportunities for women to develop their individual leadership capacity. Social networks may help develop leadership capacity, opportunity, and confidence. They can provide social support and informational resources that help navigate the leadership labyrinth or negotiate the double bind women experience. Social networks and the alliances they can create also can provide emotional support by creating a community to combat the effects of isolationism and pioneerism. They also can provide instrumental support by giving women access to resources and expertise that helps leaders solve particular problems and make informed decisions. Connecting with other women as peers and mentors can help women better realize formal and informal opportunities to develop as leaders, pursue other leadership positions, and be effective at the leadership positions they occupy. These possibilities are what led Purdue University to create Purdue Women Lead, an alliance of women leaders who participate in educational workshops, research-focused "brown bag" events, expert-led seminars, and opportunities to build alliances with other women campus leaders.

Campus Women Lead

Given the current economic challenges and competition for the best students and faculty, colleges and universities need competent, qualified leadership more than ever. Strategic efforts to increase the representation of women in upper-level administration should support existing as well as future leaders in an effort to expand the pool of targeted recruits for twenty-first-century leadership challenges. Purdue University is working to contribute such a pool. With a generous gift from a committed alumna who had a successful career as a pioneer in her own field, Purdue created the Susan Bulkeley Butler Center for Leadership Excellence. The mission of the center is to enhance collaborations and build alliances that benefit women leaders.

For its inaugural event in 2008, the Butler Center, in partnership with the Women's Resource Office, sponsored the American Association of College and Universities' *Campus Women Lead* program. Emerging out of the work by a group of veteran administrators and faculty members who participated in the National Initiative for Women in Higher Education, Campus Women

Lead seeks to help women individually, collectively, and strategically develop inclusive leadership in institutions of higher education. The program promotes "a women-led agenda for the sustained transformation of higher education for the twenty-first century" (http://www.aacu.org/campuswomen lead/).

Purdue's Campus Women Lead program was a two-day workshop facilitated by Dr. Gertrude Fraiser and Dr. Kathy Wong, who hold tenured positions at the University of Virginia and the University of Western Michigan, respectively. The goal of the workshop was to help participants understand how to increase their spheres of influence by building alliances and understanding their own and others' perspectives, values, and intentions. We invited sixty participants to share and prioritize key intervention areas and possible solutions. Faculty leaders participated on the first day and staff leaders attended the second day. For subsequent activities, faculty and staff leaders were invited to participate together, knowing that some events may be of greater interest to one group or the other. For example, faculty concerns often center on how to balance administrative opportunities with the research and teaching that brought them to the academy. Staff members appear more concerned with promotion opportunities within their sometimes limited spheres of influence. Both groups, however, share concerns about work/life balance, isolation, support, and leadership opportunities. Over the course of the two days, we came to see that each group, while working in different day-to-day environments, faced comparable challenges regardless of where on campus they worked. Moreover, each group had informational resources and expertise necessary for the other to succeed at the same university. As noted in an earlier assessment of the event:

> In those two days, we knew we had created something special. We thought we had successfully selected participants when sixty campus women leaders quickly acknowledged their invitations. But we knew we had filled an unmet need when nearly every person arrived at 8 a.m., after travelling through knee-deep snow and blizzard winds, to take part in a program none had ever heard of. With BlackBerries in hand and cell phones buzzing, some participants said they could stay only for the morning. By the end of the day, almost all attendees remained in the room. Inspired by insightful and sensitive conversations ... participants

committed to continuing the work they had started after the workshop's end. (Sypher & Pope, 2009, para. 11)

The discussions over these two days revealed that participants wanted to "work together more," to learn "how to move from ideas to action" with "more knowledge about leadership." They wanted "more opportunities for 'how to' " and welcomed the opportunity to interact with other women knowing that "they weren't alone." The Butler Center provided a platform for launching a collective effort to promote alliances that support women's talent for and interest in leadership opportunities.

From Campus Women Lead to Purdue Women Lead

With Campus Women Lead, the various Purdue offices came together to leverage their resources and respective expertise, increase the potential impact of the program, and better realize their shared goals of promoting educational opportunities for women. Consistent with the charge from Campus Women Lead to view the workshop as the start of an ongoing process rather than a one-off event, the outcome of these collective efforts was the creation of *Purdue Women Lead*, an alliance to create a leadership community where women could learn from one another and grow. The Butler Center and the Women's Resource Office launched *Purdue Women Lead* to provide support to women in formal leadership positions at Purdue, targeting women at the director level and above for its initial efforts. The goal is to encourage women leaders to build alliances, develop spheres of influence, and better understand the institutional landscape.

In its first year, we structured Purdue Women Lead activities in direct response to issues participants shared in our initial two-day gathering. They expressed an interest in having a "time to connect with other women on campus," have "open and honest discussions," "share similar experiences," and "build alliances." The opportunity "to interact with other professional women" offered sufficient motivation for many to continue to attend subsequent events, to invite others to join, and to suggest the kind of activities that would interest them. They wanted to further develop themselves as leaders, have more "best practices time," and learn "specific strategies" to balance the rewards and challenges at work and home. In response to this feedback, we offered monthly workshops, seminars, keynote speakers, webinars, and faculty research presentations on a range of topics.

For example, in the late spring and fall of 2008, luncheons gave participants the opportunity build networks and learn from women researchers on Purdue's campus. Topics included *Adult Child and Parent Relationships, Civility in the Workplace*, and *Work–Life Balance*. In the spring of 2009, Purdue Women Lead hosted a webinar series on women and leadership led by Purdue alum Rebecca Shambaugh, president and CEO of SHAMBAUGH Leadership. These webinars were free to participants who came during lunch to discuss such topics such as building networks, communication skills, conflict resolution, and change management.

In the summer of 2009, a focus group of women participants helped plan Purdue Women Lead projects for the subsequent academic year. Also, women who had not been invited to the initial Purdue Women Lead program expressed interest in participating as news of the events spread. These women also offered suggestions to help set our direction for future programming. The most common theme in suggestions from both groups was an opportunity to meet with other women leaders in more informal settings. Developed in response to this desire, a reception was held at the home of the Butler Center Director at the beginning of the new academic year. It drew the largest number of Purdue women leaders of any event to date. Attendees were delighted to have the opportunity for an informal gathering to meet and talk with other women leaders about topics ranging from professional to personal. The event gave women from different areas and levels of the university the chance to converse and build connections rarely found in the confines of their daily routines. Perhaps one of the longest-lasting imprints of this event, consistent with responses to Campus Women Lead and many other PWL events, is that participants now have a greater network of peers to rely on, whether it be for advice, support, or to get something instrumental accomplished in their work.

From the initial sixty women at the Campus Women Lead workshop, we invited an additional sixty women, most of whom were invited by other participants or heard about it via word of mouth. This doubled our initial participant numbers in just one year, with numerous women continuing to express interest in developing their leadership capacity through educational and relational events.

Reflecting on Lessons Learned

Purdue Women Lead is a work in progress. With much qualitative evidence to demonstrate its short-term success, additional assessments and time will reveal how successful the program is in developing and supporting women leaders. Entering the third year of the program, key emphases involve addressing the growing the number of participants, developing activities of interest and advantage, and assessing the benefits of the program and what can and should be done to further strengthen it. The growing interest in Purdue Women Lead from groups both inside and outside of Purdue suggests its potential benefits are heightening the awareness and recognition of women leaders and meeting their needs for growth and development and connection with other women in similar positions. For those interested in developing inclusive leadership programs, we have found the following benefits of Purdue Women Lead that might have transferability to other similar programs.

Providing the Opportunity to Form Connections

Women who are leading or interested in leading want to connect with others because they realize the importance of building relationships that matter. In describing what they gained or learned as a result of participating in Purdue Women Lead, many of the participants talked about cultivating new relationships, expanding their networks, and recognizing that "I am not alone." The most common theme from the first two-day event in 2008 was excitement about simply being in the same room with other women leaders on our campus. Due to Purdue's size and diversity, our women leaders tend to be organizationally and geographically dispersed; their locations and responsibilities are arranged in such a way that provides little opportunity to meet face-to-face. Moreover, so much of our work is done electronically. We often know someone only from e-mail. Providing leaders with networks often allows for greater success because they get to know people who can provide informational resources and social support necessary for problem solving, reality checks, and mentorship. Purdue Women Lead has created a context in which smart, creative, interesting women can connect with others. One unique component of Purdue Women Lead is that these networks are institution specific. Most leadership programs for women focus on leadership more generally.

While Purdue Women Lead includes discussions of general leadership issues, it also engages the particular context of Purdue to make leadership development more accessible and applicable to the everyday world of Purdue women leaders.

Know Who You're Not

When we first solicited input on the scope and focus for Purdue Women Lead, some women suggested that Purdue Women Lead should be an on-campus women's lobbying group. However, others resisted and felt this function might dilute the group's initial mission. The decision was made to keep the focus on education and alliance building to help leaders succeed. While the group would not shy away from raising concern about women's issues, we found success in narrowing our focus at least initially on a particular audience with particular educational and social support needs.

Greater Inclusion and Targeted Specialization

Women need leadership development opportunities at all stages of work life, not just when one reaches or is within reach of particular job titles or roles. To enable a strategy of long-term inclusive leadership success, we need to develop leadership capacity in women at all levels, from the undergraduate student to the university president, in order to ultimately increase women's representation and success in leadership positions. When we launched Purdue Women Lead, we intentionally selected those women in current leadership roles to participate, in part because their own stories told us they needed this program to improve their work environment. In truth, it was also because we needed to start somewhere, and inviting women at the director level and above was a manageable way to kick off the program. However, since the time of our first event in 2008, our numbers have grown because women across the university have asked to participate or PWL members have invited other women in their departments to join our events.

Even as more women participate, we also recognize the need to allow women in similar roles to network and peer mentor each other, which is what led us to launch our newest program for women department heads. Women department heads are a small minority and while several have been in place for several years, others are brand new to their roles, and until now there has never been a venue for them to get together. Gathering all the women department heads for lunch once a semester, we provided these women with an opportunity to ask questions of each other, discuss best practices, and explore common challenges and problem-solving strategies.

Managing Growth and Sustaining Legitimacy

As with any program, there are continuing challenges to be addressed and met. Two key issues are (a) managing growth and (b) sustaining legitimacy. First, what happens if we continue to be successful? Although the growth of Purdue Women Lead is an optimistic sign, we also recognize the issues inherent in supporting an ever-growing participant pool. First, we must allow for those women at certain levels to have access to their peers with opportunities to discuss issues of concern with some level of confidentiality. The women's department head lunches are such an initiative. However, we must also allow women in mid-level leadership roles to have access to top administrators and each other to develop mentoring networks even while recognizing the already demanding lives of women in top leadership positions. The demands to meet the needs of specific groups at specific times in their careers call into question whether we can continually adjust and design our programs to meet the needs of a diverse participant pool or whether we should stay small and focused and work with women leaders already in position.

Second, how do we sustain the legitimacy of Purdue Women Lead in order to achieve our goal of inclusive leadership? Improving and enhancing assessment protocols to incorporate a longitudinal review of the tangible and intangible benefits of program participation is necessary. Moreover, are we doing what we need to be doing to achieve this goal? The initial answer is "no." To date, we have focused on developing the leadership already in place. Will these programs help other women decide to take on leadership positions? The answer is not clear. In five years' time, will we see any increase in the number of women leaders at the director's level and above? Will we learn that women who do step from faculty or staff roles to administrative positions feel more confident in their abilities? Will we see more women leading from within, regardless of their formal roles on campus? These are the questions we must begin to apply to our work now to better assess Purdue Women Lead in the years to come. Although increasing the number of underrepresented leaders is one goal, measuring the confidence, skills, and success of those already in leadership positions is another. Continuing to refine our mission and goals and assess the degree to which they are met will be critical to the long-term legitimacy of the program.

Conclusion

Looking at numbers and statistics tells us part of the story about women's leadership in higher education. While the number of women receiving PhDs has increased, this does not directly correlate to an increase in women leaders throughout higher education. The labyrinth that women must navigate from graduate student to university president and everywhere in between is built both through institutional climate and culture as well as more individual-level concerns about work life environment and access to social networks and leadership support. One way to help manage the challenges facing those working through the leadership labyrinth is to offer programs that provide support and access to social networks that offer opportunities to grow and learn. Purdue Women Lead is one program addressing these issues locally; Campus Women Lead is one of the array of national programs engaged in the same work.

As mentioned earlier, we need more institutional models serving a broader range of employees across the spectrum of their career. Men must also be included in discussions to enlist them as change agents and supportive mentors who can promote women's leadership and help women leaders succeed. Furthermore, special consideration must be given to intersections of gender and race, as well as other identities, to determine the best ways to assist women of color, women of diverse religious backgrounds, and all women in navigating and simplifying the leadership labyrinth. The solutions are many and in some ways unique to the institutions. What is certain is programs such as those described here must flourish to increase the potential for more women leaders and more success in their leadership opportunities.

References

American Council on Education. (1986). *The American college president.* Washington, DC: American Council on Education.

American Council on Education. (1996). *The American college president.* Washington, DC: American Council on Education.

American Council on Education. (2007). *The American college president: 2007 Edition.* Washington, DC: American Council on Education.

American Council on Education. (2010). *Gender equity in higher education: 2010.* Washington, DC: American Council on Education.

Birnbaum, R., & Umbach, P. (2001). Scholar, steward, spanner, stranger: The four career paths of college presidents. *Review of Higher Education, 24*(3), 203–18.

Buzzanell, P. M. (1995). Reframing the glass ceiling as a socially constructed process: Implications for understanding and change. *Communication Monographs, 62,* 327–54.

Chliwniak, L. (1997). Higher education leadership: Analyzing the gender gap. *ASHE-ERIC Higher Education Report, 25*(4). Washington, DC: George Washington University.

Ciulla, J. B. (2000). *The working life: The promise and betrayal of modern work.* New York: Random House.

Committee on Science, Engineering, and Public Policy. (2007). *Rising above the gathering storm: Energizing and employing America for a brighter economic future.* Washington, DC: National Academy Press.

Cox, M. F., Cekic, O., & Adams, S. G., (2010). Developing leadership skills of undergraduate engineering students: Perspectives from engineering faculty. *Journal of STEM Education, 11,* 22–33.

Eagly, A. H., & Carli, L. L. (2007a). Women and the labyrinth of leadership. *Harvard Business Review, 85*(9), 63–71.

Eagly, A., & Carli, L. (2007b). *Through the labyrinth: The truth about how women become leaders.* Boston: Harvard Business Press.

Ehrenberg, R. G., Jakubson, G., Martin, M. I., Main, J. & Eisenberg, T. (2009). *Do trustees and administrators matter? Diversifying the faculty across gender lines.* IZA Discussion Paper No. 4664. Available at SSRN: http://ssrn.com/abstract=1530668.

Etzkowitz, H., Kemelgor, C., & Uzzi, B. (2000). *Athena unbound: The advancement of women in science and technology.* Cambridge, UK: Cambridge University Press.

Hartley III, H. V., & Godin, E. E. (2010). *A study of chief academic officers of independent colleges and universities: Who are they? Where do they come from? What are they doing? Where do they want to go?* Washington, DC: Council of Independent Colleges.

Ibarra, H. (1997). Paving an alternative route: Gender differences in managerial networks. *Social Psychology Quarterly, 60,* 91–102.

Ibarra, H. & Hunter, M. (2007, January). How leaders create and use networks. *Harvard Business Review,* 40–47.

King, J., & Gomez, G. G. (2008). *On the pathway to the presidency: Characteristics of higher education's senior leadership.* Washington, DC: American Council on Education.

Kouzes, J. M., & Posner, B. Z. (2002). *The leadership challenge* (3rd ed.). San Francisco: Jossey-Bass.

Kellerman, B., & Rhode, D. (Eds.). (2007). *Women and leadership: The state of play and strategies for change.* San Francisco: Jossey-Bass.

Mason, M. A. (2009). A bad reputation. *Chronicle of Higher Education, 55*(22). Retrieved July 10, 2010, from http://chronicle.com/article/A-Bad-Reputation/44843/.

Murphy, M. C., Steele, C. M., & Gross, J. J. (2007). Signaling threat. How situational cues affect women in math, science, and engineering settings. *Psychological Science, 18,* 879–85.

National Research Council. (2010). *Gender differences at critical transitions in the careers of science, engineering, and mathematics faculty.* Washington, DC: National Academies Press. Retrieved July 10, 2010, from http://books.nap.edu/openbook.php?record_id=12062&page=R1.

Purdue University. (2008a). *Purdue data digest 2007–2008.* Retrieved July 10, 2010, from http://www.purdue.edu/datadigest/archive.html.

Purdue University. (2008b). *2008–2014 New synergies: Purdue University's strategic plan.* Retrieved July 10, 2010, from http://www.purdue.edu/strategic_plan/documents/StrategicPlanBrochure.pdf.

Ragins, B. (1998). Gender gap in the executive suite: Ceos and female executives report on breaking the glass ceiling. *The Academy of Management Executive (1993–2005), 12*(1), 28–42.

Rhode, D. L., & Kellerman, B. (2007). Women and leadership: The state of play. In B. Kellerman & D. L. Rhode (Eds.), *Women and leadership: The state of play and strategies for change.* San Francisco, CA: Jossey-Bass.

Ryan, J. (2006). Inclusive leadership and social justice for schools. *Leadership and Policy in Schools, 5*(1), 3–17.

Stanley, C. A. (2006). *Faculty of color: Teaching in predominately white colleges and universities.* Bolton, MA: Anker.

Sypher, B. D., & Berkelaar, B. (2010, April). *An examination of the pathways to academic administration: Academic disciplines, prior positions and time in position for nationally ranked and CIC provosts and presidents.* Research report presented at the Committee on Institutional Cooperation Academic Leadership Program, Seminar III at Purdue University. West Lafayette, IN.

Sypher, B. D., & Pope, K. (2009). From Campus Women Lead to Purdue Women Lead: A new program for inclusive leadership. *On campus with women, 38*(1). Retrieved July 2, 2010 from http://www.aacu.org/ocww/volume38_1/feature.cfm?section=2.

Touchton, J., Musil, C., & Campbell, K. (2008). *A measure of equity: Women's progress in higher education.* Washington, DC: Association of American Colleges and Universities.

West, M., & Curtis, J. (2006). AAUP faculty gender equity indicators 2006. *American Association of University Professors.* Retrieved July 2, 2010, from http://www.aaup.org/NR/rdonlyres/63396944-44BE-4ABA-9815-5792D93856F1/0/AAUPGenderEquityIndicators2006.pdf.

11

Relationship Building and Higher Education Women: Stories and Observations

Penelope M. Earley, Jane H. Applegate, and Jill M. Tarule

In two earlier works (Applegate, Earley, & Tarule, 2009; Tarule, Applegate, Earley, & Blackwell, 2009), we explored aspects of gendered leadership, using narrative analysis to identify and describe themes that characterize women leaders. The first study of women higher education leaders identified several themes: the importance of proximate and nonproximate support networks; the power in being marginalized; the intersection of personal and professional lives; and the ability to nurture power (Tarule et al., 2009). A second study (Applegate et al., 2009) further documented challenges for women in education, including experiences of both K–12 leaders and emerging leaders in postsecondary education. From these narratives a new theme—visibility—emerged. That is, in some instances, women were made to feel invisible, whereas in others they chose to use invisibility as a leadership tool. A related and disturbing theme was the consequence of surplus visibility (Patal, 1992, in Applegate, Earley, & Tarule, 2009). Surplus visibility occurs when a woman is elevated into a role held previously by a man and perhaps because of the newness of the situation, every detail of the woman's life and decision making receives extraordinary, and often negative, scrutiny. We note media attention to women presidential and vice presidential candidates as examples of surplus visibility.

Continuing our inquiry on women as leaders, in the current study we turn to how women leaders build and sustain relationships. Women often are identified as concerned with relationships and many works on leadership—both how-to books and empirical studies—suggest relationship building is essential for a successful leader (see, for example, Fullen, 2001; Gardner, 2007; Hanh, 2007; Kellerman & Rhode, 2007; and Wheatley, 2006). Despite work that differentiates female and male leadership styles, we find little in the literature that describes the ways in which relationship building is reflected in the actions of senior women leaders. The works of Eagly and Johannesen-Schmidt (2001), Eagly, Johannesen-Schmidt, and van Engen (2003), and Eagly (2007) have been useful in framing our thinking about the need to study and develop relationship theories pertaining to women leaders. Eagly and colleagues suggest women's leadership is often described in communal terms: concern with the needs of others, nurturing, sympathetic, and the like; whereas male leaders are seen as agentic: forceful, independent, daring, self-confident, and assertive (Eagly & Johannesen-Schmidt, 2001, p. 782). Drawing on the political science and organizational theory literature, these two authors identify three leadership categories: transformational, transactional, and laissez-faire. Eagly et al. (2003) explored these three categories in further detail using a meta-analysis and determined that women were more likely to exhibit characteristics of transformational leaders. These include willingness to consider new perspectives and problem-solving strategies, a focus on mentoring, and attention to individual needs.

Eddy (2009) directly addresses gender differences in leaders' relationship building, suggesting that, "Men realize the value of relationship building, traditionally a female characteristic, but have the advantage of still being seen as [a hero leader] at the same time" (p. 24). She continues, "men . . . often used relationships to foster and build on their hero image. . . . women, instead used relationships to foster more of a fit within the institution, with an eye toward the development of community" (p. 24). In essence, one can argue that for women, relationship building is central to being a successful leader, whereas for men, it is a tool to achieve personal or organizational goals (p. 25).

Even though the capacity to build and maintain good relationships in the workplace can be viewed as critical for transformational and other leaders, it still is not uncommon for a woman leader to be accused of being too concerned about how others are reacting to her leadership, too concerned with being liked, and not adhering to the classic advice given to new leaders, "If you want to be loved, get a dog." Women leaders have been identified as having a style that is "more democratic and participative, compared with men's more autocratic and directive styles" (Carli & Eagly, 2007, p. 139). It is acknowledged that democratic, participatory processes require establishing good workplace relationships, but the question of interest to us is how women leaders approach this task.

For this study we invited five senior women higher education leaders, including current or former university deans, provosts, vice presidents, or presidents, to provide a description of a critical event in their work in which the process of building relationships was a significant factor. As Carter (1993) observes, narratives and the analyses of them are both objects of inquiry and a method to study them. Narrative inquiry, as described by Marshall and Rossman (2006) " . . . assumes that people construct their realities through narrating their stories." (p. 117). The addition of our own narrative inquiry analyses of these stories adds interpretive depth that holds promise as a contribution to an expansion of gendered leadership theory. To that end, we three authors analyzed each of the stories. We then pooled our individual findings and through a process of consensus identified themes that illuminate relational leadership.

We begin with a summary of the five critical incident vignettes. We note that when invited to describe an event, each woman observed that the difficult part of the task was deciding which event of many to describe. One vignette, Diane's, recounts how a woman used relationship building to neutralize a negative member of a university task force. The others, Madeline, Polly, Rosalind, and Susan, recount events involving their roles as leaders. Three of these women describe leadership challenges when they moved to a new university as a senior administrator. Two informants, Susan and Polly, struggled to lead from a deficit position, that is, a more senior leader at their university either did not support their efforts or, in the case of Susan, challenged and undermined her.

Five Women's Stories

Diane's Story: The Minority Report

Diane is a former administrator and now a member of the faculty at a large public institution. She was invited by the provost to be part of a five-person task force to gather information from each academic unit for the university's new strategic plan. Each task force member was a senior member of the faculty who had served in one or more administrative roles. Two were women, three were men. The task force was charged to design a system to gather information from across the campus, to analyze the data, and to create a synthesis for the president to include in her report to the Board of Regents.

At the first task force meeting, one of the members, Bob, said he would ask a few of his campus colleagues their opinion on the new strategic plan and further suggested that because he would contact people he knew, he could get the information and write the final report in a few days. Diane felt that gathering input from a broader group of faculty and administrators would better reflect the pulse of the faculty and help build a sense of community on campus. Bob was adamant that his approach was best and continued to remind everyone that given his thirty years at the university, he had a better sense of history than anyone else in the group.

Both Bob's and Diane's proposed approaches were submitted to the provost, who indicated he wanted input from the entire campus, not just part of it. Bob was irritated and argued that the task force members should resign in protest. His attitude bothered the other four members. At that point Diane redirected the conversation away from who supported which approach to a discussion of the expertise that each task force member brought to the assignment. Through her quiet, professional leadership, she was able to reinforce the value of each person. By doing this, she began to build a team and became the de facto leader of the group.

Over the next six months, the task force gathered data. But at every point along the way, Bob publicly or privately criticized the group and its work. As might be expected, four of the five members of the task force developed a sense of ownership in the process that they believed generated excitement about the future of the university across campus. All task force members participated in the writing and editing of the report, but at the end of the day, Bob decided to write a minority opinion. In it he recounted his dissatisfaction with the process and what he perceived as a lack of attention to the history of the institution. The report with the minority opinion went to the provost and from there to the president. Four task force members were disappointed when she submitted the strategic plan to the Board of Regents and only a one-paragraph summary of the task force report was included.

Months later, the president told Diane that she was delighted with the report and the careful way it captured the voices of faculty and administrators. However, she felt it was not politically wise to send the report to the Regents with Bob's minority opinion. Arguably, everyone won and everyone lost. Diane was able to build an energized team to gather the opinions of the faculty and administrators. Her leadership style and sense of enthusiasm were contagious and the faculty were pleased to have their opinions seriously considered. Bob also won. He wanted to derail the work of the task force and, ultimately, he did because the report did not go beyond the president's desk. As a result, the campus lost an opportunity to demonstrate to the Board of Regents that the faculty and staff wanted and could be participatory members of a campuswide effort to enhance the work and reputation of the university.

Madeline's Story: Undermined from Within

Madeline spent six months visiting the campus before she moved to the provost position. Getting to know people in the administration led her to suspect that, initially, her relationship with Charles might be difficult. Charles, she learned, had been an internal candidate for her position and had served as interim provost for the past year. Knowing from her own experiences that her arrival might be difficult for him, Madeline scheduled a meeting to clear the air. Since he now had to report to her, she thought it might help for the two of them to acknowledge, together, that this kind of transition of power may be hard and troubling. She went on to express her hope that they would have a good working relationship and knew that she would need his knowledge and institutional history. Charles was curt, asserted that everything was fine, and cut the conversation short. Madeline was surprised by his response, but she chose to believe that, indeed, everything would be fine.

But things were not fine. There were too many incidents when his apparent hostility toward her made learning the new job harder. Charles would not respond to her requests for information or when he did, he provided only partial information that did not include sufficient detail for her to understand the issue fully or to make a reasoned decision based on evidence. In addition, he would sometimes launch into what felt like a lecture to her about how she should act.

At one public meeting with other university administrators, Charles responded to a question Madeline asked with a long and, for her, irrelevant lecture, implying she did not know what she was talking about. Later, some of the other administrators shared that they were uncomfortable with the content and tone of his actions. It seemed that Charles's challenges, and possibly some outright sabotaging of her efforts, were increasing. She worried that she would not be able to construct the collegial professional relationship the two of them needed to advance the goals of the university. She also recognized that as the new leader, she needed positive working relationships with everyone who reported to her and knew that Charles's actions were not invisible to them.

Meanwhile, Madeline assessed the administrative organizational structure and decided that it needed to change to accomplish what she envisioned for the university. The change would impact current positions, including Charles's. Madeline felt that she needed to tell Charles about her vision and to forewarn him that when reorganization occurred, his position would be affected. She also realized that there could be a new role for Charles as a senior member of the administrative team. Madeline chose to address this change in her regularly scheduled meeting with Charles to convey that this was not to address their difficulties but rather to address her developing vision for the university. Upon hearing her ideas, Charles did not want to discuss his position at all. Instead, he critiqued her proposed structure and for the next few weeks repeatedly tried to show her how it would not work. Madeline noted his ability to once again sidestep engaging with her by dismissing her and her ideas. His behavior immobilized her for a few days as she tried to figure out if there was a way to mend this relationship. Increasingly it seemed that she was going to have to terminate him and sought advice from an attorney. A week later, in an unscheduled meeting, Charles acknowledged that he knew that sometimes he could be difficult. Albeit brief, the conversation represented for Madeline the beginning shreds of the dialogue she felt was needed for them to move forward and to work together effectively.

Polly's Story: A Politician's Ward

Having been a dean and vice president for academic affairs at SCC, a state university, Polly interviewed for new jobs with confidence. Her SCC experience had been a success. One of her proudest accomplishments was the collaboration she created among the vice president and the deans, which was particularly effective in budget planning and resource allocation. Her effectiveness was captured by one professor who told her, "You have the whole place thinking in new ways."

Polly was delighted to be invited to interview at PNS, an urban campus, whose recently departed president had led the university to national and local prominence. As she was considering the position, a university president told her, "It's the most interesting provost's position in the country." But her idealized view of the campus was challenged in the first interview she had with the deans and the president's executive council. It was the most unruly group she had dealt with in all her interviews. Two deans quarreled openly about whose faculty was paid the least, while two others tangled with the chair of the search committee over a budget issue. Fielding increasingly hostile questions from the group, she felt she had not been among such a group of unruly "boys" since teaching a high school social studies class, many years earlier.

Despite doubts, she took the job. Immediately, she was visited by both faculty and non faculty who had been receiving favors from the previous provost. One group, editors of a regional journal in the discipline of the previous provost, wanted their $70,000 a year budget enhanced. Another visitor, also with personal ties to the former provost, wanted to ensure his yearly $30,000 stipend to facilitate university/community partnerships, although he was unable to tell her what partnerships he facilitated. He did mention that his wife had multiple sclerosis. She reflected on these meetings, "My god, this place is run like some sleazy politician's ward!"

To address the "begging system," she sought to institute a transparent budget process and to build a team with the deans. With a hefty budget surplus that year, and despite the fact that the president had had no budget process the preceding year, he agreed to her request for a universitywide budget process and to stop dealing with budgets requests in an ad hoc manner. The deans were leery, but as a comprehensive budget was developed, they realized that their academic units actually benefited. Other attempts to create a new culture included scheduling regular lunches with each dean and a series of *deans' informals,* monthly gatherings in a club during which there was no agenda and an agreement of confidentiality.

The hard-won, carefully crafted budget process was dropped when cuts became necessary and the campus reverted to the culture of "inside deals and old boys' networks." About this time, Polly met with a campus visitor who reported that a senior dean had said to him, "Here the provost is staff to the president." It captured for her why transparency and collaboration had been so challenging and ultimately unsuccessful.

Rosalind's Story: Closing the Engineering Program

Rosalind described an event when she became provost of a small public comprehensive university in the Midwest. She values shared governance and asserts that building understanding and trust is a daily effort, but once established, those relationships are sturdy enough to be drawn on when there is hard or difficult work to be done. Therefore, academic program planning and similar decisions should be placed in the broader context of developing strong relationships with faculty members and the various faculty bodies.

An early challenge was the future of the underenrolled engineering program. Historically, engineering was seen as a potential niche for the campus, located in a region with significant manufacturing operations. However, this program never developed the strength necessary to sustain it, although community members often commented on the need for more engineers. Working closely with the chair of the academic planning committee, a review was conducted of all academic programs, identifying programs that required additional resources and those that were underutilized. Engineering was at the top of this list.

She recounted a two-year process during which she involved faculty and administrators in the engineering program to consider a variety of options, including what might be done to bolster the program. At the same time, major budget reductions intensified the pressure to discontinue institutional support for small, underenrolled programs. She worked to involve faculty in determining the future of the program. Many difficult issues needed to be resolved. Would there be positions in other university units for engineering faculty if the program were discontinued? How would the university care for students already enrolled in engineering?

Rosalind realized that a senior member of the engineering faculty was angry and defensive about the scrutiny given engineering. She spent carefully planned time to develop a strong working relationship with him, wanting him to understand that his opinion and contribution to the university were respected. Eventually he came to understand that both of them would have liked the situation to be different but that there was no option but to close the program. One difficult issue was to find an appropriate place for the engineering professor to continue his career. Rosalind approached the chair of the physics department, who agreed to invite the engineering professor to join that department. Although initially wary, Rosalind explained that, "He shared with me that he was glad to move to a department where he was so well regarded. And, he thanked me for the respect with which I handled the entire matter."

Reflecting on this experience, Rosalind felt her relationships with individual faculty members, many of whom were seen by their colleagues as leaders, were very important to the final outcome. Allowing time for full discussion in many quarters, an important component of the organizational culture, was certainly a factor, as was creating a context in which all faculty members who were directly impacted by the decision could say that they were treated well, even if they did not support the outcome.

She concludes, "For me, it is the web of relationships that make organizations, and perhaps also their leaders, function. Dealing with people and making decisions in one arena impacts many others, sometimes in ways that cannot be anticipated. It is the relationships that hold everyone together and make it possible to move things forward. And, it is these relationships that keep me coming to work every day."

Susan's Story: Ambushed

Susan is a dean of education and the highest-ranking female administrator on her campus. She described receiving an e-mail calling her to a meeting with the provost and president. The e-mail mentioned that "Given our precarious economic condition, we must be active in looking forward to ways that we can further develop the College and University." She was alarmed not only by the content of the e-mail but also because the president had a history of criticizing members of his administrative team based on anecdotal or flawed information. The meeting was held in a large formal conference room set up so that she was forced to sit in a way that made her feel as if she were on trial.

The president spent over an hour presenting charts that showed declining trend lines and minimal details on how or when figures had been pulled. Susan was not offered any time to present contextual information, nor was there any discussion of how she might work with the president and provost to address the data and subsequent perceptions. She was told not to share the data with others. She left the meeting angry and feeling betrayed. The following day she spoke with the provost to explain her discomfort at the antagonistic rather than collaborative tone of the meeting. Although he acknowledged her concerns, he offered no support.

Susan worked diligently to develop a presentation that answered points missing from the first meeting. Two weeks later, in the same conference room, she presented her data to the same administrators. She tried to check her defensiveness at the door while specifically highlighting the details and contextual information not included in the president's presentation. She concluded with a list of solutions and a draft that defined the evidence of what it would look like if the teacher preparation program retained its moniker of the premier teacher preparation program in the state.

After agreeing upon next steps, Susan began to plan how to immerse the provost front and center in each step and the actions needed to address the president's negative perceptions. She felt that whatever steps were taken to elevate the program in the president's eyes needed to be a joint effort between the provost's office and her own. Susan and the provost co-hosted a luncheon that honored the program's longstanding history and reputation and announced steps that the university would take to support their continued strength as a leading teacher preparation program. Susan continued to involve the provost and to brief him regularly. A year later, Susan had the satisfaction of providing an updated set of data that showed the progress made within twelve months.

Adding Our Perspectives

All of the vignettes prepared for this study were longer in their original form and were summarized for the purpose of this chapter. The summaries above capture essential details of the events and later, in the analysis, we add the voices of these women leaders through the use of quotes from the longer versions of their stories. To preserve confidentiality, the names and identifying circumstances were changed. We believe there are more lessons to be learned from these five rich vignettes than we have space to analyze. With that in mind, we divide our analysis into two parts. The first is a discussion of the role circumstances or context played in each woman's use of relationship building. In the second, we turn to the elements we concluded were consistently important in how these five women viewed, built, and sustained relationships.

Power Plays, Blockers, and Warning Signs

Leadership never is context free. Rosalind observes it is important to build positive, trusting relationships before difficult decisions must be made. But even in ideal circumstances, events may conspire to undermine a leader's success—whether the leader is female or male. We identified three contextual factors within these five stories, individuals who are intent on making power plays, negative forces that blocked, or attempted to block, forward progress, and warning signs that the situation at hand may be more difficult than originally anticipated.

Power Plays and Power Players

Looking at the experiences of Diane and Madeline, each was forced into the position of having to lead and build relationships in an environment in which one individual engaged in power plays, attempting to gain authority and/or to cast himself as a hero, as the person who had the best information, the most extensive knowledge of the university's history, and the organizational skills to do the job. We see in the story of Diane that when Bob was not successful in getting his way, he engaged in a number of behind-the-scenes maneuvers to sabotage the efforts of the task force and ultimately, by writing a minority report, he succeeded in diminishing the report's impact. In the case of Diane, because everyone on the task force was a senior professor, they all had equal power. Thus, when she became the de facto leader, she had the support of three of her colleagues but no administrative tools to sanction Bob's actions.

Madeline, on the other hand, faced open hostility from Charles, a man who was a lower-level administrator than she. His actions " . . . continually challenge[d] [my] decisions and ideas" in public settings, threatening to undermine her work and her new position of authority. Diane was in a situation where the task force would disband in six months; however,

Madeline was in a permanent leadership role. As such, her relationship building needed to be transparent and collaborative because these relationships had to stand the test of time and become part of the culture of the university. As Rosalind observed in her story, "Trust is developed through the course of daily events." Madeline's attempts to build a collaborative culture were undercut by Charles's behavior. Madeline speculated that Charles "was feeling furious at her and vulnerable for having been unable to get the affirmation he was seeking." This description could also apply to Bob, who became increasingly angry when the task force members did not accept his ideas.

Both Madeline and Diane recognized that a confrontation with their nemeses would escalate rather than resolve the situation. Diane was able to simply ignore Bob and work with the remaining members of the task force. Because Charles was a part of her administrative team, Madeline could not avoid him. Instead she offered opportunities for conversation and ultimately there was a breakthrough of sorts. Nevertheless, although she was grateful when Charles acknowledged that he was difficult to work with, she wondered if an improved relationship "would really pan out or if the next time that we had to meet or disagree, the old responses would return and they'd be back in the same dysfunctional place."

Because a university provost or president determines if a dean will stay or be removed, Susan was in a vulnerable position when her president and to some extent the provost behaved as power players—that is, individuals who are in a position of authority and who believe their role entitles them to criticize those administrators below them and do so without an obligation to gather solid information first. Because she was not new to the university, she had " ... spent considerable time attending the president's cabinet and witnessed four occasions when my president formed a negative perception about a woman's leadership capacity and the reputation lasted until the person either left, retired, or was dismissed." Nonetheless, forewarned was not forearmed. Susan could not forestall what she felt was an ambush. Her strategy to deal with a president who tends to act before gathering necessary information was two-fold. She first provided evidence that would correct or at least counter the president's perceptions. She then worked to build a strong working relationship with the provost. Because criticism was leveled both at Susan and at her college, she felt betrayed and very angry. Wisely, in subsequent meetings with the president and provost, she deliberately " . . . checked her defensiveness at the door," realizing that in a contentious situation, the president always would win.

Blockers and Negative Forces

Each of the five women confronted negative forces or blockers. For Susan, Madeline, and Diane, the blockers were humans who used personal power or power tactics in an attempt to challenge their leadership. Polly faced a cultural blocker that enabled deans and others to engage in begging rather than strategic budgeting. The culture was a powerful force that hit her in the first meeting with the deans:

> I had not been among such a group of unruly "boys" since I taught a freshman social studies class in a wealthy suburban high school two decades earlier. The class met following lunch and the 25 boys and six girls were nearly impossible to control. What, I asked myself, explained such behavior?

Rosalind quickly identified her potential blocker, a senior member of the engineering faculty who did not want to see the program closed. By recognizing a blocker, involving him in the discussions about the fate of the program, and " . . . respect[ing] his many contributions to the university," she was able to avoid a situation in which the faculty member might have resorted to power plays. The difference between events as related by Rosalind and by Susan is stark. Rosalind, a provost, described her leadership style as:

> From day one, a high priority for me was forming strong relationships with the faculty, both in groups and as individuals. I have found that shared governance is most effective when understanding and trust is developed through the course of daily events, so that these may be drawn upon when a problem or crisis arises.

The seating arrangements in the room in which Susan's president and provost presented unfavorable information about her college revealed that those administrators did not acknowledge or value relationships. Susan wrote:

The meeting room was set in a very large hollow square and the other three administrators were already seated, one to the right, one to the left, and one straight ahead, all at least 15 feet apart from each other. I assumed a seat on the remaining fourth side of the hollow square closest to the door and mentally reflected on the interrogation style of the meeting arrangement for an agenda that was suppose to focus on solutions. I considered my own leadership style and the way in which I would have set up the meeting format where I could be within arm's reach of the person with whom I was meeting.

As Rosalind asserted, having invested in establishing positive relationships and in community building, when the difficult decision to close the engineering program needed to be executed, she was able to do so without rancor. Reflecting on this event, she wondered:

Could I have forced a decision earlier, and just moved the faculty members involved? Perhaps, but not without damaging relationships with key faculty who were influential in many parts of the university, relationships that were critical in moving other parts of the agenda forward.

Early Warning Signs

Three of the women described events that occurred shortly after moving to a new position. Madeline and Polly struggled to enact change and neutralize blockers. Rosalind faced a failing department and appeared to avoid public rancor on her campus by making relationship building a first and high priority so when the decision was made to close the engineering department, she was able to find new and welcoming assignments for the senior faculty who were displaced.

It is of interest to us that both Polly and Madeline's vignettes describe observing what might be problematic undercurrents at their universities before they were offered a leadership position. Polly wrote, that "My idealized view of the campus was challenged" in her job interview with top administrators:

This was the most unruly group I met in more than 20 interviews I had in the three years I searched for a presidency or vice presidency. The dean of education and the dean of fine arts quarreled openly about whose faculty was paid the least.

Similarly, Madeline introduced her description of her trials working with Charles by admitting that she " . . . suspected in the early visits to the institutions, before [I] had formally taken the job that this was going to be a difficult relationship."

We do not know what all these women thought before they entered their institutions, but why, we wondered, did these two bright, perceptive women decide to take positions that might prove to be particularly difficult? We have a sense of Polly's motivation, who reported seeking advice from colleagues and that "A former university president told me, 'it's the most interesting provost's position in the country.' " Moreover, the former president of the university was credited with bringing national visibility to the institution. Madeline's narrative does not address her decision-making process. However, we speculate that she persisted in attempting to forge a "productive working relationship with Charles" because the total university context persuaded her she could make the position work. Her story concludes with uncertainty amidst a glimmer of hope. Similarly, Polly thought she could change the culture at her university by employing strategies that were successful in her previous job. However, when the university faced budget cuts, her plan for a comprehensive budgeting process ended. She concluded, "The culture of inside deals and the old boys' network combined with a weak president was so strong that once resources declined, the campus reverted back to where they have been."

Institutional culture and context exert powerful forces on building and maintaining relationships. Polly reminds us that sometimes leadership strategies do not transfer from one context to another. The attitudes of Susan's president, Bob, and Charles demonstrate that individuals who enjoy using power plays likely will not be persuaded to change through dialogue alone. Finally, if a leader moves into a position where she suspects there will be significant challenges, developing collaborative relationships may take more time than she expects and opportunities may come in unexpected forms.

Time, Flexibility, Opportunity, and Persistence

In addition to the lessons associated with the environment or context, there are four themes in the stories that emphasize an aspect of how these women went about building effective relationships. Each theme presented below suggests a lesson about what matters and what is critical in creating effective relationships at work.

The Rule of 1,440

There are exactly 1,440 minutes in a day; no more. Building and maintaining relationships take time. Rosalind identified early in her position the need to make wise use of diminishing resources. "Slowly, the dean and I began to connect ongoing conversation to resource allocation. I got to know the department chair quite well [too]. . . . The chair, the dean and I had ongoing conversations regarding the future of the program." After two years of dialogue with all of the affected parties, Rosalind was able to close a program with minimal adverse results and she reflected, "I think that my relationships . . . were very important to the final outcome. Allowing time for full discussion in many quarters, an important component of the organizational culture, was certainly a critical factor."

Madeline was startled by the amount of time it took for her relationship with Charles to begin to show potential for the kind of " . . . relationship she wanted with the person in his role: a collegial professional relationship in which dialogue supported exploration and creativity while also providing data and the institutional history." Instead, she met defensiveness rather than cooperation until she wondered if investing time in relationship building would ever be productive. "A few weeks later she was in his office on a quick errand and got a strong sense that he wanted to talk about something." She again opened the communication door to him and he walked through, initiating the level of communication she had wanted from the beginning. Perhaps he needed time to adjust to a shift in his role and to come to terms with it.

The Strong Tree Bends in the Wind

Recognizing alternative leadership styles and being flexible enough to meet others where they are so problems can be solved is a second element in the search for solid relationships. Clearly, in Susan's case, she was blindsided by the data and the approach taken by her provost. She quickly saw that their styles were different and she knew that if she were to forge a relationship where she could be heard and respected, she would need to meet the provost on his ground using the language (data) that he would understand. Although she " . . . felt [her] blood pressure rise and her defensiveness reach an all-time high," she masked her feelings and began thinking strategically of a way she could shape the enrollment argument differently. She drew on her communication skills, calling the provost and requesting a meeting. She sought support from the institutional research office and she began shaping her message with more detailed data. Finally, she included additional details and contextual information and brought her own list of solutions to the table. Knowing a presentation alone would not be sufficient to counter negative impressions, she " . . . continued to involve the provost in each step of our strategy and to brief him regularly on our progress."

Polly also recognized that to build relationships in her new institution, she would have to think differently about the leadership styles at work on her campus where processes and styles were quite different from those with which she was most comfortable. Seeing her leadership as process oriented rather than product driven, Polly needed to address the budget from two vantage points, that of the institutional president and that of the deans. In presenting her position to her president, she requested a universitywide budget process where there had been none. The deans needed to be convinced that there was more to be gained by working together as a team than by each dean standing on his or her own:

> In addition to building a team around a budget process, I tried various ways to get to know the deans. I had regularly scheduled lunches with individual deans in order to hear what was on their minds. I instituted a series of deans' "informals." We gathered monthly for a glass of wine in one of the city's private clubs. We had no agenda and agreed that what was said in the room, stayed in the room.

There Must be an Opportunity in Here Somewhere

A third element in relationship building is the ability to grasp the unexpected opportunity. In Diane's story we see how a member of a committee can assert a position that created conflict and how Diane's actions made it possible to:

redirect the conversation away from who supported which approach to a discussion of the expertise that each task force member brought to the assignment. Through her quiet, professional leadership she was able to reinforce the value of each person. By doing this she began to build a team and became the de facto leader of the group.

By doing this, Diane created an opportunity for task force members to feel positive about their work and as a result moved forward with their work, ignoring the negative background noise from Bob.

By establishing an academic planning committee, Rosalind created an opportunity for faculty to have input into decisions about the fate of small programs. This was critical to her goal of faculty buy-in and support for her ultimate decision about engineering:

> My approach to this issue was quite general at first. Working closely with the chair of the academic planning committee, we conducted a review of all academic programs, identifying those that required additional resources as well as those that were underutilized. Members of the committee were quite vocal about programs where small numbers of students resulted in light teaching loads. The inequalities for faculty members were a matter for continuing discussion.

As the process moved from the formal review through hours of informal meetings and conversations, she was able to see the opportunity for action. She concludes:

> Dealing with people and making decisions in one arena impact many others, sometimes in ways that cannot be anticipated. It is the relationships that hold everyone together and make it possible to move things forward. And it is these relationships that keep me coming to work every day.

The Little Engine that Could was Right

Relationship building is not a tool to gain advantage nor is it something to do on Tuesday, then check off the list. Good relationships are an investment that, as we observed in Rosalind's story, will yield results during difficult times. Like the train in the children's story, *The Little Engine that*

Could, had to keep moving to make it up the mountain, relationship building and maintaining cannot stop but must be integral to the professional life of a successful leader.

Rosalind defines relationships as central to why she wants to remain a provost. "I am," she asserts, "far more interested in building relationships inside an organization and making things change as a result of a shared understanding of the need to move in a particular direction." Leaders who value building and maintaining relationships will be persistent in their efforts to build strong alliances that promote working together toward a shared vision, a common goal. Belenky, Bond, and Weinstock (1997) draw on the literature on black women's leadership to identify skills needed for the development of people and communities. Calling it a "tradition that has no name," these leaders "ask good questions and draw out people's thinking. They listen with care. To better understand what they are hearing they try to step into the people's shoes. . . . [T]hen they look for ways to mirror what they have seen, giving people a chance to take a new look at themselves." (p. 14).

Diane's ability to integrate Bob's dissenting voice ameliorated conflict so that the team could begin to form and to work on the task at hand. Rosalind explained it is critical to create "an environment where each of the faculty members who were directly impacted by the decision could say they were treated well, even if they did not support the outcome." Being treated well, feeling heard, feeling valued—all contribute to the development of sustained working relationships and to the capacity for all to be able to negotiate issues and conflict toward achieving better decisions. When leaders create and nurture these relationships, each member of the team will have an attitude that, "I think I can."

Creating these positive, lasting relationships and outcomes often relies on developing a dialogue. Madeline seeks to establish the dialogue with her colleague Charles by first having a clearing-the-air conversation, albeit ineffective. Diane leads her group to focus on gathering information from across the campus, which allows their work to move forward, whereas Susan asserts the importance of the quality of the dialogue in relationships when she describes how she approaches a challenging meeting: "I frequently review related information prior to a discussion and try to anticipate what else should be shared or whose perspective is missing from the dialogue." Rosalind reflects that "allowing time for full discussion in many quarters" was critical in the process of closing a program while sustaining good relationships with and among those affected. Polly engaged the deans in an extended discussion about how the budget process should and could work and notes that as time went on, the dialogue among herself and the deans "finally got to the point where we could discuss . . . differing views." Both Diane and Polly teach us that dialogue is hardly always easy or without conflict. But by finding ways to maintain the relationships through thick and thin, their approach to leadership engages others in a way that is markedly different from engagement in a command-and-control, authoritarian environment.

But creating and allowing a multifaceted dialogue toward building sustained relationships and groups also takes time. Polly invested evening time as a way to create dialogue toward sustained relationships with the deans, inviting them to gather off campus with an agreement that there was no agenda and "what was said in the room, stayed in the room." Although she felt their conversations progressed, she noted that this group seemed to never relax together as a group, that they "never let their hair down and joked" as another group she had worked with had been able to. For these five women leaders, a critical aspect of their leadership was being persistent about creating and facilitating healthy, sustained relationships.

Some Final Observations

In closing, what are the lessons from these five leaders about how to cope with the contextual forces and processes for creating, maintaining, and sustaining lasting relationships? First, institutional culture and context exert powerful forces on building and maintaining any relationship in higher education. Although contexts vary, women must be aware and mindful of institutional history and how that history becomes interpreted. Second, recognizing power and all of its facets is critical for a woman leader, and relationship building has to account for elements of power. Whether the relationship is with a person in a higher position of power, with a colleague of equal stature, or with a person who reports to the leader, elements of position, politics, and persuasion must be considered if barriers are to be overcome. Third, all work environments have challenging relational dynamics. Whether they are apparent in taking on a new role or whether they are discovered along the way, we need relationship-building strategies to help us negotiate the minefields that exist in higher education and elsewhere. Finally, having good communication skills, taking time to listen, and being patient and flexible all are attributes we observed in these women leaders. As we learned from Polly, who successfully built relationships in one institution, the same strategy had a different result in another one. Susan has begun a multiyear effort to change the perceptions of her president and Madeline believes there may be an opportunity to build a positive working relationship with Charles. But their stories are unfinished and, optimistically, we believe they will succeed. Yet, pragmatically, we recognize it may not be so.

References

Applegate, J., Earley, P., & Tarule, J. (2009). Support for women leaders: The visible and the invisible. In C. Mullen (Ed.), *The handbook of leadership and professional learning communities* (pp. 151–60). New York: Palgrave.

Belenky, M., Bond, L., & Weinstock, J. (1997). *The tradition that has no name: Nurturing the development of people, families and communities.* New York: Basic.

Carli, L., & Eagly, A. (2007). Overcoming resistance to women leaders: The importance of leadership style. In B. Kellerman & D. L. Rhode (Eds.), *Women and leadership: The state of play and strategies for change* (pp. 127–48). New York: Wiley.

Carter, K. (1993, February). The place of story in the study of teaching and teacher education. *Educational Researcher, 22*(1), 5–12.

Eagly, A. (2007). Theoretical rationale for sex differences and similarities in leadership style. *Psychology of Women Quarterly, 31*, 1–12.

Eagly, A., & Johannesen-Schmidt, M. (2001). The leadership styles of women and men. *Journal of Social Issues, 57*(1), 781–97.

Eagly, A., Johannesen-Schmidt, M., & van Engen, M. (2003). Transformational, transactional, and laissez-faire leadership styles: A meta-analysis comparing women and men. *Psychological Bulletin, 129*(4), 569–91.

Eddy, P. (2009). Leading gracefully: Gendered leadership in community colleges. In D. Dean, S. Bracken, & J. Allen (Eds.), *Women in academic leadership: Professional strategies, personal choices* (pp. 8–30). Sterling, VA: Stylus.

Fullen, M. (2001). *Leading in a culture of change*. San Francisco: Jossey-Bass.

Gardner, H. (2007). *Five minds for the future*. Boston: Harvard Business School Press.

Hanh, ThichNhat (2007). *The art of power*. New York: HarperCollins.

Kellerman, P., & Rhode, D. L. (Eds.). (2007). *Women and leadership: The state of play and strategies for change*. San Francisco: Wiley.

Marshall, C., & Rossman, G. (2006). *Designing qualitative research* (4th ed.). Thousand Oaks, CA: Sage.

Tarule, J., Applegate, J., Earley, P., & Blackwell, P. (2009). Narrating gendered leadership. In D. Dean, S. Bracken, & J. Allen (Eds.), *Women in academic leadership: Professional strategies, personal choices* (31–49). Sterling, VA: Stylus.

Wheatley, M. (2006). *Leadership and the New Science*. San Francisco: Berrett-Koehler.

12

Complexities of Female Leadership for the Novice Leader in Higher Education Settings

Tanisca M. Wilson

Female leadership has been a topic of interest to researchers for quite some time. Research that explain differences in male and female leadership styles is plentiful (Bensimon, 1989; Chliwniak, 1997; Marion, 2002). Despite theoretical explanations about women leaders, novice female leaders can still struggle with navigating the political and ethical terrains in higher education settings. Higher education is an ever-changing environment that demands visionary leaders who understand that its culture is rigid, inhibiting, and progressive. For the purposes of this chapter, novice female leaders are defined as women who have been in higher education for five years or less and who have authority to evaluate, supervise, hire, or terminate others. These women can be successful leaders when they recognize and know how to overcome the complexities of female leadership.

Although there is no one-size-fits-all theory, Lussier and Achua (2004) point out three variables that can have a significant impact on a leader: the leader's personality and preferred style, the followers' preferred style, and the environment in which the leader is situated. According to Gardner (1990), leadership is the process of persuasion by which an individual (or leadership team) induces a group to pursue objectives held by the leader. But, for novice female leaders, this simple definition of leadership can still present issues for women because it does not give suggestions for how women should lead nor does it address the issues that are unique to females. To influence peers, subordinates, and other constituents, novice female leaders must have a clear understanding of the political and organizational structure in which they work. There are four suggestions that may prove beneficial to the success of the amateur female leader: (1) Learning the culture of the institution in which she works, (2) observing where opportunities and limitations exist in the organization, (3) building meaningful relationships with superiors and staff, and (4) networking and forming alliances with the appropriate people.

How to Undertake and Lead Change

The culture of an organization is its collective essence, and, in a sense, its personality. From a change perspective, the culture reflects the interrelationship of shared assumptions, beliefs, values, and behaviors that are acquired over time by its members (Conner, 1993). Culture change in organizations can be very difficult, but success cannot be sustained in an organization unless there are some appropriate changes to culture. Although scholars do not agree on what specifically constitutes organization culture (Smircich, 1983), they acknowledge that organizations have cultures and that culture produces patterned behaviors that influence meanings people attach to organizational events. When undertaking change in an organization, the female leader needs to understand the history of her organization, the pattern of the behaviors of people, the symbolic meanings of specific events, and her position as the change agent. It is within an organization's culture that women can meet with the most resistance to their efforts to make a positive impact on an organization. Some cultural conflicts that can exist for women leaders in higher education settings are:

- Women are expected to not be firm, assertive, or as aggressive as their male counterparts. If they are, they are unfavorably perceived by others.
- Women are not expected to exhibit their feminine traits in male-dominated settings. For example, they are expected to wear black or dark colors to meetings, to only speak when asked, and to not resist the majority vote.

- Staff, peers, and others show more respect for directives given by male leaders than female leaders.

- Women leaders are viewed as tokens, and they are not taken seriously by their superiors, staff, or peers.

- Women leaders are perceived as emotional beings who anger easily and make decisions based on emotions, not facts.

To determine if these cultural conflicts exist in an organization, a good idea is to probe into the history of your department and especially your position within the organization. Ideally, some of the questions about an institution's history can be answered in an interview. But realistically, most cultural conflicts are not discovered until one has agreed to take the position. The department directors, especially males, are excellent candidates for such an inquiry. Ask questions such as:

- What major projects have been undertaken in this department to help the institution with its strategic goals? This question will help to determine if the organization or your department is accustomed to dealing with change. If the department has been stagnant in progressive change, it could be an indication that the organization is resistant to change and that the organization is used to operating according to the status quo.

- Who led those projects and what concerns arose about them? This question can help to determine if the strategic approach of the department was successful or not successful. Also, it can help leaders avoid possible pitfalls in the future.

According to Lick and Kaufman (2000), two-thirds of change efforts fail because of leaders' actions, or a lack of them, for the following reasons:

- Leaders have not reframed their own thinking and that of their institution relative to major change.

- Leaders have implemented a strategic planning approach that is incomplete and inadequate for the systematic change required.

• Leaders have not provided or implemented a detailed and structured transition plan for identifying and implementing change.

As a "newbie" to leadership in higher education, a woman must recognize that observation is a key tool for success. Observing the culture, people, and behaviors of an organization allows for planning a success strategy. Know the key players in your organization and be mindful that a key player does not have to be someone with a fancy title. A key player could be someone who has a major influence in the community and not necessarily in your organization. Know the influencers and know the followers. Know the history of the program, department, or organization in which change should be created. Some people resist change not because it is not needed but because the change is occurring to something they initiated.

The relationship between leadership and organizational roles reveals that leadership is not confined to certain roles in an organization (Ogawa & Bossert, 2000, p. 53). For the novice female leader, this means that she does not have to be limited in the changes she needs to initiate, manage, or follow through on because of her newness to an organization. However, it is wise for her to understand her position as a "newbie" and to know when the timing is appropriate to be a change agent. For the female leader, knowing when to act as well as what to act on and to whom to present the actions are critical for successful leadership. To acquire skill for such an action, women must have an intimate understanding of the culture of their organization.

Avoiding Political and Ethical Pitfalls

The relationship between sex-role stereotypes and leadership is complex and has not been fully defined. However, older research studies have made connections between sex- role stereotypes and self-concepts (Broverman, Vogel, Clarkson, & Rosenkrantz, 1972; O'Leary, 1974). According to these studies, many women internalize societal sex-role stereotypes and attitudes. In educational settings, this could still be the case and could possibly present traps for failure for novice female leaders. Historically, women, even those in leadership positions, have been expected to be mild mannered, agreeable, and easygoing. This expectation comes from women as well as men. In political organizations, women who frequently display mild-mannered attributes when the situation calls for assertiveness can find themselves in a political demise. Higher education institutions are political organizations, some more than others. Politics deal with power, conflict, and coalition (Bolman & Deal, 2003). This, in and of itself, can present an issue for the novice female leader. The historical account of women and power puts women at a disadvantage because women have struggled to acquire power, or more simply put, women have struggled to have the power of independency that is equal to their male counterparts. Another possible disadvantage for the "newbie" who must learn how to survive and be successful in political organizations is the fact that she is new and may not have had the opportunity to form alliances with the appropriate people.

In their explanation of a political framework, Bolman and Deal (2003) explain that politics is the practice of allocating scarce resources, which contributes to conflict in organizations. How and to whom those resources are allocated comes down to one thing: power. There are eight variations of power: (1) position power is authority that comes with titles (Maxwell [1993] contends that this variation of power is the least influential); (2) information and expertise is the power of knowing how to get information to solve important problems; (3) control of rewards is the ability to deliver jobs, money, political support, or rewards; (4) coercive power is the ability to constrain, block, interfere, or punish; (5) alliances and networks that help to get things done; (6) access and control of agendas is power given to individuals who are intimately connected in political systems; (7) control of the meaning and systems is power exercised by elites who have the ability to impose meaning that defines identify, beliefs, and values; and (8) personal power is the ability of individuals to use charisma, energy, stamina, political skills, and good communication to accomplish a vision.

Position power is the most likely source of power that a novice female leader will have as a newbie in leadership. The authority that accompanies the position must be visible in order for the leader to be taken seriously by peers and subordinates. The longevity of a leader's success is dependent on how well she exercises her authority and the rapport she builds with her constituents. Autocratic leadership, cracking the whip, is a common mistake of new female leaders, and this style of leadership, as well as coercive power, should be used sparingly. Both can be detrimental when on the political turf because your staff can be your main source of support or resistance when political stakes are high. In any leadership position, the goal is to acquire personal power, but to do so will take time and experience.

It is unrealistic to assume that a leader can exclude herself from the practice of politics. Female leaders in higher education must know how to survive the political terrains of their organizations, even if they do not like it. Simply put: know the game even if there is no desire to play it. To avoid political pitfalls in your organization, know what the scarce resource is and examine your stake in it. For example, a scarce resource could be the opportunity to acquire a company vehicle for your department, a grant that can only be given to one department, or an opportunity to hire more staff for your department. As a novice female leader, always know your role in the stakes. It could be that you are needed just for support. If this is the case, it is advisable to consider if the alliance being formed can be beneficial to your future interests. For example, if the group or individual you are supporting has the right intentions, and if the group or individual could be of assistance to you in the future, then create a bargaining opportunity. In layman's terms, be sure the group or individual knows that your support is a "You owe me one." In the game of politics, do not give and lose the opportunity to get. However, there will be times when the scarce resource is of little or no importance to you. In such cases, exclude yourself. As a novice female leader, it is not wise to have frequent involvement in the political area because it could hurt your chances of promotion in the future. In the world of politics, which is an integral part of higher education institutions, there is no guarantee that those who gain power will use it wisely or justly. The exercise of power is a natural part of society, and those who use it as a constructive and productive possibility to help institutions become more just and efficient are the political winners.

Networking

Although politics is a complex phenomenon, it is not without its positive characteristics. Networking is essential to the success of novice female leaders, not only for political implications but also for alleviating feelings of isolation. Networking is the art of building relationships. According to Bolman and Deal (2003), the first task in building networks is to figure out whose help you need. The second step is to develop relationships so people will be there for you when you need them. Basically, you need friends and allies to get things done and to get their support, you need to cultivate relationships. As a novice female leader, realize that you will not have success at building relationships with everyone.

When developing a networking strategy, have clear intentions for the individuals or groups for which you will interact. If your intention is to network for political reasons, Kotter (1985) suggests these steps:

- Identify relevant relationships; not all relationships need to be politically motivated to be relevant.

- Examine your interests and goals and assess who might resist, why, and how strongly.

- Develop, if possible, relationships with potential opponents to facilitate communication or negotiation.

- Embrace gender and cultural differences as well as professional and personal commonalities.

When skillfully executed, building networks can be an exciting experience for novice female leaders. Realize that networking is different from bargaining and it is not advisable to do both simultaneously. Networking not only gives you a chance to get to know others, but it also gives others a chance to get to know you. Networking is an opportunity to open yourself up and show who you are as an individual as well as a leader.

Bargaining and Negotiation

Unlike networking, where the experience can exclude political implications, bargaining and negotiation are part of political skill (Bolman & Deal, 2003). Negotiation is defined as a process in which two or more parties are in conflict and attempt to come to an agreement (Lussier & Achua, 2004). However, previous research studies (Lussier & Achua, 2004; Marion, 2002) show that women have not been as successful at bargaining as their male counterparts. Bargaining and negotiation can happen at any time with any level of staff in an organization. Sometimes there will be time to plan a bargaining strategy and other times there won't be. According to Lussier and Achua (2004), negotiation should include the following steps: (1) develop rapport and focus on the obstacles, not the person; (2) let the other party make the first offer; (3) listen and ask questions to focus on meeting the other party's needs; and (4) do not be too quick to give in and be sure to ask for something in return, because those who ask for more get more.

Ethics and Politics

When engaged in organizational politics, it can be tempting to be unethical, but do not be. Lussier and Achua (2004) define ethics as "standards of right and wrong that influence behavior" (p. 48). As a novice female leader in higher education, it will not be uncommon to feel pressure to go along with the majority, even when the majority is wrong. But because ethical behavior is a major part of politics that is often ignored, it would be wise to stand firm on what is right when pressured to support unethical decisions. An agreeable personality can lead to following the crowd in either ethical or unethical behavior, so it is essential for female leaders to know when to be assertive. Three factors influence ethical behavior: (1) personality and traits, (2) moral development, and (3) the situation.

As leaders, we bring to organizations our attitudes and leadership traits. It is our attitudes and beliefs that shape our leadership and communication styles. When engaged in political warfare, it is important to focus on the resource and not the task of hurting people. When gaining the resource becomes personally hurtful to an individual or group, ethical leaders choose doing what is right over doing what is popular. Moral development refers to understanding what is right from wrong. According to Lussier and Achua (2004), there are three levels of right and wrong. The preconventional level is choosing right from wrong based on self-interests, the conventional level is when one seeks to live up to the standard of others, and the postconventional level is standing up for what you perceive is right regardless of others' ethics. In high-pressure situations, some leaders will forget their ethics and put their own interests first. For example, you know that one of your employees is being sexually harassed by your male boss. You know what he is doing is wrong, but you know that if you report him, it is likely that he will retaliate and fire you. So, what do you do? Do you ignore the harassment? Do you encourage the employee to report him but to leave your name out of it, or do you report him based on the fact that it is the right thing to do?

Leaders who exhibit ethical behavior gain the trust of their constituents. In doing so, they are more likely to have stronger alliances, which helps to build their personal power of influence. Trust is an important commodity to female leaders because it will make others, male and female alike, feel safe around them. As a result, the female leader who has gained the trust of others will become privileged to information from different sources. She will be respected as a trusted leader others will come to depend on for leadership.

How to Cope with the Pressures of a New Leadership Position

Leadership is a high calling and it can be a daunting task for the novice female leader. Whether the leadership position is that of an assistant director, director, provost, or chancellor, each position requires skills and expertise to effectively get things done. As well, each position faces some of the same leadership challenges: effective communication, positive rapport with staff, superiors, and constituents, and the execution of political skill. In addition to the common challenges, female leaders may also face competition from their male counterparts. This section of the chapter stems from the author's personal experience in a leadership position.

Know and be true to thy self. Know your strengths and weaknesses as a person, as they will become your strengths and weaknesses as a leader. For example, you may be known to fly off the handle with your friends when you hear something you do not like. However, as a leader, this should not be done. To cultivate respect from your boss, your peers, and your staff, you have to learn how to stay calm even when you feel like exploding. Once you discover your weaknesses, take the necessary steps to minimize them.

Balance your roles. Many novice female leaders assume leadership positions in addition to their roles as mother, wife, and/or student. Each role has its own set of demands that must be met. The pressure of these demands can sometimes cause stress and force female leaders to feel out of balance. As a newbie in leadership, you may be tempted to bring your work home in an attempt to stay on top of your tasks or to impress your boss. This is highly discouraged if you have a family. There is a time for work and a time for family and a time for fun. Using your time wisely will not only relieve you of stress, but it will also help you to stay alert in your different environments. When at work, dedicate your time to work. When at home, dedicate your time to family. When free time presents itself, have a little fun, or use the time to do your homework if you are a student. Do not make trade-offs with your time. Keep everything in its proper perspective.

Wear your leadership skin. Do not be timid when expressing your ideas. When you speak, speak with confidence. When you give directives, hold those for carrying them out accountable for the task. Make decisions that are yours to make and do not pass them on to your boss. If you are unclear about direction, ask your boss about it. Do not send your staff to your boss unless your boss prefers it that way. If he or she does, you need to have a conversation with him or her about the extent of your authority. Do not shed confidence in the presence of your male counterparts, no matter how macho they act. Be confident in who you are as a leader and do not diminish the value of your position, ever.

Stand firm with staff. As a new leader, you may find that your staff will challenge you on your decisions or purposely ignore your directives in an act of defiance. These actions can be viewed as staff not accepting your leadership, or your staff could be testing you. In either case, hold them accountable. Depending on the nature of the staff member's action, take the appropriate disciplinary action. Ignoring their behaviors will only make it worse. As the leader, your disciplinary actions must be fair and ethical, regardless of what you feel like doing. The punishment must fit the crime, and you should never make a decision when you are upset about an employee's actions. Take time to calm down and remember the golden rule: do unto others as you want them to do unto you.

Know your job. Successful leaders know their jobs, and that entails knowing their boss. For newbies, this can take time because the job description never tells the whole story. As a leader, especially if you are in an assistant's position, learn your boss's language. If he or she says, "Are you available to attend a meeting on my behalf?" Make sure the question means what you think it means. Because it could mean, "I need you to attend this meeting on my behalf." The difference is the former gives you the option of not attending the meeting. The latter does not. Know what is expected of you from your boss as well as your staff. Expectations can change, so do not miss an opportunity to learn if you and your boss or if you and your staff are still on the same page. Know the scope of your role and your limitations. Your position is entitled to only so much authority. Know where it begins and where it ends.

Do not be a yes woman. You may feel inclined to agree with every idea your boss has because he or she is the boss and you are afraid of being seen as confrontational or resistant. It is not good leadership to agree with everything your boss says or does because he or she is the boss. If your boss wants to bounce ideas off you, be honest with him or her if it is not a good idea. Find a way to say it respectfully. If you become a yes woman, eventually, your boss will stop asking for your opinions because he or she knows you will agree. In disagreeing with your boss, be careful to not become confrontational. Just simply outline why you believe the idea may not be the best one. When you do this, base it on facts and experience, not on how you feel. When you are honest with yourself and your boss, you can feel good about doing your job. However, if you go along to get along, you may not feel satisfied with yourself.

Take advantage of opportunities to grow and develop as a leader. Experience is a good teacher and learning from seasoned leaders is a good way to perfect your own leadership. Conferences, symposiums, books, and journal articles about women in leadership can be helpful to a novice leader. Seek out a mentor who shares your interests and who has extensive leadership experience. Be sure your mentor has a proven track record of being successful. It is advisable for female leaders to seek out other female leaders because they may better understand the obstacles of females in leadership.

Women have made tremendous progress in acquiring leadership positions. Despite these strides, women still face major obstacles in leadership positions. Fortunately, enough women have traversed the leadership track and they are in positions to train, assist, and enable other female leaders to make a difference. The foibles of leadership are common to male and female alike, but the challenges that are unique to female leaders have been well documented in the literature, and women leaders must make a concerted effort to continue to rise above these challenges. The success of our society is dependent on leaders who can fearlessly undertake and lead change, skillfully execute political tactics for the betterment of citizens, and transform what is into what should be. Women have risen to the challenge of leadership, and despite inequity and inequality in some industries, they continue to make a positive impact in their leadership positions.

References

Bensimon, E. M. (1989). A feminist reinterpretation of presidents' definitions of leadership. *Peabody Journal of Education, 3*(66), 143–56.

Bolman, L., & Deal, T. (2003). *Reframing organizations: Artistry, choice, and leadership* (3rd ed.). San Francisco: Jossey-Bass.

Broverman, I. R., Vogel, S. R., Clarkson, F. E., & Rosenkrantz, P. S. (1972). Sex-role stereotypes: A current appraisal. *Journal of Social Issues, 28*(2), 59–78.

Chliwniak, L. (1997). *Higher education leadership: analyzing the gender gap*. ASHE-ERIC Higher Education Report, *4*(25). Washington, DC: Graduate School of Education and Human Development, George Washington University.

Conner, D. (1993). *Managing at the speed of change*. New York: Villard Books.

Gardner, J. W. (1990). *On leadership*. New York: Free Press.

Kotter, J. P. (1985). *Beyond power and influence*. New York: Free Press.

Lick, D., & Kaufman, R. (2000). Change creation: The rest of the planning story In J. Boettcher, M. Doyle, & R. Jensen (Eds.), *Technology-driven planning: Principles to practice* (Chapter 2). Ann Arbor, MI: Society for College and University Planning.

Lussier, R., & Achua, C. (2004). *Leadership: Theory, application and skill development*. Eagan, MN: Thomson Press.

Marion, R. (2002). *Leadership in education: Organizational theory for the practitioner*. Long Grove, IL: Waveland Press.

Maxwell, J. C. (1993). *Developing the leader within you*. Nashville, TN: Thomas Nelson Inc.

Ogawa, R. T., & Bossert, S. T. (2000). *Leadership as an organizational quality*. San Francisco: Jossey-Bass.

O'Leary, V. E. (1974). Some attitudinal barriers to occupational aspirations in women. *Psychological Bulletin, 81*, 809–26.

Smircich, L. (1983). Concepts of culture and organizational analysis. *Administrative Science Quarterly, 28*, 339–58.

13

The "Borderlands" Experience for Women of Color as Higher Education Leaders

Patricia Arredondo

Introduction

A few years ago, I became aware of a powerful book by Gloria Anzaldúa, *Borderlands/La Frontera* (1987). In her honest and descriptive style, Anzaldúa eloquently and painfully chronicled the role conflicts for Latinas with intersecting identities of ethnic and racial heritage, sexual orientation, class, and occupation, just to mention a few. On the Mexico–Texas border where she grew up, the borderlands experience was more than a metaphor; it was a daily experience driven by culture-bound expectations of her as a Mexican-American, a woman of color, and a lesbian. Another writer and poet, Julia De Burgos, expressed sentiments about not being who she could be in a male-dominated society that pigeonholed her based on gender and class. Her classic poem, *Yo misma fui mi ruta* (I Was My Own Path; 1953) is a sentiment of senior women of color captured in qualitative research studies and reflections that will be shared in the chapter.

As is reported in the literature about women and women of color, leadership roles in traditionally white male institutions are fraught with multiple unwritten rules and deficit expectations based on our identity and perceptions of our competence. Understandably, role conflict, power plays, regressive interactions, and other nonprofessional behaviors will take up a woman's psychic and physical energy and detract from her leadership priorities. The higher education context for leading is complicated and nuanced interpersonally and sociopolitically, and this requires ongoing examination and discussion. As was voiced by one colleague, "expectations for excellence and the culture of collaborative leadership in key relationships" (personal communication, October 1, 2010) are necessary to support her talent engagement and leadership as a woman of color.

To write this chapter is both personal and professional and based on my commitment to the advancement of women and women of color in senior leadership roles in higher education. As a counseling psychologist, organizational consultant, and the highest-ranking Latina academic in two research universities (as of 2011), I was very amenable to write the chapter on women of color in higher education. Similar to my professional colleagues and friends whose voices are shared throughout this chapter, I have not had a traditional route into senior roles. Yet, as will be discussed, navigating a nonlinear path often affords women like me multiple "borderlands" and new doorways to reinforce a sense of perseverance and self-efficacy.

Approaches and Research Foci

Studies of women of color in roles of college and university presidents, school principals, and superintendents and faculty have been undertaken primarily by women of color (Enríquez-Damián, 2009; Muñoz, 2010; Turner, 2002). A qualitative research design is the lens most often used to gather women's voices about their life journeys leading to a presidency and/or how they have managed in these exclusive leadership roles. For faculty women of color, quantitative studies have addressed the glass ceiling for Asian Americans (Lee, 2002) and obstacles to success for African American women (Nichols & Tanksley, 2004). Opinion statements lament the miniscule numbers of Asian American presidents (Saigo, 2008) and the decline of African American college presidents (Chenoweth, 2007).

Findings from empirical research and individual commentaries indicate there is insufficient attention to women of color for senior roles and to change this practice, effective developmental practices are required within individual institutions. For example, a culture for leadership development for persons of color is often mentioned. Mentorship and role models are other themes that resonate in women's accounts with utility for their practices as leaders and also enablers to full participation and respect in their institution. The narratives tend to yield findings that can be reframed for institutional benefit because the lessons learned by individual women can become instrumental for value-added organizational practices. Such observations will be shared throughout this document.

Overview of the Chapter

In the sections that follow, there will be discussions about women of color in higher education and our intersecting identities, the culture and climate of higher education institutions and relevant meta-theories, leadership models and strategies, and resources to achieve goals as a woman of color senior leader. I will discuss psychological and organizational culture paradigms that can be used as lenses for examining pervasive structural and institutional barriers affecting plans for women of color, the intersectionality of identity, and women's sense of well-being as professional leaders. In the final section of the paper, resources for senior leadership development will be presented. Women's reflections, invited to comment for this chapter, will be sprinkled throughout. I will also introduce my own experiences and at times write in the first versus the third person.

In no way will I provide the final word on the topic; rather, I hope to share perspectives based on my own scholarship, others' research, and literature that influences my thinking and leadership practices. The prevailing questions are: *How prepared are institutions to support and ensure the success of women of color in leadership roles?* and *What must the woman have in her leadership toolkit to continue to navigate the higher education borderlands world?*

Women of Color in Higher Education: Context and Different Realities

The Civil Rights Act (1964) legislated access to equal education, employment, housing, and other basic rights to women, people of color, and others historically marginalized. Affirmative Action policies became the tool for enacting the civil rights legislation with the intent of equity, albeit in an uneven and even detrimental way for the person who was to benefit. The woman of color had to prove that she was more than a "twofer," a check-off on an affirmative action report because of her dual minority

278 Women as Leaders in Education

status. The culture of gender and racial prejudice was not eradicated by new policies. At times, for example, my legitimacy as a junior professor was questioned because it was known that I was an Affirmative Action hire. Turner (2002) describes the experiences of women of color living with marginality in higher education, often in "no-win" situations because of their race and ethnicity.

With the election of President Barack Obama in 2008, discourse about a postracial society in the United States has emerged. There is speculation that this will lead to an increase of opportunity and representation of people of color as senior leaders. Another part of the national context, however, is the increase in race-based hate crimes. It is reported that the number of hate crimes in the United States increased and in 2009, reportedly there were 932 hate groups and 309 nativist extremist groups (Southern Poverty Law Center, 2010). The nativist groups focus on immigrants and other groups because of perceived heritage and religion. The sociopolitical landscape, however, must be factored into discussions of senior women of color leadership because our visibility may make us targets based on others' conscious and unconscious fears and prejudices.

In the United States, moreover, the social construct of race led to hierarchical status among groups based on gender and race/ethnicity in particular. In his research of fifty-plus nations, Hostede (1984) found that historical and national values influence institutional values and practices of individualism versus collectivism, masculinity versus femininity, high and low power distance, and high to low uncertainty avoidance. His data indicate that the United States has national values biased toward masculinity and individualism, and these have become enculturated in educational and workplace settings' policies and practices. Thus, women in general will be assessed by the white male norm of dominance, transactional behavior, and appearance (Cheung & Halpern, 2010; Eagly & Carli, 2007) and not necessarily proven performance. Women of color, regardless of their heritage—African, American Indian, Asian/Pacific Islander, Latina, and multiple heritages—will generally have lower ascribed status in comparison to white women and men independent of their earned position. Consequentially, negative stereotypes and low expectations often create self-fulfilling prophesies in the eyes of the majority individual (Arredondo, 2003; Sanchez-Hucles & Davis, 2010; Valverde, 2003).

Women of color may also be senior administrators in institutions with a specific affiliation or dimension of identity—faith-based, historically black college and university, Hispanic-serving institution, tribal college, and/or women's college. Here too, the woman of color is often the exception and subject to multiple types of scrutiny by different groups not accustomed to having women like her in roles of authority and decision making. Even in the ethnic-specific institutions, men historically have held the senior administrative and faculty roles.

Based on prevailing practices, women of color are not expected to be leaders, and to have such individuals in an organization creates dissonance and sometimes backlash. When certain groups in the country are the targets of marginalization because of their cultural heritage, appearance, and religion, women of color cannot escape the halo effect.

Organizational Context Culture and Climate

The relative "fit" for women of color in senior roles will be affected by the institutional culture, climate, and prevailing practices. Valverde (2003) contends that universities have historically been traditional and conservative and maintain the status quo. The traditionalism of colleges and universities typically means a hierarchical, governance-based system, more de facto privilege for white men as faculty and administrators, working conditions that are not family oriented, and a tenure and promotion system that favors scholarship over teaching and service and does not readily accommodate women's professional and family goals.

Obstacles of systemic racism and sexism and lack of a critical mass of black women in predominantly white institutions are also visible and invisible conditions that keep the bureaucracy intact (Henry & Glenn, 2009). A study by the Wellesley Center for Women found that the critical number for women's impact on a governance board is three (Kramer, Konrad, & Erkut, 2006). Supreme Court Justice Ruth Bader Ginsberg illuminates the point in her statement about how litigators often mistook her for Justice O'Conner. With the addition of Justices Kagan and Sotomayor, this will unlikely occur, she noted (Lithwick, 2010).

Assuming that most higher education institutions are traditional and conservative, what must women of color know about how they are affected and affect the prevailing culture? What lens or paradigms about organizational behavior will become part of one's toolkit?

Organizational Climate and Behavior

In the early 1980s, Sandler and Hall first described the chilly climate affecting women in college classrooms. This spawned additional research and publications on the experiences of women faculty in traditional male disciplines and in departments that otherwise do not value women (1986). In an organization with a chilly climate, women are made to feel unwelcomed and marginalized through silence and other forms of negative behavior such as not being included or invited to a planned meeting. The chilly climate creates a work atmosphere fraught with tension, uncertainty, and frustration for the woman. For a woman of color, the climate can be even chillier because she is the anomaly in the organization and often the target for exclusion. She may be overlooked for coffee invitations, not sought after when a meeting ends, not included for informal social gatherings, and so forth. Unless a woman of color has a network or an accepting supervisor of color with whom to share experiences, she may find that the climate in her work setting may become too much of a burden.

The chilly climate can also feel like a psychic prison (Morgan, 1997), a metaphor used to describe a type of organization. Attributes of the psychic prison include favored ways of doing things (meaning new ideas or practices are not acceptable), unconscious and protective or defensive behaviors, organizational anxiety, and other psychological phenomena. When new ideas are introduced by a newcomer such as a woman of color, a "circling of the wagons" behavior may result. According to one of my colleagues, the woman of color may become caught in "historical conflicts and a culture of mistrust," thereby impeding new ideas she is trying to introduce (personal communication, October 1, 2010). Change, discomfort, and unpredictability are generally the reasons for the manifestation of any of these characteristics. Ingrained interpersonal behavior with ethnic minorities may be difficult practices to change for white colleagues.

In *Successful Diversity Management Initiatives* (Arredondo, 1996), I discussed a systems methodology to deliberately and authentically have more diverse work settings. I also addressed some of the effects of introducing diversity: "Organizational change upsets the dynamics of power and politics" (p. 12). When a woman of color becomes an organizational leader, she affects the organization's homeostasis. "We have always done it this way" statements, according to a colleague, "interfere with her ability to introduce new ideas and slows progress" (personal communication, July 18, 2010). Just one person can upset the status quo, others' sense of comfort, and, depending on the nature of the relationship, reciprocity and equity. As a senior administrator, I have always been the minority based on heritage, gender, and other nonacademic career experiences and therefore I am on the alert about how to manage relationships with different types of individuals. The same cannot be said for my generally white peers, superiors, and assistants, and I can detect their discomfort. If a direct report is a white person, particularly a white woman, there are generally subtle tensions and I have to negotiate these, not she.

A woman of color who enters the organization as a senior leader precipitates a range of reactions, both conscious and unconscious. Others may become wary or openly resist change. Lack of previous formal experiences with an administrator of color may also stir unfounded fears, anxiety, and hostility. "Does she think I am racist?" "How should I talk to her?" "Will she expect more of us than we do?" Because of historic issues of affirmative action, employees in a psychic prison will question the woman of color's authority. "Is she qualified?" In spite of glowing credentials, she may be mistrusted and held up to scrutiny. Self-protective behaviors by others in the organization are not within the control of the woman of color, but she must be able to recognize them. Excessive questioning of the woman in front of others, patronizing comments, and other forms of defensive behavior like silence rather than open exchanges in a meeting are manifestations of an organization as a psychic prison. In contemporary psychology, these behaviors are called microaggressions, forms of interpersonal insults, both verbal and nonverbal.

The Culture of "Whiteness" and "Niceness"

In all workplace cultures in the United States, including higher education settings, "whiteness" is another prevailing structural and interpersonal dimension of power, perceptions, and expectations. According to Warren, "Whiteness is invisible or unmarked as an ethnic or racial category within this culture" (1999, p. 186); it is self-evident and normative. Being of color means one is a VERG—visible ethnic racial group member (Helms, 1990). Unlike whites in higher education, senior women of color do not have white privilege or a "set of unearned assets" (Macintosh, 1989). Continuing with this line of discussion, Warren indicates that "White identity can be situational but not so for women of color" (p. 196). She cannot be herself and go about carrying out her responsibilities as a senior administrator because everyone is watching and perhaps waiting for her to err. In a psychic prison-type organization that is hierarchical, with favored ways of doing things and loaded with unwritten rules, certain behaviors may not be accepted because of the individual in charge.

In his study of Latinas/os in educational and political settings, Alemán (2009) reported on the politics of "niceness." Women's consideration of others through niceness, respect, and decorum suggests they may not express dissatisfaction with the status quo and/or behave by being too appeasing and agreeable. If this behavior is reinforced by institutional superiors, it is a way of keeping the woman of color in her place and controlling her voice. Turner (2002) also refers to the concept of "ambiguous empowerment": mixed messages about how to behave.

Women of Color Affected by Double Standards and Double Binds

The higher education environment has historically been white male dominated, classist, and slow to change. Though it is seen as a setting for intellectual discourse and the advancement of new knowledge, women of color often find it less than affirming of their intellectual talent (Eagly & Chin, 2010; Myers & Turner, 1999; Turner, 2002). The climate of an unhealthy organization introduces numerous land mines such as hypocrisy, deficit thinking about people of color by everyone from students to faculty, low expectations that lead to self-fulfilling prophecies, and "white ignorance" (Valverde, 2003, p. 39). If a woman of color is underestimated, she will likely be relegated to assignments where she has no direct reports or budget responsibilities. As a result, she will not acquire the skill sets for administrative advancement. If the individual's supervisor behaves in exclusionary and other nonsupportive ways, the woman will likely have feelings of disappointment to betrayal (Valverde, 2003). The concept of "ambiguous empowerment" (Turner 2002) also seems apropos for these examples because women experience contradictions felt when those to whom they report respond in discriminatory or dismissive ways.

Over the years, I have heard from women of color in senior roles, such as vice presidents, vice provosts, and deans, lament their shock and frustration with their superiors, individuals largely responsible for their hiring. This often begins when the new hire is introduced only to certain administrators or stakeholders, left to fend for herself on a new campus, or otherwise told to make sure she connects with other people of color on campus. In these situations, the woman is not welcomed to the community of administrators appropriately and it is fair to say, disrespect in different forms becomes the modus operendi. These are additional examples of microaggressions.

Intersecting Identities

The reality of multiple identities has been discussed as it relates to women of color (Arredondo, 2003; Eagly & Carli, 2007; Sanchez-Hucles & Davis, 2010). Although women of color have more than gender and ethnicity or race as identity attributes, these are the dimensions that readily become the focus of stereotyping and attributions. How often do we say, "She is an African American woman" but we do not say she is a "white woman." Because white is the norm, there is no reason to describe the white woman. Perceptions, attributions, and expectations of women of color are influenced by gender and racial/ethnic stereotypes. The intersection of multiple identities is impossible to tease apart.

In a classic article, Fiske (1993) proposed that individuals with power in an organization control stereotyping of those with less power. Accordingly, women of color are ready targets for such stereotyping because they are unknown entities, have outsider status, and are assumed to have little to no real power. Consider how often people of color, including senior women, are asked to sit on committees to represent local or their "constituencies" viewpoint. Even as a senior administrator, I recognize requests/assignments to serve on citywide, social service councils because of my ethnic identity. Although a person of color is not necessarily the most appropriate representative, in the mindset of certain administrators, this is the person to designate from the university. For women of color in career advancement, questions about window dressing and tokenism may naturally ensue as well as double binds if one rejects certain appointments.

In the early 1990s, a colleague and I developed a schema to capture the holistic essence of individuals' pluralistic identity, also termed *intersectionality* (Eagly & Carli, 2007; Sanchez-Hucles & Davis, 2010). The Dimensions of Personal Identity (DPI) model (Arredondo & Glauner, 1992) is a contextual and developmental model indicative of the multidimensionality of all individuals, not just senior women of color. The connection between fixed dimensions (A), historical and contextual factors (C) not always within one's control as with budget cuts, and more fluid factors (B) introduces opportunities for institutional leadership. The model can also be used to reveal relationships in the workplace based on occupational stratification. For women of color who are unique senior administrators, it is possible that tokenism occurs and that stratification further promotes isolation and/or marginalization. If an institution only congratulates itself for hiring women of color as deans, provosts, or chancellors, it will unlikely fail to notice how other organizational practices such as power relations and low expectations remain unchanged.

Agars (2004) argued that gender stereotypes affect women's advancement in organizations. He discussed performance evaluations and the role of sexism and stereotypes in the preferential treatment and selection of men over women. Although his study was not in a higher education setting, the findings may still have applicability to women of color in higher education. Valverde (2003) suggested that underrepresentation of leaders of color can be attributed to "poor recruitment, minimal hiring, and weak retention due to an unsupportive environment" (p. 38). One can only wonder about the role of stereotyping, tokenism, and other embedded institutional practices that actually hinder the advancement and success of senior women of color.

Power and Privilege

Because gender is an "ascribed status characteristic," it always suggests more status, privilege, and resources for men (Ayman & Korabik, 2010). Ironically, women of color administrators are often told that they intimidate their peers, men and women alike. This seems like a lot of power to give to a person who is generally a numeric minority and for whom there are low expectations. Fiske's research on the power of stereotyping can again be invoked to explain additional differences between white women and women of color. Sanchez-Hucles and Davis point out that stereotypes about white women are generally not about their identity but about their skills. For women of color, the initial stereotypes are about identity.

Alexiou (2005) discussed a case study of "Monica" at the heart of gender power in a learning organization. Because a learning organization is conceptualized as a model for collaboration, inclusiveness, and development of staff, the analysis yielded a different set of experiences for the woman of color protagonist and career-tracker, Monica. In short, although Monica followed the script of the organization, producing data that were in keeping with her assignment, an assessment of her performance rendered it insufficient. Male gender power prevailed, putting Monica in her place. Alexiou pointed out that women of color are a "product of a network of discourses and power relations" (p. 27), rendering us targets of control and subordination, another example of an organization as a psychic prison.

Women of color are the ones who literally move between two or more worlds. Of course, we have learned how to coexist with white people and other ethnic minorities as well. The borderlands/la frontera, as characterized by Gloria Anzaldúa, is the daily experience of senior women of color—and their peers have no idea. In predominantly white institutions, it is the woman of color who has more experience engaging with others who do not share her heritage.

> Not having enough women and people of color around the table, in this instance around the table of deans, creates challenges. The challenge, though, has been greater for my male colleagues than it has been for me. I'm used to operating an environment where I am the underrepresented person. They're not used to working with a peer at their level, certainly who's a female and a person of color. That's a change for them, and it's an adjustment for them. (personal communication, July 16, 2010)

Negotiating Prejudice with Transformational Leaders

The intersection of identity and race/ethnicity is one inevitable reality for women of color as it relates to leadership in general (Eagly & Chin, 2010; Sanchez-Hucles & Davis, 2010) and higher education leadership

(Arredondo, 2003; Henry & Glenn, 2009). This theme has been discussed primarily by women of color. Ironically, the majority are psychologists by training or women with doctoral degrees in higher education administration. Perhaps we have noticed more through the lens of multiculturalism and ethnic and racial identity models than we learned about and write about. For women completing doctoral work on the topic of careers for women of color in higher education, they report witnessing the treatment of their faculty and women in administrative roles. Of course, our lived experience as women of color in higher education also motivates our voice on identity conflicts and other challenges in the academy.

Discussion of the intersection of multiple identities has emerged through the multicultural psychology literature (Arredondo, 2002; Sue & Sue, 2003). Women of color, not included in the feminist discourse evolving from the Civil Rights movement, have had to raise the issue that white, heterosexual males and females do not have to be the norm. When it comes to experiences in university settings, there will be a difference between white women and women of color. White women may experience sexism and classism, but women of color will be recipients of sexist, racist, and classist interactions. Contributing to these multiple experiences with isms are stereotypes and stereotype threat (Steele, 2000). The latter concept suggests that individuals incorporate the stereotype about them and behave accordingly. Thus, if the prevailing stereotype a woman of color accepts is that she can only be successful in a leadership role with ethnic minority groups, she may exclude herself from other settings.

Here are two case examples that had positive outcomes because of the women's supervisor. Two women of color were selected, after a search, for the position of academic dean and vice president for student affairs in large public and predominantly white universities. Both reported to presidents of color, an African American man and woman respectively. As might be expected, these women were the highest-ranking persons of color next to the president in the university and were seen as "insiders." Regressive behavior ensued. Individuals, particularly white men, agreed to participate in meetings initiated by the dean or to take responsibility for an activity and then conveniently forgot to follow through. The vice president for student affairs had inherited many projects that her predecessor had not completed. This meant late hours and critical decisions in order to make progress on unfulfilled obligations. Criticism ensued and she became the target of overt criticism while her predecessor, who still remained on campus, was seen as the benevolent former vice president. The success of these women five years later can be attributed to many factors, including their astuteness about the prevailing organizational culture that did not support women of color, maturity as individuals and professionals, and open and honest relationships with their presidents. Their presidents had also entered these environments and understood the climate of marginalization and disrespect regardless of their rank. Through their guidance and encouragement, the women were validated and knew that hard decisions would be fully supported.

The preceding examples reflect behavior of leaders embedding and transmitting culture change. By setting an example that they pay attention to their senior women of color, presidents and provosts model and reinforce behavior expected of other managers and staff. Organizational change and leadership require deliberate actions, including role modeling, teaching, and coaching (Schien, 1985). The provost and president who want their direct reports to succeed will schedule periodic coaching and catch-up sessions. If this does not happen for senior women of color with their immediate supervisors, it is a request to be made. Culture can also be affected by leader behavior. Observing formal interactions between the president and provost and senior women of color at meetings or other academic gatherings can have multiple benefits for the women because of what is signaled to other staff. Ultimately it is positive leader behavior that will contribute to the advancement of women of color in higher education.

Leadership Perspectives

There is no shortage of books on the topic of leadership theories/models, styles, and attributes, generally reporting case studies of how to lead and sustain successful organizations. *Good to Great* (Collins, 2000) and *How the Mighty Fall* (Collins, 2009) are two examples of in-depth analyses of corporations and principles that contribute to greatness. Embedded throughout these texts are assumptions about leader behavior, particularly planning and decision making. Most examples feature white men as the leaders.

Definitions of leadership continue to evolve with structural changes in historically hierarchical, bureaucratic organizations to ones that are flatter, more organic, and even women led. The study of leadership is not new, but the focus on women and women of color is fairly recent. Early theorists defined leadership primarily from a white male corporate perspective. Being autocratic and operating from command and control, transactional behavior was deemed normative. Early examples were the Theory X and Y (McGregor, 1960) and achievement-oriented models. Theory X and Y were predicated on the need to control employees and get them to perform. Alternatively, individual leaders' need for achievement and power was proposed as the basis to motivate the individual's style of a more authoritative model (McClelland, 1975). Other touted models of leadership include situational leadership (Hersey, Blanchard, & Johnson, 2007), transformational and integrative leadership styles (Avolio, 2007) and charismatic leadership (Conger & Kanungo, 1987), all seen as more people friendly, less heavy handed, and engendering greater collegiality. These models have been proposed by men about men in traditional hierarchical settings.

More female style examples of leadership have also emerged. They are considered "female" because of their collectivistic or communal attributes. To engage employees, these types of leadership styles are described as interactive, employee centered, participatory, "good" coach and teacher, and "enlightened" parent (Eagly & Carli, 2007). These styles seem to be associated with a woman's more preferred or intuitive styles but can work against her if she is deemed too soft or friendly. However, when men are more interactive, they are given more affirmation and complimented for demonstrating caring and nurturance. In these various models, the objective of leaders is to inspire, motivate, and get results. Also notable in all models are built-in assumptions about the sex of the leader. Men are still the favored and expected leaders.

Incorporating the topic of diversity (ethnicity, gender, race, and sexual orientation) in leadership conversations is fairly recent and generally based on headcount (Chin, 2010). The topic of women of color in leadership roles in higher education has been given voice primarily by presidents/chancellors, provosts, and other senior administrators as was previously mentioned. In these examples, the focus is on achievement, negotiating challenges structurally and interpersonally, and always being goal oriented.

Women and Women of Color as Leaders

With the implementation of Affirmative Action policies, more white women entered corporations. One of the classic texts at the time, *Men and Women of the Corporation* (Kanter, 1977), described structures and processes that supported and impeded women's advancement. These included having new opportunities, assuming roles with power, and connections to power. All three factors continue to be relevant to today's organizations, including higher education. However, change has been slow. Regardless of the apparent progress of women in the workplace as college presidents/chancellors and provosts, the culture of gender prejudice still exists (Eagly & Carli, 2007) with a lack of equal access to leadership. Contributing to double standards for women is ambivalence about women's skills and styles of interacting. Women's verbal and nonverbal behaviors are not readily accepted and any form of self-promotion is frowned upon (Eagly & Carli, 2007). Though men can brag about their accomplishments and merely express their opinions, for women to do so is risky.

Valverde (2003) observed that much depends on the track that individuals are assigned or shepherded toward—deliberately or not. He describes these in higher education as mainline/traditional or sidetracked based on stereotypes. Because sponsorship in white institutions of higher education is controlled by white men, there is more likelihood that a stereotype track may ensue for women of color. This has many meanings, from being given assignments that focus particularly on issues of institutional diversity or people of color to community outreach and service-oriented roles. For a new leader of color, the initial response may be appreciation to demonstrate capabilities in areas where others have not tread or that work needs to be done—partnership with public schools with majority students of color, community agencies in underserved neighborhoods, and so forth. Before long, however, this individual may become pigeonholed.

Discussions with women of color colleagues in senior administrative roles in higher education highlighted the necessity of being on mainline/traditional tracks in order to have their talent and leadership skills fully engaged. "Because of the decentralized nature of this campus, I am called upon to lead myriad activities" from faculty and staff development, fundraising, and budget oversight to strategic planning (personal communication, July 18, 2010). Another colleague stated, "I have a president who really believes in utilizing the talents of everyone, regardless of gender, race, ethnicity or other types of differences. He does it by example and he holds his leadership and direct reports to that standard" (personal communication, July 16, 2010).

Leadership for and by Women of Color

Why should leadership for women of color be any different than leadership behavior of other women, white men, and men of color? One simple answer is that we are different and second is the fact that the salience of race always trumps gender identity for women of color. Multidimensional identity creates a complexity that may make us hard to figure out. When people state they are surprised I am Latina and, more specifically, Mexican American, I take that as code that I do not meet their stereotyped images of Latinas. We carry our heritage, gender, and other dimensions of our integrated identity (relationship status, spirituality, sexual orientation) with us, and these identity factors are indistinguishable. We are one cultural being embodying a number of identity attributes. Previous discussions have pointed out that leadership is not naturally attributed to women, let alone women of color. So how do we make progress and make a difference as institutional leaders? Mentorship is one of the routes.

Transformational leadership is proposed as the model that works best for women of color in higher education (Valverde, 2003). If transformational leadership were recognized, the work of the woman of color might be considered as essential to culture change for the institution. She is leading by example and enacting stated institutional priorities with and through others. Transformational leaders facilitate and influence. According to Valverde (2003), through their behavior, the leaders of color educate and model for other institutional staff and various stakeholders the value of collaborations to meet shared goals with cultural and political brokers.

Lessons Learned and Resources for Women of Color

Discussions thus far seem to suggest that women of color must be formidable, courageous, and highly self-confident to persist as leaders in higher education. As Julia de Burgos, feminist and social justice advocate, poetically stated, women *have to be and create our own pathways.* The nontraditional, nonlinear route of most women of color leaders has been more atypical than typical. That is, some started in community colleges, assumed responsibility for parents as well as their children, and went against family wishes to achieve their dreams. Current studies by and about women of color in higher education inform strategies and practices that are instructive. These reflections are about personal and professional commitments, values based and with intentionality to make a difference in the lives of others. The goal, through these accountings, is to describe the landscape of historical and foundational drivers, motivational factors, examples of perseverance, and attributes of women who can be viewed as successful achievers.

Practices that Promote and Develop Women of Color

In her study of Latina community college presidents, Muñoz (2010) inquired about impactful influences on career success, strategies to manage barriers, and challenges and organizational climate and practices that hindered or supported careers. As with participants in other studies of women of color leaders in higher education, these women indicated that professional development programs and membership in professional associations were influential in their preparation process. But there was more than institutional and academic socialization discussed; these women also described formative early experiences with responsibility and leadership in their homes and communities. Early developmental encounters also introduced them to several mentors, generally other women, who set expectations of them even as precollege adolescents. These presidents learned about achievements and how the engagements they were having, generally in their communities, were needed. As the women reflected on their pathways to leadership roles in higher education, they noted that they were motivated to keep helping and also experienced reciprocal benefits—the same experiences they had as senior leaders. In other words, they possessed a servant leadership worldview.

As I read examples provided by Muñoz, I recalled my own early examples of mentorship by other women outside of the home and school. In this instance, my mentor was a missionary nun from Puerto Rico, Sister Gracia, working with the newly arrived Puerto Rican families in my neighborhood. First, I was drawn to the new church because of its Spanish-speaking practices, something new to me and very different from the bilingual English-Slavic church and school I attended. Perhaps the second reason to venture about the five or six blocks away was because of my cultural curiosity. Once Sister Gracia learned that I wanted to help, she gave me responsibility to "sign up" families for services and engage them in more formal processes involving paperwork. Though I was only thirteen at the time, this did not seem to be a concern to her. She knew of my willingness and empowered me to take on many tasks and risks. Caring was the common denominator for me and she recognized this intention.

Of course, being a senior leader, depending on the level, presents women with unique challenges. How did the community college presidents overcome barriers and challenges? The women indicated they were prepared, had the appropriate credentials and credibility, and were proactive, persistent, goal oriented, and willing to take risks (Muñoz, 2010).

In her qualitative study about constructing mentors, Méndez-Morse (2004) learned that the Latina educators found sources of mentorship to meet particular needs. In other words, "They assembled a mentor by putting together separate talents of various individuals in a manner that facilitated their professional growth" (p. 582). She identified three mentor categories: familial, distant, and professional. Mentors were found primarily in three areas—home, school (K–12) and university, and career settings. Mothers were mentioned by these women as their strongest and primary mentors. Distant mentors were individuals the women had worked with and still counted on for consultation and support after they had moved on to new positions. Overall, the mentor relationships were more informal and less structured; however, they were readily available upon request.

Once again, I introduce the voices of my colleagues who shared examples of institutional practices they have been able to influence to improve the organizational culture. One vice provost spoke about her use of data to inform colleagues for several purposes. The first was to influence the distribution of university scholarships and the second to inform search committees for senior level higher. Data can be persuasive. Another colleague reported that she was in a position to identify and support nontraditional leaders such as junior faculty members, outstanding staff, and individuals with technical expertise. From her position, this senior administrator of color was able to invite, reward, and "support others' innovation and resourcefulness" (personal communication, July 18, 2010).

Other leadership roles, serving as chair of high-level search committees for the campus, and representing the institution at systemwide meetings are generally appointments approved by the chancellor/president. Thus this dean has exposure to others across the system and on her campus, indicating trust from the top. This type of nonverbal message conveys confidence in the woman. As Kanter (1977) found, being empowered and assuming assignments with power speak volumes about the woman's contributions to institutional priorities.

Developmental Programs with Promise

Advancing historically underrepresented individuals into senior campus roles is becoming increasingly essential as the projected turnover of sitting university presidents in the next five years is reported to be 92 percent (Gladys Johnson, personal communication, June 12, 2010). Two higher education associations with goals for the preparation of persons of color and women are mentioned herein. The Millennium Leadership Institute (MLI), a program of the American Association of Colleges and Universities (AASCU), was established in 1999 by a group of African American college presidents. With the class of 2010, the program has produced 370 protégés. It is also reported that fifty-seven graduates have assumed presidencies and chancellors. The Bryn Mawr Higher Education Resources Services program (HERS) established in 1976 has focused on preparing women for senior roles and typically enrolls U.S. women of color. HERS also has an active program with South Africa. Other developmental programs for senior administrators are hosted by the American Council on Education, among others.

Identity-Specific Associations

In my review of ethnic- and racial identity-specific professional associations in higher education, I identified one for black/African American women, another for Hispanic/Latina/o women and men, and a third for American Indians in higher education, although there may be others. None of these associations had goals to prepare higher education administrators specifically. The American Association of Hispanics in Higher Education (AAHHE) has programs for early and mid-career faculty. The Association of Black Women in Higher Education (ABWHE), established in 1978, promotes "the intellectual growth and educational development of Black women in higher education" and the removal of barriers to "achieving their full potential" (retrieved from the website on August 21, 2010, http://www.abwhe.org). The web page for the American Indian

Higher Education Consortium (AIHEC) leads to a strategic plan prioritizing student engagement, accreditation of its colleges, sustainability, and strengthening communities (retrieved from website on August 21, 2010, http://www.aihec.org/). Of interest on the AIHEC main page was the announcement of American Indian presidencies. Cassandra Manuelito-Kerkvliet assumed the presidency of Antioch University-Seattle in 2007 and continues in that role as of this writing. Remarkably, she became the first American Indian woman to become president of a university that was not within the tribal college system. She had previously served as the president of Diné College, located on a Navajo reservation in Arizona. Luana K. Ross, women's studies professor at the University of Washington, was selected to be president of Salish Kootenai College, replacing the only president of Salish Kootenai College in place since 1979. I found no associations specific to Asian/Pacific Islander women in higher education.

Concluding Thoughts

As women of color, we learn about initiative, adaptability, and responsibility in many settings and enact these behaviors in a white world. Our mindfulness about the racial and gender context is shaped from our childhood and we come to recognize these conditions in all types of organizations, from schools and universities to volunteer settings. By the time women of color become senior administrators, they have passed through many gauntlets and know that there will always be more to negotiate. We know the "borderlands" experiences for women of color as higher education leaders.

Perhaps in the next ten to fifteen years, women of color in higher education administration will not be a rarity. As reports and studies indicate, women have the courage, knowledge, and willingness to lead. However, the culture of gender bias and suspicions about the credibility of women of color will remain unless institutional leaders, such as those described by my colleagues, make our advancement a priority. I remain hopeful.

References

Agars, M. D. (2004). Reconsidering the impact of gender stereotypes on the advancement of women in organizations. *Psychology of Women Quarterly, 28,* 103–11.

Alemán, Jr., E. (2009). Through the prism of critical race theory: Niceness and Latina/o leadership in the politics of education. *Journal of Latinos and Education, 8*(4), 290–311.

Alexiou, A. (2005). A tale of the field: Reading power and gender in the learning organization. *Studies in Continuing Education, 27,* 17–31.

American Indians in Higher Education Consortium. (n. d.). http://www.aihec.org/.

Anzaldúa, G. (1987). *Borderlands/La frontera.* San Francisco: Spinsters/Aunt Lute.

Arredondo, P. (1996). *Successful diversity management initiatives.* Thousand Oaks, CA: Sage.

Arredondo, P. (2002). Mujeres Latinas-santas y marquesas. *Cultural Diversity and Ethnic Minority Psychology, 8,* 1–12.

Arredondo, P. (2003). Resistance to multiculturalism in organizations. In J. S. Mio & G. Y. Iwamasa (Eds.), *Multicultural mental health research and resistance: Continuing challenges of the new millennium* (pp. 83–104). New York: Brunner-Routledge.

Arredondo, P., & Glauner, T. (1992). *Dimensions of personal identity.* Boston: Empowerment Workshops, Inc.

Avolio, B. J. (2007). Promoting more integrative strategies for leadership theory-building. *American Psychologist, 62,* 25–33.

Ayman, R., & Korabik, K. (2010). Leadership: Why gender and culture matter. *American Psychologist, 65*(3), 157–70.

Chenoweth, K. (2007, July 13). African American college presidents in decline. *Higher Education News and Jobs.* Retrieved August 6, 2010, from http://diverseeducation.com/article/8499/.

Cheung, F. M., & Halpern, D. F. (2010). Women at the top. *American Psychologist, 65,* 182–93.

Chin, J. L. (2010). Introduction to the special issue on diversity and leadership. *American Psychologist, 65,* 150–54.

Civil Rights Act of 1964, as amended, 42 U.S.C. § 2000E *et seq.* (1964).

Collins, J. (2000). *Good to great.* New York: HarperCollins.

Collins, J. (2009). *How the mighty fall.* New York: HarperCollins.

Conger, J. A., & Kanungo, R. N. (1987). Toward a behavioral theory of charismatic leadership in organizational settings. *Academy of Management Review, 12*(4), 637–47.

De Burgos, J. (1953). *Yo misma fui mi ruta* (I was my own path). Retrieved July 16, 2010, from http://www.arlindo-correia.com/120205.html#YO _MISMA_FUI_MI_RUTA.

Eagly, A. H., & Carli, L. L. (2007). *Through the labyrinth*. Boston: Harvard Business School Press.

Eagly, A. H. & Chin, J. L. (2010). Diversity and leadership in a changing world. *American Psychologist, 65,* 216–24.

Enríquez-Damián, E. (2009). *Leadership among Latina women in education: Challenges and rewards*. Unpublished doctoral dissertation, Arizona State University-Tempe.

Fiske, S. (1993). Controlling other people: The impact of power on stereotyping. *American Psychologist, 48*(6), 621–28.

Helms, J. E. (Ed.). (1990). *Black and white racial identity attitudes: Theory, research and practice*. Westport, CT: Greenwood.

Henry, W. J., & Glenn, N. M. (2009). Black women employed in the ivory tower: Connecting for success. *Advancing Women in Leadership Journal, 27*. Retrieved August 6, 2010, from http://advancingwomen.com/awl/ awl_wordpress/black-women-employed-in-the-ivory-tower-connecting -for-success-2/.

Hersey, P., Blanchard, K. H., & Johnson, D. E. (2007). *Management of organizational behavior: Leading human resources*. New York: Prentice Hall.

Hostede, G. (1984). *Culture's consequences*. Newbury Park, CA: Sage.

Kanter, R. M. (1977). *Men and women of the corporation*. New York: Basic Books.

Kramer, V. M., Konrad, A. M., & Erkut, S. (2006). *Critical mass on corporate boards: Why three or more women enhance governance*. Wellesley, MA: Wellesley College Center for Women.

Lee, S. M. (2002). Do Asian American faculty face a glass ceiling in higher education? *American Educational Research Journal, 39*(3), 695–724.

Lithwick, D. (2010, September 6). The female factor: Will three women really change the court? *Newsweek, 19.*

Macintosh, P. (1989, July/August). White privilege: Unpacking the invisible knapsack. *Peace and Freedom,* 1–4.

McClelland, D. (1975). *Power: The inner experience.* New York: John Wiley.

McGregor, D. (1960). *The human side of enterprise.* New York: McGraw Hill.

Méndez-Morse, S. (2004). Constructing mentors: Latina educational leaders' role models and mentors. *Educational Administration Quarterly, 40,* 561–90.

Morgan, G. (1997). *Images of organization* (2nd ed.). Thousand Oaks, CA: Sage.

Muñoz, M. (2010). In their own words and by the numbers: A mixed-methods study of Latina community college presidents. *Community College Journal of Research and Practice, 34,* 153–74.

Myers, S. L., & Turner, C. S. (1999). *Faculty of color in academe: Bittersweet success* (1st ed.). Upper Saddle River, NJ: Pearson Education.

Nichols, J. C., & Tanksley, C. B. (2004). Revelations of African-American women with terminal degrees: Overcoming obstacles to success [Electronic version]. *Negro Educational Review, 55*(4), 175–85.

Potok, M. The year in hate and extremism. Southern Poverty Law Center (2010, spring). Issue Number 137.

Saigo, R. (2008). Why there still aren't enough Asian-American college presidents. *Chronicle of Higher Education, 55*(5), B60-62. Retrieved August 6, 2010, from Academic Search Complete database.

Sanchez-Hucles, J. V., & Davis, D. D. (2010). Women and women of color in leadership: Complexity, identity, and intersectionality. *American Psychologist, 65*(3), 171–81.

Sandler, B. L., & Hall, R. M. (1986). *The campus climate revisited: Chilly for women faculty, administrators, and graduate students.* Washington, DC: Association of American Colleges, Project on the Status and Education of Women.

Schien, E. G. (1985). *Organizational culture and leadership.* San Francisco: Jossey-Bass.

Steele, C. M., & Aronson, J. (1995). Stereotype threat and the intellectual test performance of African-Americans. *Journal of Personality and Social Psychology, 69,* 797–811.

Sue, D. W. & Sue, D. (2003). *Counseling the culturally diverse* (4th ed.). Hoboken, NJ: Wiley.

Turner, C. S. (2002). *Diversifying the faculty: A guidebook for search committees.* Washington, DC: Association of American Colleges.

Valverde, L. A. (2003). *Leaders of color in higher education.* Walnut Creek, CA: AltaMira.

Warren, J. T. (1999). Whiteness and cultural theory: Perspectives on research and education. *The Urban Review, 31,* 185–203.

14

Beyond Quid Pro Quo: Undergraduates and "Consensual" Sex with Professors

Billie Wright Dziech

When editor Jennifer Martin contacted me about writing a chapter for *Women as Leaders in Education,* I suspect she hoped for a work that would provide insight into the advances women have made in bringing the issue of sexual harassment to the attention of the higher education community and making it more responsive to students who have been discriminated against because of both hostile environment and quid pro quo harassment. In the case of the latter, I think she also must have wished for a genuine "leader," one who could provide definitive advice about ways in which to meet the challenges of a culture in which we can no longer make simplistic, easily generalized assumptions about young women's values and behaviors or about methods for ensuring that faculty members and institutions will act conscientiously and professionally in dealing with students.

What I am absolutely certain she did not expect is a work that would begin with an "I'm not sure I know" disclaimer. But the truth is that I really am uncertain where we are headed and what we must do on campuses where casual sex is an undeniable reality, where some faculty members condone or take advantage of that reality, and where some university officials dismiss sexual contact between faculty members and undergraduates as primarily a nuisance that threatens their reputations and finances.[1] The one point of which I am confident is that this issue of so-called "consensual" sex demands far more attention than it currently receives.

These days *The Chronicle of Higher Education* seldom carries advertisements for conferences on sexual harassment, and the media tend to focus only on sexual abuse by schoolteachers.[2] There was a time, of course, when "sexual harassment" was a major concern of educators and the public alike. Back in the 1970s when books like *The Lecherous Professor* and Michele Paludi's *The Leaning Ivory Tower* were published, the women's movement was in full swing, and what came to be known as "hostile environment" sexual harassment emerged as a focal point in discussions of campus life. Fed up with gender discrimination, we thought we knew everything then. We understood that words could hurt and that unspoken prejudices could limit educational and workplace opportunities for females. So we began to conduct research and talk and write about our experiences and findings; and slowly but surely, the legal system and a sizable portion of the public began to recognize what some called the "victimization" of females when they were subjected to crude sexual jokes and anecdotes, unwanted touching, offensive gestures, and demeaning nicknames.

---

[1]Undergraduate and graduate student "consent" exists, and both frequently qualify as quid pro quo harassment. However, factors such as smaller age discrepancies and greater and more immediate professional risks make graduate student "consent" more complex and deserving of separate attention. Thus this article will concentrate only on undergraduates and professors.

[2]Sexual misbehaviors by schoolteachers have received considerable attention, whereas information on college professors' misconduct is limited. A five-year study (2001–2005) by the Associated Press found 2,570 cases in which various kinds of sexual harassment by teachers occurred. This number includes verbal and other types of abuse and does *not* suggest that all teachers were involved in "consensual" cases. However, the paucity of information on colleges and universities reinforces the theory that offending professors are seldom discovered and/or that their behaviors are kept secret by students, colleagues, and institutions. Thus an observation about the AP investigation may be even more applicable to higher education.

The AP investigation found efforts to stop individual offenders but, overall, a deeply entrenched resistance toward recognizing and fighting abuse. It starts in school hallways, where fellow teachers look away or feel powerless to help. School administrators make behind-the-scenes deals to avoid lawsuits and other trouble. And in state capitals and Congress, lawmakers shy from tough state punishments or any cohesive national policy for fear of disparaging a vital profession (Irvine & Tanner, 2007).

Higher education was forced to respond to new laws declaring the actions of its employees illegal if they engaged in behaviors severe or pervasive enough to create "intimidating, hostile, and offensive" environments. During those early years, hostile environment harassment seemed the more complex of the two types because bright lines between professorial language and gestures were sometimes difficult to draw. What might seem a simple compliment about a student's appearance to one could be highly offensive to another, so contentious debates about free speech raged on campus as well as off. The disagreements have never really stopped, but by now most college professors act with restraint because they recognize the foolhardiness of flouting hostile environment law.

Quid pro quo harassment was and is another matter. Few will dispute that an individual in authority has no right to predicate a student's grades or recommendations on her (or his) provision of sexual favors, but the problem has never been that simple. When cases reach institutional complaint stages, colleges and universities must theoretically protect not only their own interests but also the rights of students and faculty members. Thus they become, in a sense, prosecution, defense, judge, and jury. More troubling still is that when they have previously acted in favor of one side or the other and a case enters the court system, their sole concern and strategy becomes self-protection.

Quid pro quo sexual harassment involves a unique form of chaos in which self-interest and educational, legal, and moral philosophies collide. In the last quarter century or so, student culture has changed in ways we did not foresee, faculty advocacy for unlimited rights to "consensual" sex with students has become more public, and institutions have responded in diverse ways that frequently place their mission and policy statements in conflict with their desires to protect their reputations and resources. The result is that students bringing complaints may stand on shakier ground than in the past as the credibility of quid pro quo sexual harassment is increasingly tested.

Students

There was a time when we could with a fair amount of accuracy argue that "consensual" relationships between undergraduates and professors resulted from the victimization of naïve coeds coerced into sexual liaisons with more experienced, manipulative professors. But today we live in a world where many or perhaps most young women resist the victim label; and while that is understandable and even commendable, a new form of naiveté characterizes some who believe themselves to be so sophisticated that they can, without repercussions, handle the vagaries of an ambiguously defined sexual culture known as the hookup.

The evolution of hookup culture can be traced by reviewing social historian Beth Bailey's *From Front Porch to Back Seat: Courtship in Twentieth-Century America* (1988). Bailey notes that during the calling era or first decade of the century, males of the middle and upper middle classes would visit or "call on" respectable young women of similar positions at their homes, where they would spend time with them and their families under the watchful eyes of the women's mothers, who might permit them a small degree of privacy if they were certain their daughters were interested in the male visitors. Women's public presence and freedom increased rapidly in the second decade of the century as more and more attended college and took jobs. The invention of the automobile made it possible or perhaps inevitable that the young would no longer be willing to submit to parental oversight. And so, Bailey observes, dating spread until approximately the mid-1920s, when it became a "universal custom" (Bailey, p. 19).

In *Hooking Up: Sex, Dating, and Relationships on Campus*, Kathleen Bogle (2008) contends that World War II and its aftermath changed the norms of dating for the majority of America's young. The war took its toll on the number of eligible bachelors on campus, and the subsequent economic boom gave the young greater financial stability so that "going steady" and eventual marriage seemed more viable and attractive. Deprived of definitive research on the sexual behaviors of American youth, we cannot be certain about the number who engaged in intercourse during these eras; yet Bogle concludes that "as the twentieth century progressed, greater sexual intimacy emerged, but for those in the mainstream this sexual intimacy was generally restricted to intimate relationships where a likely outcome was marriage" (Bogle, 2008, p. 20).

Then came the Baby Boom generation of the 1960s and with it, changes that rocked the foundations of American youth culture. Nowhere were these changes more intense and sweeping than college campuses.

As children, Boomers experienced post-war optimism and adoring parents groomed to have the perfect family life. As they grew-up, Boomers enjoyed constant attention from a child-obsessed, idealistic America and naturally grew to focus on themselves. At the same time, parents of Boomers amassed sufficient resources to send them to college in record numbers, prolonging the childhood stage and helping to foster the idealistic perspectives that permeated the 60s and 70s. (Ritchie, 2002, p. 29)

Like their male counterparts, college women were part of a generation that, rightly or wrongly, has generally been characterized as narcissistic, nonconformist, and rebellious. Availability of the birth control pill made sexual relations much less threatening for young collegians who might otherwise fear becoming pregnant, and the women's movement with its stress on female equality helped fuel a sexual revolution. Although they would later divide on issues concerning pornography, hookup culture, and student–professor physical intimacy, early feminists argued that women had as much right to assert their sexuality as males. On this point at least, their views elicited little disagreement from college men, who were all too eager to help further such rights.

A serious impediment, however, was what most considered an outmoded campus tradition called *in loco parentis*. Meaning "in place or instead of a parent," the term describes institutions' legal responsibilities to protect the interests of students while they are not under parental care. Time had led to the belief that the most frequent "danger" from which young women needed protection was the carnal desires of young men, so a complex system of regulations and separate residences had evolved to keep the two apart. Independent collegians in the waning years of the twentieth century were not about to be bound by such restrictions, and same-sex dormitories sprang up as rapidly as curfews fell. Colleges and universities had never mastered the art of controlling students' study habits, let alone their sexual drives, so they had no regrets about relinquishing a task few had desired in the first place.

College increasingly came to mean freedom from the restraints of home; on campus, students lived in a culture all their own, a culture in which the music and images of Woodstock became the symbol for a generation besotted by drugs and sex. Whether the symbolism was illusion or reality, an accurate or deceptive portrayal of an entire generation matters less today than the fact that peer culture then, as now, exerted an enormous influence on the young. What college students believed to be true of their peers increasingly became the reality as more and more condoned or adopted the sexual behaviors of their peers. Formal dating had met its demise, and hookup culture was born.

Recognition of changed sexual mores persisted from the late 60s through the latter part of the century, partially because the public and educators grew increasingly concerned about the threat of HIV/AIDS to collegians. But by the 1990s, the term *hooking up* had made its way into student jargon, and the phenomenon of casual sex so intrigued researchers that many focused exclusively on it. Two early examinations of hookup culture, one academic and the other an article in the popular press, probably had the greatest impact.

In " 'Hookups': Characteristics and Correlates of College Students' Spontaneous and Anonymous Sexual Experiences," Paul, McManus, and Hayes (2000) reaffirmed earlier studies and offered a definition of *hookup* that clarified the term for the academic community:

> . . . a sexual encounter, usually lasting only one night, between two people who are strangers or brief acquaintances. Some physical inter-action is typical, but it may or may not include sexual intercourse. Such experiences are usually spontaneous (i.e., something that "just happens"); alternately, the goal of hooking up is planned by the target of the hookup or the individual with whom the hookup occurs is unknown. . . . In addition, hookups are usually anonymous in that the partners are strangers or only brief acquaintances and rarely continue to build a relationship, let alone see each other again. (p. 76)

That definition, with some minor alterations and additions, has remained for a decade the description of a behavior both collegians and academics had known for much longer to be true. But it was Janet Reit-man's 2006 *Rolling Stone* article, "Sex and Scandal at Duke," that shocked a public less familiar with the American campus. Since then, Duke has enjoyed a dubious reputation as the poster child for uncontrolled sexual expression, but the weight of subsequent statistical and anecdotal research demonstrates that hookup culture has been alive and well on other campuses for years.

Exact figures on the extent of students hooking up, especially in the case of intercourse, are difficult, if not impossible, to discover. Some conclude that the practice is widespread (Feldman, Turner, & Araujo, 1999; Grello, Welsh, Harper, & Dickson, 2003; Kahn, Fricker, Hoffman, Lambert, Tripp, & Childress, 2000; Lambert, Kahn, & Apple, 2003), while others believe it is exaggerated (Taneja, 2010). What matter most, however, are students' perceptions of peers' behaviors; and most appear to find it pervasive. For example, a 2001 study, "Hooking Up, Hanging Out, and Hoping for Mr. Right: College Women on Mating and Dating Today," commissioned by the Independent Women's Forum, found that 91 percent of college women believe hookup culture defines their campuses.

Contemporary parents and campus personnel alike have sought explanations for this conduct that exceeds even the excesses of the '60s and '70s. It can be explained in part, of course, by the hypersexualized atmosphere in which the young have grown up, but the underlying cause may be more complex. Tracing the relationship between hookup culture and student development, Arnold (2009) contends that contemporary adolescence "now reaches far beyond the teenage years" (p. 4) and extends from approximately 18 to 28 years of age. She cites the work of Jeffrey Arnett (2004), who defined this new developmental phase as "emerging adulthood" (p. 4).

> With minimal duties to others and considerable autonomy to run their own lives emerging adults tend to be self-focused. The period of emerging adulthood is . . . characterized by feeling in-between childhood dependence on parents and adult self-reliance: young people themselves define full adulthood as some future time in which they will accept full responsibility for themselves, make independent decisions, and reach financial independence. Finally, emerging adulthood is an age of possibilities in which individuals see themselves as free from the past, optimistic about the future, and able to transform themselves. (Arnett, 2004, p. 4)

As in the case of the *Rolling Stone* article, work written for popular consumption attracted greater attention. In Tom Wolfe's widely read novel, *I Am Charlotte Simmons*, a friend of the protagonist attempts to explain why hookups are acceptable:

College is like this four-year period when you can try anything and everything—and if it goes wrong, there's no consequences.... College is the only time your life, or your adult life anyway, when you can really *experiment*, and at a certain point, when you leave, when you graduate or whatever, everybody's memory like evaporates. You tried this and this and this and this, and you learned a lot about how things are, but nobody's gonna remember it. It's like amnesia, totally, and there's no record and you leave college exactly the way you came in, pure as rainwater. (Wolfe, p. 168)

If we are to take her at her word, if one sees the college years as a last chance to experiment without consequences and if the most likely testing ground is sex, it is not difficult to understand why some students assent to and even welcome physical intimacy with professors. In a culture where any kind of sexual behavior is tolerated, age discrepancies between partners have little relevance beyond their effects on physical attraction, so why not hook up with a history professor? After all, points out Coté (2006),

In the context of freedom without guidance, people can exercise the choice to pursue a life course totally devoid of traditional social markers, with or without exerting much mental effort, by simply selecting a number of default options now available in youth culture, by which they follow the paths of least resistance and effort, as in the imitation of the latest fashion and music trends. (Coté, p. 92)

The vast majority of research and publication examining the effects of hooking up concludes that it is detrimental to females (Grello, Welsh, & Harper, 2006; McIlhaney & Bush, 2008; Paul, McManus, & Hayes, 2000; Stepp, 2007); and anyone who has witnessed the "morning after" of a faculty–student hook up or relationship is unlikely to see the typical female student as undamaged or, as some claim, an empowered victor in the struggle for gender equality.

My own first experience with the then-phenomenon was listening to a sobbing freshman honors student from a small town in Ohio. Her roommates had been telling her that "no one (was) a virgin anymore," so when she was "feeling cool from a few beers at a party and this cute guy kept looking at (her)," she went to his apartment and had intercourse with him. What upset her most, she said, was that she "thought he really liked (her) but he wouldn't even walk (her) to the dorm afterwards."

The emotions are even more complex when they involve a professor. Not long ago I was asked to consult with attorneys for a very bright young woman who had had a brief affair with one of her professors. The institution obviously knew he was guilty because he had had a long record of aberrant behavior and had no qualms about publicly stating that he believed members of his profession had a right to have sexual relationships with students. The woman came from a background that could only be described as "horrific." She had a history of molestation, drug abuse, homelessness, and lack of parental and family care.

When she attempted to extricate herself from the affair, the professor became threatening, and the college took her concerns so seriously that it provided her with a guard while she was on campus. The professor was eventually dismissed; but the law states that an institution can be held responsible if it knew or should have known about an employee's inappropriate behaviors, so she sued the college because she believed her situation would not have occurred if the institution had previously acted responsibly. Like many who have been involved in "consensual" situations, she lost the case.

Not long afterward she wrote to me:

> I'm still confused. I don't understand why no one else can understand what happened, especially when I have been honest, desperately hoping that the law worked and honesty would win. Now, I don't know what to do. I feel a great need, that desperation, to make something of this, to help others, to get my story out, for it not to be "pushed under the rug" with everything else. Although it has almost burned what was left of any trust I had in the world and the way that it works, I feel much better to not have this court case over my head any longer. It feels great to not have to fight and for no one to be able to say that I am looking for a "paycheck," as the College's attorney said.
>
> I think that many people just don't understand, and I get that. I have this need to help them understand. I want to get into some sort of activism. I'm not sure if there is some sort of group out there like me or an organization that I can become active in. I want to change things, not only for me, but for all the others anything like this has, or will,

happen to. I just don't know where to turn and am hoping you may know where I should be reaching out.

How should I answer? Should I say I wish I had been able to warn her that far too many judges and juries assume she made a choice and has to live with it? Should I admit I don't know of any support systems because most students who find themselves in her situation are too humiliated, too frightened of repercussions to file complaints or be identified? Should I tell her that there are educators who think she is "fair game" and even some who understand collegians' "reasoning" about hookups and are eager to present themselves as "default options?"

Professors

Determining the numbers or percentages of faculty members who engage in sexual relations with students has always been, at best, a guessing game. Early surveys found 17 percent to 25 percent of professors claiming to have had "consensual" sex (Fitzgerald, Gold, Omerod, & Weitzman, 1988; Glaser & Thorpe, 1986); but those percentages do not take into account the number of nonrespondents, respondents who denied the behavior to protect themselves, or those who exaggerated it to fit a macho stereotype. Nor can they provide an accurate measurement of academics who are repeat offenders, engaging in sex with multiple students and burdening their colleagues with a negative stereotype that they do not deserve.

Rather than attempting to measure the immeasurable, it seems to me we now have more to learn by focusing on rhetoric emanating from contemporary academics who feel no inhibitions or sense of absurdity in arguing that their rights to bed students are analogous to religious and political freedoms or that sexual intercourse is the means by which we express our humanity and the spark that ignites our desire to learn.

In *Romance in the Ivory Tower: The Rights of Liberty and Conscience*, Paul Abramson (2007), UCLA psychology professor, uses the Ninth Amendment to make a case for intimate relationships between professors and students. His distinguished career in psychology appeared daunting when I first heard of his book. After all, who am I by comparison? An English professor who began writing about sexual harassment because of her experiences with students is no match for an expert in human sexuality, I thought; and MIT Press that published his work is no slacker either. Then I read the book and, after that, the press description of *Romance in the Ivory Tower*:

> Allen Ginsberg once declared that "the best teaching is done in bed," but most university administrators would presumably disagree. Many universities prohibit romantic relationships between faculty members and students, and professors who transgress are usually out of a job. In *Romance in the Ivory Tower,* Paul Abramson takes aim at university policies that forbid relationships between faculty members and students. He argues provocatively that the issue of faculty–student romances transcends the seemingly trivial matter of who sleeps with whom and engages our fundamental constitutional rights.
>
> By what authority, Abramson asks, did the university become the arbiter of romantic etiquette among consenting adults? Do we, as consenting adults, have a constitutional right to make intimate choices as long as they do not cause harm? Abramson contends that we do, and bases this claim on two arguments. He suggests that the Ninth Amendment (which states that the Constitution's enumeration of certain rights should not be construed to deny others) protects the "right to romance." And, more provocatively, he argues that the "right to romance" is a fundamental right of conscience—as are freedom of speech and freedom of religion.
>
> Campus romances happen. The important question is not whether they should be encouraged or prohibited but whether the choice to engage in such a relationship should be protected or precluded. Abramson argues ringingly that our freedom to make choices—to worship, make a political speech, or fall in love—is fundamental. Rules forbidding faculty–student romances are not only unconstitutional but set dangerous precedents for further intrusion into rights of privacy and conscience.

I may not be a genius in the field of sexuality, but as an English professor, I do know that inaccuracies in a book's description matter. Long years of dealing with the issue of sexual harassment have also taught me a few simple facts. For instance, to state that "many" universities "prohibit" or "forbid" relationships between professors and students is false. Some and, hopefully, many institutions by the twenty-first century have begun to *discourage* such intimacies, but few have been willing to issue prohibitions. Instead they have taken the path of least resistance and written discouragement policies that are typically vague and have limited authority. Moreover, convincing institutions to do even this little has been a long and arduous process, primarily because of opposition from educators obsessed with faculty rights.

The assertion that "professors who transgress are usually out of a job" is factually, as well as grammatically, incorrect. It is common knowledge that all forms of sexual harassment, including intimate relationships between students and professors, are rarely reported. When they are, the institutional inclination often is to doubt the veracity of the accusation. This is a major reason why so few come forward. When a complaint occurs and offending faculty members do admit to sexual liaisons with collegians, few are summarily dismissed, as they might be if they were in the workplace. Fear of adverse publicity more often results in such individuals being asked to retire or leave quietly, bolstered by generous severance agreements from institutions relieved to be rid of them.

At the heart of the quid pro quo argument is the phrase "consenting adults," which MIT's press uses to describe students as well as professors. To insist that a nineteen- or twenty-year-old brain functions in the same way as that of a forty-year-old is to dispute all that magnetic imaging technology and neuroscience have taught us about the human brain. Whether the brains of collegians are not fully developed until the mid-twenties, as studies like that of Bennett and Baird (2006) claim, or develop too quickly as Berns, Moore, and Capra (2009) theorizes, those of us who have taught college students and/or raised children know from experience that the young are prone to risky decision making and faulty reasoning. In the dark ages of brain science, the "consenting adult" argument might have been worth debating. In 2010, it has become a moot issue.

Abramson may argue "ringingly that that our freedom to make choices— to worship, make a political speech, or fall in love—is fundamental," but ultimately most reasoning citizens, especially those paying college tuition, doubt that the nation's founders equated religious and political freedom with the so-called "right" to bed college students. It is true that institutions' discouragement or prohibition policies are predicated in large part upon fears of being sued by a rejected coed, but those of us who have dealt firsthand with the aftermath of student–professor sex know that only rarely do professors "fall in love" with students, that sex rather than "romance" is usually the motivation, and that "who sleeps with whom" is seldom a "trivial matter" to undergraduates or their families.

Jane Gallop, Professor of English at the University of Wisconsin–Milwaukee, fits Abramson's profile as both student and professor exercising her Ninth Amendment right to have sex when and with whom she pleases. Her book, *Feminist Accused of Sexual Harassment*, followed formal charges brought against her by two female students in 1993. Amazon.com's book review excerpts contain an entry from *Library Journal*, which notes that "only a few pages are devoted to the facts of the case. . . . What could have been an original and enlightening discussion of a serious issue becomes a portrait of unprofessional behavior glibly sketched." Less restrained, Richard Kimball (1997) calls it "subacademic sensationalist trash."

The book is, as Gallop herself admits, disjointed, fluctuating between distant and recent past, between theory and personal experience. According to her account, she was originally charged with sexual harassment and then found "guilty of violating university policy because (she) engaged with one of (her) students in a 'consensual amorous relation' " (Gallop, 1997, p. 34). The substance of the two complaints is lost in verbal obfuscation that attempts to differentiate sexual harassment from Gallop's having French kissed a student before a group of onlookers at a bar. She says of the kiss:

> We both were known to enjoy making spectacles of ourselves, and this opportunity for professional exhibitionism was bound to turn us on. . . . It was a performance. By that, I do not mean that I wasn't really kissing her or that I didn't find it sexy. What I mean is that we didn't just happen to be seen kissing, but we kissed like that because we were being watched. And it was precisely the knowledge of being watched that made it sexy. (Gallop, 1997 p. 91)

Gallop complains about the "confusion" of facts in the case:

> While there were indeed two complaints against me, I had kissed only one student and that student didn't go to the affirmative-action office to complain that I'd kissed her. She went to complain that I tried to

sleep with her and that, when she turned me down, I started rejecting her work. She filed her complaint in tandem with another student who made almost identical claims against me, even though I never kissed *her*. Both women charged me with classic quid pro quo sexual harassment. (Gallop, 1997, p. 94)

I talked with one of those women who contacted me on a few occasions to discuss the event and its aftermath; and while she deserves her privacy and has, hopefully, moved on with her life, it is worth nothing that she found the experience to be anything but "trivial." What frustrated me following our conversations is the knowledge that Duke University Press, the publisher of *Feminist Accused of Sexual Harassment*, probably wouldn't have paid second notice to a manuscript she or the other woman submitted describing that time in their lives.

Gallop reiterates her pleasure in being an "exhibitionist" and describes several incidences in which she had sex with students. She begins with an account of living briefly with one of her older graduate students, who left her for another woman. She describes feeling "rejected and quite alone" (Gallop, 1997, p. 45) until a former undergraduate and "cute kid" (Gallop, 1997, p. 45) "stopped by (her) apartment . . . to cheer (her) up by sleeping with (her)" (Gallop, 1997, p. 45). She adds:

> I was glad he had come by and immediately took to the idea . . . We had sex on several occasions over the course of the next year or so. This was, however, not at all a romantic relationship; all the sex was very casual. For example, about a year later he stopped by in just the same way he had the first time: it was my birthday, and, in view of the occasion, he wanted to make sure I got laid. The thought was sweet; I appreciated and accepted his offer. . . . But his real devotion to me was intellectual. He took every course he could with me during the rest of his time in college. (Gallop, 1997, p. 45)

She then explains her relationships with a lesbian couple enrolled in one of her classes:

> In the middle of that semester, they broke up. Late one weekday evening soon after, the tough, curly-haired one showed up at my apartment

with the express purpose of seducing me. . . . Since I found her very sexy, I was thrilled to let her seduce me. . . . A year later (the other student) found occasion to invite me to spend the night with her. Diane was soulful and very beautiful; I was extremely flattered and more than happy to accept her invitation. (Gallop, 1997, p. 48)

Gallop is careful to observe that she eventually fell in love, stayed with photographer Dick Blau, and hasn't slept with a student since 1982, about the time institutions began making policies discouraging "consensual" sex between professors and students. Her latest book, *Living with His Camera* (2003), is a combination of her commentary and Blau's photographs of Gallop and their children. One picture shows her and her son lounging naked together.

Despite the turn to family life, Gallop still recalls happy memories from her graduate school days when she "wanted ever so badly to sleep with" (Gallop, 2003, p. 41) her dissertation advisers, both of whom rejected her advances "more than once" (Gallop, 2003, p. 41). Eventually, however, she prevailed and had intercourse with "each separately, to be sure, but oddly, coincidentally, in the same week" (Gallop, 2003, p. 41).

In describing herself in relation to the two, she appears blissfully unaware that she and they epitomize the classic sexual harasser and target. (Even though the latter term would disturb her, Gallop might prefer it to "victim," since she appears unable to comprehend that the initiator of sex can simultaneously act as a dehumanized object for another's use.) Her language in depicting the incidents is as much that of a wide-eyed freshman as it is an aging college professor.

I had sex but once with each of them. Neither of these became "relationships." It was just what is called "casual sex," although there was nothing casual about my relation to either of them. Their opinion of me already mattered profoundly; their teaching had forever changed the way I understood the world.

To be honest, I think I wanted to get them into bed in order to make them more human, more vulnerable. These two had enormous power over me: I don't mean their institutional position but their intellectual force. I was bowled over by their brilliance; they seemed so superior. I wanted to see them as like other men. Not so as to stop taking them seriously as intellects (I never did), but so as to feel my own power in relation to them …

Sexual harassment creates an environment that is hostile to a student's education. My experience was the opposite. I was in an environment extremely conducive to my education, a heady atmosphere where close personal contact intensified my desire to learn and my desire to excel. I learned and excelled; I desired and I fucked my teachers. (Gallop, 2003, p. 42)

Unfortunately (or fortunately, depending upon one's point of view), the experience of at least one of the two participating professors was less enthusiastic than Gallop's. When he was identified and asked to write a blurb for her book, Cornell's Richard Klein responded, "For decades I have felt guilt and shame for having performed toward her in a way that was unprofessional, exploitative, and lousy in bed" (Kimball, 1997). Perhaps, after all, he recognizes the pathetic need of an individual who conflates sex with humanity:

We fight against sexual harassment precisely because it is dehumanizing. But the ban on consensual relations is dehumanizing too. Telling teachers and students that we must not engage each other ultimately tells us that we must limit ourselves to the confines of some restricted professional transaction, that we *should not treat each other as human beings.* (Gallop, 2003, p. 51)

I have read that statement again and again and have never ceased wishing to respond, "Dogs and pigs also 'engage one another' in sex but that doesn't mean they are treating one another other as human beings." Abramson and Gallop are hardly representative of the academic profession as a whole, but the fact that they and others like them are taken seriously is disquieting. They suggest a profession totally self-indulgent and out of control. Others in the workforce conceal behaviors that too many in higher education are willing to tout or tolerate. What corporate CEO, union president, small business owner, schoolteacher, or clergyperson could retain a position after publicly insisting that he or she had the right to have intercourse with subordinates? Who would employ a manager who recorded for public consumption his random sex acts with former supervisees? The image of unbridled faculty hedonism and self-interest is easily transferred to students, which makes it all the more difficult for them to extricate themselves from quid pro quo situations and to obtain fair hearings on campus or in the courts.

Institutions

Quid pro quo issues place institutions in extremely difficult positions, so some have recently recognized the importance of clarifying policies on "consensual" faculty–student sex. Doing so requires the ability to withstand condemnation from various faculty members, students, and outsiders. For instance, Yale University set off a maelstrom of criticism in 2010 when it adopted the long-considered and easily understood prohibition:

> Undergraduate students are particularly vulnerable to the unequal institutional power inherent in the teacher–student relationship and the potential for coercion, because of their age and relative lack of maturity. Therefore, no teacher shall have a sexual or amorous relationship with any undergraduate student, regardless of whether the teacher currently exercises or expects to have any pedagogical or supervisory responsibilities over that student.

Institutions and individuals alike have become accustomed to opposition and hysteria as a result of their support for bans. Dank and Albuquerque's Internet article "Banning Sexual Asymmetry on Campus" (1998) uses a familiar tactic. Citing a study claiming only one out of 521 University of Massachusetts students admitted to a sexual relationship with a professor, they conclude:

> The proponents of banning with their familiar arguments about protecting innocent female students, sound frighteningly reminiscent of 19th-century Puritans. To avoid the wrath of these new Puritans, most persons involved in intimate asymmetric relationships on campus have closeted themselves. They are not only hiding from the extremists, but also from academic bureaucrats who have the responsibility of enforcing university policies which have codified the new Puritans' procrustean moral agenda. The new Puritans have been remarkably successful in imposing this agenda on campus, because the professoriate and

university administrations have been singularly unwilling to challenge all the loose facts and tired stereotypes emanating from this group. (Dank & Albuquerque, 1998)

Asymmetric relationships is a curious phrase to describe faculty–student sexual relations since the term means "unequal," and the last thing the authors want is to suggest student–professor inequality. Moreover, results of the study they cite are remarkably inconsistent with others. Nevertheless, when they remark that professors engaging in "consensual" sex with students "have closeted themselves," they are correct. The corollary to this statement is that if concealment characterizes professors, it is also descriptive of students intimidated by revealing participation in improper behaviors with faculty members. Dank and Albuquerque's use of the term *Puritanical* is a pejorative generally employed to describe those who support bans. I recall being asked on occasion if the label bothers me, and I think my response has been like that of any professional who has been witness to quid pro quo harassment. If *Puritanical* is used as an epithet to imply someone suspicious of physical pleasure, then the user knows little about the Puritans or me. If it is employed to suggest that an individual is concerned about discipline and morality, both of which are, in my opinion, inherent in professionalism, then I am more than willing to be thus characterized. Fortunately, more and more institutions are coming to the realization that they have little choice when it comes to banning faculty–student sex. Discouragement policies have too many loopholes that offenders' and complainants' attorneys alike can use in court, and defeats mean loss of both revenue and reputation. Yet despite efforts to end "consensual" sex, there is no guarantee that it will disappear if it is prohibited by institutional policies:

Although bans cannot prevent amorous relationships, they do . . . establish legal and ethical positions for faculty, administrators, and institutions. They communicate to the campus a required standard of behavior. They send a message that faculty and students disregard at their own risk and, in so doing, alleviate the potential for problems at the institution's expense when "consensual" affairs sour. Prohibition is not prevention, but it does offer a safeguard, and that is the best that beleaguered institutions can hope for as they struggle with more complexities and challenges than ever before. (Dziech and Hawkins, 1998, p. 135)

I would like to write that efforts like those to enforce prohibition policies have convinced me colleges and universities invariably act with concern for students who bring justifiable internal complaints and legal cases. But that would be a lie. I cannot claim that I have been involved in enough cases to contend that the institutional behavior I witnessed is characteristic, but then again I would probably not have been consulted if the college or university had accepted responsibility for what it knew or should have known in each circumstance.

The most egregious is a case in which a young undergraduate had a brief sexual encounter with a professor who was taking and providing students with drugs. On the night the student went to break the association off, she overdosed and died in his apartment. When he finally placed a call to police, he initially denied knowing her name. Later others would report on what they allege to be his long history of both rape and quid pro quo behavior. A few years before the death occurred, another student had formally accused him of trying to have her touch his genitals; but the college had dismissed the case as a he said/she said situation, even though the investigator admitted to believing the student.

The death resulted in a cursory investigation by the institution. Asked to recount details of the process, most officials had "no recall" or "couldn't remember" what they had said or done. This was basically the case because the college has a practice of not recording or word-for-word transcribing investigatory interviews. The professor was ultimately dismissed, but at this point in time the institution has refused to admit any legal responsibility. This is only one example of an institution's refusing responsibility and recompense; and even though death is an extreme result of "consent," institutional behavior in this instance is not. Colleges and universities often take the "hard line" and fight to protect their finances and "good names." Winning is easy when students lack resources to employ attorneys or when they are labeled as gold diggers.

At times institutions take what appears on the surface to be a more ethical stance and decide to settle with young women arguing that they were manipulated into and damaged by sexual encounters with professors. This practice also has its dark side, and I have been a part of it. Inherent in many settlements are gag orders or agreements that facts of the case and its resolution will not be publicly disclosed. Consultants who give depositions in quid pro quo and other types of sexual harassment cases are often held to such restrictions. What gag orders mean is that institutions achieve at least half and perhaps the most important of their goals, which is to protect their reputations even when their reputations do not deserve defense.

The Internet's Answers.com gives four definitions for the term *secret*. It is a word with the power to disturb me because three of its four meanings depict so accurately the state of sexual harassment on the American campus. They make me wonder how we could have come so far by the twenty-first century and yet failed so many of the young women (and sometimes young men) in our charge.

If I place them in the following order, the first two definitions of *secret* describe a simple fact that applies to far too many colleges and universities: (1) the existence of much sexual harassment is "kept hidden from others or known only to (themselves) or to a few" and (2) for institutions, the secrecy is a "method or formula on which success (protecting reputation and finances) is based." But it is the third definition that most truthfully depicts the secret of institutional behavior regarding sexual harassment on campus: it is (3) "something that remains beyond understanding or explanation."

I have agreed to be "gagged" on occasion because I knew it could contribute to closure for people who had been damaged by members of my profession, but I also know that silence will increase the danger for other students, especially in cases of quid pro quo harassment. Silence furthers the illusion that there are no perils in professorial–student sex and that professors never misuse their power to demand sex from students or to retaliate when they try to extricate themselves. Silence tells professors that every young woman is fair game and that, institutional policies aside, they will never be judged. Silence prevents the public from realizing that the "ivory" tower built with its money is not so pure after all.

Arnold concludes her discussion of hookup culture:

> College students understand and enact their relationships and sexuality within the framework of their own developmental positions. . . .
> Most undergraduates lack the mature competence and cognitive complexity to analyze and withstand normative peer behavior. The

realities of postponed adult commitments, time pressure, and ambiguous social values encourage no-strings experimentation and shallow connections to sexual partners. The meaning-making structure of most undergraduates is not yet sufficiently developed to reflect outside of the immediate environment in order to understand the larger forces that construct contemporary social norms. (Arnold, 2009, p. 8)

She observes, correctly, that attempts by higher education to improve students' identity development, self-image, relational skills, sense of autonomy, and ability to deal with cognitive complexity may enable them "to reflect on their cultural assumptions and analyze their personality (so they will be moved toward) conscious decision-making" (Arnold, 2009, p. 9).

Yet in the final analysis, controlling sexual relations between undergraduates and professors depends on adults with the personal integrity, professionalism, and courage to withstand opposition. As long as a minority of academics employs the hackneyed civil liberties defense to justify the unjustifiable, as long as some colleagues and institutions cover for themselves and friends and employees, the problem will persist. Some professors will suffer because of their own insistence on perpetuating a behavior that the public and higher education alike deplore. But most injured of all will be young women who are "more sinned against than sinning" (Shakespeare, *King Lear*, Act 3, scene 2, 57–60), who emerge from sexual relationships with professors having discovered that "consent" is not real after all, that sex is not what makes us adult or human, that sometimes it leaves us "burned . . . of any trust (we have) in the world and the way that it works."

References

Abramson, P. (2007). *Romance in the ivory tower: The rights of liberty and conscience.* Cambridge, MA: MIT Press.

Arnold, K. (2009). *College student development and the hookup culture.* Unpublished manuscript. Retrieved from www.bc.edu › schools › Lynch School › faculty › faculty by name (Permission to use granted).

Bailey, B. (1988). *From front porch to back seat: Courtship in twentieth-century America.* Baltimore: Johns Hopkins University Press.

Bennett, C. M., & Baird, A. A. (2006). Anatomical changes in the emerging adult brain: A voxel-based morphometry study. *Human Brain Mapping*, *9*, 766–77.

Berns G. S., Moore S., & Capra C. M. (2009). Adolescent engagement in dangerous behaviors is associated with increased white matter maturity of frontal cortex. *PLoS one, 4*(8), e6773.

Bogle, K. A. (2008). *Hooking up: Sex, dating, and relationships on campus*. New York: New York University Press.

Coté, J. E. (2006). Emerging adulthood as an institutionalized moratorium: Risks and benefits to identity formation. In J. J. Arnett & J. L. Tanner (Eds.), *Emerging adults in America: Coming of age in the 21st century*. Washington, DC: American Psychological Association.

Dank, B. M., & Albuquerque, K. de (1998). Banning sexual asymmetry on campus. *Electronic Journal of Human Sexuality, 1*. Retrieved on March 4, 2011 from http://www.ejhs.org/volume1/bdank.htm.

Dziech, B. W., & Hawkins, M. H. (1998). *Sexual harassment in higher education: Reflections and new perspectives*. New York and London: Garland Press.

Feldman, S. S., Turner, R. A., & Araujo, K. (1999). Interpersonal context as an influence on sexual timetables of youth: Gender and ethnic effects. *Journal of Research on Adolescence*, *9*, 25–52.

Fitzgerald, L. F., Gold, Y., Omerod, M., & Weitzman, L. M. (1988). Academic harassment: Sex and denial in scholarly garb. *Psychology of Women Quarterly*, *12*, 329–40.

Gallop, J. (1997). *Feminist accused of sexual harassment*. Durham and London: Duke University Press.

Gallop, J. (2003). *Living with his camera*. Durham and London: Duke University Press.

Glaser, R. D., & Thorpe, J. S. (1986). Unethical intimacy: A survey of sexual contact and advances between psychology educators and female graduate students. *American Psychologist, 41*(1), 43–51.

Grello, C., Welsh, D., & Harper, M. (2006). No strings attached: The nature of casual sex in late adolescents. *The Journal of Sex Research, 43*, 255–67.

Grello, C. M., Welsh, D. P., Harper, M. S., & Dickson, J. W. (2003). Dating and sexual relationship trajectories and adolescent functioning. *Adolescent and Family Health, 3*, 103–12.

Institute for American Values. (2001). Hooking up, hanging out, and hoping for Mr. Right: College women on mating and dating today. Report for Independent Women's Forum.

Irvine, M., & Tanner, R. (2007). Thousands of teachers cited for sex misconduct. *USA Today.* Retrieved from … www.usatoday.com/ … /2007-10-20-teachermisconduct_N.htm.

Arnett, J. (2004). *Emerging adulthood: The winding road from the late teens through the twenties.* New York: Oxford University Press.

Dziech, B.W. & Hawkins, M.H. (1998). *Sexual harassment in higher education: Reflections and new perspectives.* New York and London: Garland Press.

Kahn, A. S., Fricker, K., Hoffman, J., Lambert, T., Tripp, M., & Childress, K. (2000). "Hooking up: Dangerous new dating methods?" In A. S. Kahn (Chair), *Sex, unwanted sex, and sexual assault on college campuses.* Symposium—American Psychological Association, Washington, DC.

Kimball, R. (1997). The distinguished professor. *The new criterion.* Retrieved on March 24, 2011 from … www.newcriterion.com/articles … /The-distinguished-professor—3348.

Lambert, T. A., Kahn, A. S., & Apple, K. J. (2003). Pluralistic ignorance and hooking up. *Journal of Sex Research, 40*(2), 129–35.

McIlhaney, J. S., & Bush, F. M. (2008). *Hooked: New science on how casual sex is affecting our children.* Chicago: Northfield.

Paul, E. L., McManus, B., & Hayes, A. (2000). "Hookups": Characteristics and correlates of college students' spontaneous and anonymous sexual experiences. *Journal of Sex Research, 37*(1), 76–78.

Policy on teacher-student consensual relations. (2010). Office for Equal Opportunity Programs/ Human Resources/Yale University. New Haven, CT

Reitman, J. (2006). Sex and scandal at Duke. *Rolling Stone.* Retrieved November 28, 2006, from www.duke.edu/web/hookup/side.htm.

Ritchie, Karen. (2002). *Marketing to Generation X*. New York: Free Press.

Romance in the ivory tower: The rights and liberty of conscience. (2007). Cambridge, MA: The MIT Press.

Stepp, L. S. (2007). *Unhooked: How young women pursue sex, delay love and lose at both.* New York: Riverhead Books.

Taneja, R. (2010). Hook-ups not as common as most think, study finds. *The Chronicle,* Retrieved 3/4/11. from dukechronicle.com › News › University.

Wolfe, T. (2004). *I am Charlotte Simmons*. New York: St Martin's Press.

About the Editor and Contributors

Editor

Jennifer L. Martin, Ph.D., has worked in public education for 15 years, 13 of those as the department head of English at an alternative high school for at-risk students in the Detroit metropolitan area. She is also a Special Lecturer at Oakland University where she teaches in the Education Specialist Degree Program and in the Women and Gender Studies department. As an educational leader, Dr. Martin has been an advocate for at-risk students, and has received several district, state, and national awards and recognitions for her advocacy, mentorship, and research. She has served as a mentor to high school, undergraduate, and graduate students, as well as to new teachers in a variety of areas such as writing and publishing, career and leadership development, and advocacy. Dr. Martin has conducted research, published fourteen book chapters and numerous peer reviewed articles on bullying and harassment, peer sexual harassment, educational equity, mentoring, issues of social justice, service-learning, the at-risk student, and other educational topics. Dr. Martin has been an invited speaker at universities and non-profit organizations on the aforementioned topics. As Action Vice President of Michigan NOW, she engages in volunteer Title IX education and legal advocacy work. Through this work she has been asked to comment on proposed Michigan legislation on National Public Radio.

Contributors

Patricia M. Amburgy, Ph.D., is an Associate Professor of Art Education at the Pennsylvania State University. Her research interests include aesthetics, visual culture, and the history of art education. She has published articles and reviews in *Art Education, Studies in Art Education, The Journal of Social Theory in Art Education, History of Education Quarterly*, and other professional journals. She has written chapters on historical research, the history of art education, and visual culture pedagogy for *Practice Theory: Seeing the Power of Teacher Researchers* (forthcoming), *Visual Culture in the Art Class: Case Studies* (2006), the *Handbook of Research and Policy in Art Education* (2004), *Women Art Educators V: Conversations Across Time* (2003), and *Framing the Past: Essays on Art Education* (1990). She co-edited a book on the foundations of education, *Readings in American Public Schooling* (1980), and a conference proceedings on the history of art education, *The History of Art Education: Proceedings from the Second Penn State Conference, 1989* (1992). She has given numerous presentations on art education at state, national, and international conferences, including meetings of the Pennsylvania Art Education Association, the National Art Education Association, the History of Education Society, and the International Society of Education through Art. She was associate editor of *The Pennsylvania Art Educator*, a journal of the Pennsylvania Art Education Association, from 1989 to 1994. Dr. Amburgy is especially interested in the relationship of art education to the social power of women, ethnic minorities, and working class people, both in the past and in the future.

Jane H. Applegate, Ph.D., is Professor of Teacher Education/English Education in the Department of Secondary Education in the College of Education at the University of South Florida. Dr. Applegate earned her Ph.D. in Teacher Education from The Ohio State University and has served on the faculties of Kent State University and West Virginia University where she also held administrative positions before joining the faculty at the University of South Florida where she also served as dean of the College of Education. Over the course of her career she has been invested in the improvement of teacher preparation. Through the genesis of grant-funded programs at both Kent State and West Virginia University she led efforts to strengthen the education of beginning teachers by focusing attention on redesigning undergraduate curricula and focusing attention on attracting high quality students into the field of teaching. At West

Virginia University she secured over 5 million dollars from private foundations to develop university-school relationships which improved the induction and professional development opportunities for practicing teachers. At the University of South Florida she also provided leadership in teacher education reform which culminated in the development of the Master of Arts in Teaching degree for the preparation of teachers with undergraduate degrees in the liberal arts and sciences. Since returning to her role as professor, she has been actively engaged in mentoring new faculty members, particularly the development of women faculty and women becoming leaders. Currently she is studying the development of women doctoral students who are becoming teacher educators. Her research has been published in journals such as the Journal of Teacher Education, Educational Leadership, the English Journal and Scholar-Practitioner Quarterly.

Patricia Arredondo, Ed.D., is Associate Vice Chancellor for Academic Affairs, Dean, School of Continuing Education and Professor of Counseling Psychology with the University of Wisconsin-Milwaukee. Her priority scholarship areas have continuously focused on immigrants and their life change processes, Latina/o issues in counseling, multicultural competency development, and organizational diversity initiatives. Embedded in her writings and presentations is the woman factor in leadership. Her publications on multicultural competencies and guidelines are widely cited nationally and internationally. Many of her students are included as contributors to her extensive publications and video productions for training. Patricia has mentored many students and early career professionals.

Patricia was the first Latina President of the American Counseling Association. Other leadership roles include president of Division 45 Society for the Psychological Study of Ethnic Minority Issues, National Latina/o Psychological Association and Association of Multicultural Counseling and Development. She chairs the Dissertation Awards Committee for the American Association of Hispanics in Higher Education. Patricia was recognized as a *Living Legend* by the American Counseling Association for her extensive contributions to multicultural counseling. She is a Fellow of the American Psychological Association and recipient of an Honorary Doctorate from the University of San Diego. Her degrees include a doctorate in Counseling Psychology, Boston University,

Master's in Counseling from Boston College and B.S. in Spanish and Journalism from Kent State University. She is a licensed psychologist and bilingual in English/Spanish. She is of Mexican-American heritage.

Brenda L. Berkelaar (Ph.D., Purdue University) is an assistant professor in the Department of Communication Studies at The University of Texas at Austin. Her work on leadership aligns with her research on careers, technology, and learning. While at Purdue, Brenda worked at the Susan Bulkeley Butler Center for Leadership Excellence. She also consulted with the National Academy of Engineering on an interdisciplinary team focusing on the development of academic change leaders. Previously, Brenda worked as an independent organizational consultant as well as in various management and leadership positions. Her current work includes an analysis of the use of online technologies in employee selection and a four-country study of children's interests in and perceptions of careers in science, technology, engineering, and math. Her work includes a number of collaborative and individual journal articles and edited book chapters.

Joanne Cooper, Ph.D., is a Professor of Educational Administration at the University of Hawaii at Manoa. She holds a Ph.D. from the University of Oregon in Educational Policy and Management. She is the recipient of the Regents' Medal for Excellence in Teaching from the University of Hawaii and a Distinguished Teaching Award for Graduate Education from the College of Education. She has served as both Associate Dean of the College of Education as well as Chair of the Faculty Senate for the University of Hawaii and has authored five books and numerous articles, many of which focus on women leaders in higher education. She has written extensively about the condition of women in higher education, including a book on tenure for women and minority faculty, as well as lead author of publications on gender equity in *The Handbook on Gender Equity in Education* and in *Women in Higher Education: An Encyclopedia.* She co-authored *The Constructivist Leader,* which was named Book of the Year by the National Council on Staff Development. Her most recent book with Dannelle Stevens is entitled, *Journal Keeping: How to Use Reflective Writing for Learning, Teaching, Professional Insight and Positive Change.* She has served on the editorial boards of *The Journal of Research on*

*Leadership Education, the American Educational Research Journal/SIA, Advancing Women in Leadership,*and *the Journal of General Education.*

Monica F. Cox, Ph.D., is an Assistant Professor in the School of Engineering Education at Purdue University. She obtained a B.S. in mathematics from Spelman College, a M.S. in industrial engineering from the University of Alabama, and a Ph.D. in Leadership and Policy Studies from Peabody College of Vanderbilt University. Teaching interests relate to the professional development of graduate engineering students and to leadership, policy, and change in science, technology, engineering, and mathematics education. Primary research projects explore the preparation of engineering doctoral students for careers in academia and industry and the development of engineering education assessment tools. Current projects incorporate my research and teaching interests. She is a 2008 NSF Faculty Early Career (CAREER) award winner and is a recipient of a Presidential Early Career Award for Scientists and Engineers (PECASE).

Beverly Davenport Sypher, Ph.D., is Vice Provost for Faculty Affairs, the Susan Bulkeley Butler Chair for Leadership Excellence and Professor of Communication at Purdue University. She is an internationally recognized scholar, award-winning teacher and experienced administrator whose research spans organizational, health and learning contexts. Her work on civility and leadership grows out of long-standing interests in workplace communication and quality of work life issues. In 2007, she launched the Susan Bulkeley Butler Center for Leadership Excellence. The mission of the Butler Center is to develop leadership capacity through research, education and collaborations that help advance inclusion and broaden representation in academic administration. She founded Purdue Women Lead out of a partnership with the American Association of Colleges and Universities and Purdue's Women's Resource Office.

Florence L. Denmark, Ph.D., is an internationally recognized scholar, researcher and policy maker. She received her doctorate from the University of Pennsylvania in social psychology and has five honorary degrees. Denmark is the Robert Scott Pace Distinguished Research Professor of Psychology at Pace University in New York. A past president of the

American Psychological Association (APA) and the International Council of Psychologists (ICP), Denmark holds fellowship status in the APA and the Association for Psychological Science. She is also a member of the Society for Experimental Social Psychology (SESP) and a Fellow of the New York Academy of Sciences. She has received numerous national and international awards for her contributions to psychology. She received the 2004 American Psychological Foundation Gold Medal for Lifetime Achievement for Psychology in the Public Interest. In 2005, she received the Ernest R. Hilgard Award for Career Contribution to General Psychology. She is the recipient in 2007 of the Raymond Fowler Award for Outstanding Service to APA. Also in 2007, Denmark was elected to the National Academies of Practice as a distinguished scholar member. She received the Elder Award at the APA National Multicultural Conference in 2009. Denmark's most significant research and extensive publications have emphasized women's leadership and leadership styles, the interaction of status and gender, aging women in cross-cultural perspective, and the history of women in psychology. Denmark is the main nongovernmental organization (NGO) representative to the United Nations for the American Psychological Association and is also the main NGO representative for the International Council of Psychologists. She is currently Chair of the New York NGO Committee on Ageing and serves on the Executive Committee of the NGO Committee on Mental Health.

Penelope M. Earley, Ph.D., is founding Director of the Center for Education Policy and Evaluation and a professor of education policy in the Graduate School of Education at George Mason University. Before joining the GMU faculty, Earley was a vice president with the American Association of Colleges for Teacher Education. At AACTE she directed federal and state governmental relations, issue analysis, policy studies, and public relations. Dr. Earley's areas of research include federal and state education policy and governance, public policy regarding teacher education, and gender equity issues. Dr. Earley has served on a member of a number of educational advisory boards including the NCES Consultative Committee on Title II Accountability; AASCU Commission on Teacher Preparation, Accountability, and Evaluation; Teacher Mentor Project; and Coalition for Women's Appointments in Government. She has authored book chapters for *Teacher Education for Democracy and*

Social Justice, Women in Academic Leadership: Professional Strategies, Personal Choices: Vol. 2., The Politics of Education Yearbook, Handbook of Research on Teacher Education, After Student Standards: Alignment, What is a Qualified, Capable Teacher? and *Developing Language Teachers for a Changing World.* Earley is the founding co-editor of the *International Journal of Education Policy and Leadership*, an open access peer-reviewed electronic journal created through a collaborative between George Mason University, Simon Fraser University, and the Association for Supervision and Curriculum Development. She honds a Ph.D. from Virginia Tech, a Masters from the University of Virginia, and Bachelors degree from the University of Michigan.

Hannah Fisher-Arfer was the 2009–2010 Student Body President of Portland State University. Previously, she was the Outreach Director for the Disability Cultural Advocacy Association and has hosted a Portland-based commercial television show, Teen Edition. At 22, she is working toward a dual undergraduate degree in Liberal and Black Studies and is planning to attend law school after completion. Ms. Fisher serves as a student director of the Oregon State Board of Higher Education, and was appointed in 2007 by Governor Kulongoski.

Susan V. Iverson, Ed.D., is Assistant Professor in higher education administration and student personnel at Kent State University where she is also an affiliate faculty member with the Women's Studies Program. Iverson earned her doctorate in higher educational leadership, with a concentration in women's studies, from the University of Maine (2005) where she also served as an instructor in higher educational leadership (2002–2006) and women's studies (2004–2006). Her scholarly interests include gender equity, multicultural competence, citizenship, and service-learning. Iverson's recent work has appeared in *Innovative Higher Education* (2010), *Michigan Journal of Community Service Learning* (2009), *Journal about Women in Higher Education* (2009), *Equity and Excellence in Education* (2008), *Educational Administration Quarterly* (2007), and she co-edited, *Reconstructing policy analysis in higher education: Feminist poststructural perspectives* (Routledge, 2010). Prior to becoming faculty, Iverson worked in student affairs administration for more than ten years. She holds a B.A. in English from Keene State College (NH), a

M.A. in Higher Education Administration from Boston College, and a M.Ed. in Counseling from Bridgewater State College (MA).

Heipua Kaopua, M.S.W., M.Ed., is a Professor CC at Windward Community College with 20 years of counseling experience. She is a doctoral student in Educational Administration with a focus on Higher Education. Her research interests center on minority women in higher education, particularly the experiences of Native Hawaiian women faculty during the tenure process. She plans to investigate the role of Native Hawaiian values during the tenure process. She earned a B.A. in Sociology, a M.S.W. and a M.Ed. in higher education, all from the University of Hawai'i at Mānoa.

Karen Keifer-Boyd, Ph.D., is a Professor of Art Education and Affiliate Professor of Women's Studies at The Pennsylvania State University. Her writings on feminist pedagogy, visual culture, cyberNet activism art pedagogy, action research, and identity speculative fiction are in more than 45 peer-reviewed research publications, and translated into several languages. She co-authored *InCITE, InSIGHT, InSITE* (NAEA, 2008), *Engaging Visual Culture* (Davis, 2007), co-edited *Real-World Readings in Art Education: Things Your Professors Never Told You* (Falmer, 2000), and served as editor of the *Journal of Social Theory in Art Education* and guest editor for *Visual Arts Research.* She has co-edited the journal, *Visual Culture and Gender,* since 2005. Keifer-Boyd has presented at more than 50 international and national conferences, and at universities in South Korea, Taiwan, Hong Kong, Austria, Germany, Uganda, and Finland. Her research focuses on feminist strategies for teaching critical and creative inquiry with dynamic/interactive technologies. She has been honored with leadership and teaching awards including a 2006 Fulbright Lecture and Research Award in Finland from the Council for International Exchange of Scholars, the National Art Education Association (NAEA) Women's Caucus Connors Teaching Award in 2005, the Texas Outstanding Art Educator in Higher Education Award in 2001, and the Arts Administrator of the Year National Art Education Association Award for the Pacific Region in 1994.

Wanda B. Knight, Ph.D., is Associate Professor of Art Education and Women's Studies at the Pennsylvania State University. Besides university level teaching, she has taught art at all grade levels, in vastly different regions of the United States, including overseas, plus communities serving rural, suburban and urban populations. Moreover, she has served as public school principal, and museum registrar and assistant museum curator of the Albany Museum of Art in Albany, Georgia. Focusing on visual culture, cultural studies, and pedagogies of difference (i.e., class, gender, race, ability), Dr. Knight has presented in local, state, national, and international venues and has published widely in leading journals in the field of art education, including *Art Education*, *Studies in Art Education*, *The Journal of Social Theory in Art Education*, and *The Journal of Cross Cultural Research in Art Education*. Dr. Knight is chair-elect of the United States Society for Education Through the Arts. Moreover, she served as chair of the National Art Education Association's Committee on Multiethnic Concerns and chair of Penn State's Commission on Racial and Ethnic Diversity (CORED). Dr. Knight has lead initiatives that foster diversity and support fair, ethical, and inclusive teaching and learning environments. Further, her leadership and extensive work in the field have been recognized through various honors and teaching awards including "Teacher of the Year," Who's Who in American Education, the J. Eugene Grigsby Jr. Award for outstanding contribution to the field of art education, and the Kenneth Marantz Distinguished Alumni Award from the Ohio State University.

M. Cookie Newsom, Ph.D., holds a BS in Education, a MA in History and a PhD in Educational Leadership. Her dissertation addressed the achievement gap and was titled "Lessons in Black and White: White teacher questioning practices of black and white students." She was the 2008 recipient of the University Award for the Advancement of Women at the University of North Carolina at Chapel Hill where she currently serves as the Director of Diversity Education and Assessment as well as the Chair of the Black Faculty/Staff Caucus. Her research interests are black women and white women's relationships, the achievement gap and blacks in higher education. Her latest work has been on the dearth of black faculty at Research 1 institutions in America. She was a research fellow at the Library of Congress for 2002–2003 in the "Cities and Public Spaces in Cultural Context" seminar. Dr. Newsom has made presentations at many national conferences including American Education Research

Association, Mid-west Education Research Association, Patterson Research Conference, American Association of Blacks in Higher Education, National Postdoctoral Association, American Council on Education and American Association of University Professors. Dr. Newsom is married, (Wayne) and has three children (Mike, Chris, and Nikki), four grandchildren (Marrisa, Julian, Ella, and Sam) and two cats (Agatha Christie and Bucky). She is a member of Phi Theta Kappa, UNC's Leadership Institute Board, School of Nursing Multicultural Advisory Board, Institute for African American Research Advisory Board, Association of Women and Faculty Professionals Advisory Board and Chair of the UNC Diversity Education Team.

Rhoda Olkin, Ph.D., is a Distinguished Professor, California School of Professional Psychology at Alliant International University, and the Executive Director of the Institute on Disability & Health Psychology. She is the author of the book "What Psychotherapists Should Know about Disability" and the training film "Disability-Affirmative Therapy: A Beginner's Guide." Dr. Olkin has presented and published on the intersection of disability and psychology, and combined this topic with her interests in families, diagnosis, case formulation, and effective teaching of clinical psychology. She has a private practice in the SF East Bay, does expert witness work, and is currently working on her next book, "Disability Affirmative Therapy: A case formulation approach."

Michele A. Paludi, Ph.D., is the author/editor of 34 college textbooks, and more than 170 scholarly articles and conference presentations on sexual harassment, campus violence, psychology of women, gender, and discrimination. Her book, *Ivory Power: Sexual Harassment on Campus*, (1990, SUNY Press), received the 1992 Myers Center Award for Outstanding Book on Human Rights in the United States. Dr. Paludi served as Chair of the U.S. Department of Education's Subpanel on the Prevention of Violence, Sexual Harassment, and Alcohol and Other Drug Problems in Higher Education. She was one of six scholars in the United States to be selected for this subpanel. She also was a consultant to and a member of former New York State Governor Mario Cuomo's Task Force on Sexual Harassment. Dr. Paludi serves as an expert witness for court proceedings and administrative hearings on sexual harassment. She has had extensive experience in conducting training programs and investigations of sexual harassment and other Equal Employment Opportunity (EEO) issues for businesses and educational institutions. In addition, Dr. Paludi has held faculty positions at Franklin & Marshall College, Kent State University, Hunter College, Union College, and Union Graduate College, where she directs the human resource management certificate program and management and leadership certificate program. She is on the faculty in the School of Management.

Katie Pope, M.A., M.S., is the Director of the Women's Resource Office, and in partnership with the Susan Bulkeley Butler Center for Leadership Excellence, designs and implements educational programs and events for faculty and staff leaders. Through this partnership, she is responsible for providing leadership, professional development and educational opportunities, with a special emphasis on fostering inclusive leadership and promoting gender equity. Working with the Butler Center and the American Association of Colleges and Universities, she helped launch the Purdue Women Lead program. Katie has an M.A. from Indiana University and an M.S. from Iowa State University. Her research interests include the development of women's philanthropic organizations and the role of women's centers on college campuses.

Rosemary F. Powers, Ph.D., is an Associate Professor of Sociology at Eastern Oregon University. Her areas of research and teaching include education, gender and sexuality, culture, and religion. Dr. Powers earned both her doctorate and master's degree in sociology from UC-Davis; additionally she has earned a master's in values from the San Francisco Theological Seminary. She serves as a faculty director of the Oregon State Board of Higher Education and was appointed in 2008 by Governor Kulongoski.

Eugenia Proctor Gerdes, Ph.D., taught social psychology and psychology of women for fourteen years in the department of psychology at Bucknell University. Dr. Gerdes's quantitative research included experimental studies of discrimination in hiring and multivariate analyses of stress experienced by women in traditionally male work roles. Beginning in 1988, she served as associate dean of faculty for one year and then as dean of the College of Arts and Sciences at Bucknell for eighteen years.

Dr. Gerdes now has returned to the faculty as dean *emerita* and professor of psychology; her interdisciplinary courses include first-year and senior seminars on liberal arts education, commercialization of higher education, and women and leadership. Since becoming dean, her scholarship has expanded to encompass essays and presentations on higher education, including topics such as the value of contemplation, time management as a part of a liberal education, educating parents, the dean's role in protecting liberal education, effective use of associate deans, motivations for becoming a dean and for quitting, and the importance of educating students about commercialization and liberal education. Her various scholarly interests come together with her own career history in the series of qualitative studies on the status of women in higher education that is the focus of her chapter in this volume.

Jill M. Tarule, Ed.D., is a Professor of Human Development and Educational Leadership and Policy at the University of Vermont. She has served as associate provost, a dean and in other academic leadership roles in three institutions. She holds a masters and doctoral degrees from the Harvard Graduate School of Education, and an honorary doctorate from the University of New Hampshire School for Lifelong Learning. Her undergraduate degree is from Goddard College. Her research has focused on women as students and as leaders, on adult learners specifically and leadership generally, and on pedagogical innovations such as collaborative learning and cognitive developmental strategies for teaching and learning. She is co-author of Women's Ways of Knowing: the Development of Self, Voice and Mind and co-editor of Knowledge, Difference and Power: Essays Inspired by Women's Ways of Knowing and of The Minority Voice in Educational Reform, An Analysis by Minority and Women College of Education Deans, as well as many articles and chapters.

Amber L. Vlasnik, M.A., is the director of the Women's Center at Wright State University in Dayton, Ohio, assuming her role in December 2005. Vlasnik's duties include assessing the needs and status of women students, faculty and staff; advising campus leaders on issues of women and gender; advancing gender equity throughout the institution; collaborating with other campus units on issues addressing race, ethnicity, gender and sexual orientation; and promoting awareness of the diverse contributions and experiences of women through programming and advocacy, among many other tasks. Prior to her position at Wright State, Vlasnik was the manager of the Women's Center at Louisiana State University in Baton Rouge. She has served as a member of the Advisory Council of the National Women's Studies Association Women's Centers Committee, and was the founding chair of the Women's Centers Committee of the Southwestern Ohio Council for Higher Education. Vlasnik currently serves as Communications Chair of the ACE Ohio Women's Network, a state chapter of the ACE/Office of Women in Higher Education. Vlasnik holds a M.A.L.A. with concentrations in gender, law, and higher education from Louisiana State University and a B.A. in International Studies and Spanish from St. Norbert College in Wisconsin. She is currently enrolled in the Higher Education & Student Affairs doctoral program at The Ohio State University. Her research interests include the history of women's participation in U.S. higher education, campus-based women's centers, and the multiple roles and opportunities of branch campuses, both domestically and abroad.

Tanisca M. Wilson, Ph.D. is a native of New Orleans, LA and a product of the New Orleans Public School System. She has a Bachelor of Arts degree in English from Southern University at New Orleans, a Master of Education degree from the University of New Orleans, a certificate in women's ministry from the New Orleans Baptist Theological Seminary and a Ph.D. in Educational Administration from the University of New Orleans. Her working life has centered on helping at risk youth and adults. In doing so, she has taught in both traditional and non-traditional settings. In addition to presenting at several regional and national professional conferences, she has been a peer reviewer for the Journal about Women in Higher Education, has professional memberships in eight educational organizations, and she is the author of a published reflection in the International Forum of Teaching and Learning Journal. Her research agenda includes educational policy, women in leadership, and correctional and higher education systems. She has been the College-wide Assistant Director of Enrollment Services at Delgado Community College for two years. In this role, she is responsible for managing, creating, and implementing pre-entry to enrollment programs at six campus locations.

Billie Wright Dziech, Ed.D., is Professor of English and Comparative Literature at the University of Cincinnati. She is the primary author of *The Lecherous Professor: Sexual Harassment in Higher Education* and co-author of *Sexual Harassment in Higher Education: Reflections and New Perspectives* and *On Trial: American Courts and Their Treatment of Sexually Abused Children.* She has written numerous book chapters and articles in scholarly journals and the popular press. Her work has appeared and been reviewed and quoted in sources as diverse as *The New York Times, The Wall Street Journal, The Chicago Tribune, The Chronicle of Higher Education,* and *People Magazine.* She has been a guest on approximately 200 television and radio programs, including "The Today Show," "CNN," "Donohue," and "Oprah" and has lectured and consulted at colleges, universities, and businesses throughout the United States and Canada. She is the recipient of the University of Cincinnati's A.B. "Dolly" Cohen Award for Excellence in College Teaching, as well as the Honors Scholars Faculty Award given by students and staff of the university's Honors Scholar Program. Dziech is currently writing a series of children's books. She and her husband, Rob, live in Cincinnati, where they are ten minutes away from their son, daughter-in-law, and absolutely perfect granddaughter, Elizabeth.

Index